I0819948

Divining Tarot

Divining Tarot

Papers on Charles Williams's *The Greater Trumps* and Other Works

by

Nancy-Lou Patterson

Editors

Emily E. Auger

and

Janet Brennan Croft

Valleyhome Books

The Patterson Papers

Ransoming the Waste Land: Papers on C.S. Lewis's Space Trilogy, Chronicles of Narnia, and Other Works Volume I

Ransoming the Waste Land: Papers on C.S. Lewis's Space Trilogy, Chronicles of Narnia, and Other Works Volume II

Detecting Wimsey: Papers on Dorothy L. Sayers's Detective Fiction

Nancy-Lou Patterson Reviews Books By and About Dorothy L. Sayers, C.S. Lewis, J.R.R. Tolkien, Charles Williams, and Others

Divining Tarot: Papers on Charles Williams's The Greater Trumps *and Other Works*

Front cover and title page illustration credit: "Williams's Fool." Patrick H. Wynne. First pub. *Mythlore* (#36) 10.2 (Summer 1983): 3. Reproduced by permission of the artist. Further reproduction prohibited.

Back cover and last page illustration credit: "Fool" from illustrations included with the 1950 Pellegrini & Cudahy and 1962 Noonday Press edition of Charles Williams's *The Greater Trumps*. Courtesy of Farrar, Straus and Giroux, LLC.

First Printing 2019
Divining Tarot: Papers on Charles Williams's
The Greater Trumps *and Other Works*
Hardcover ISBN 978-1-987919-08-0
Paperback ISBN 978-1-987919-10-3
Epub ISBN 978-1-987919-09-7

Table of Contents

List of Illustrations

Abbreviations for Charles Williams's Fiction

WH *War in Heaven.* 1930. London: Faber and Faber, 1947.

MD *Many Dimensions.* 1931. London: Faber and Faber, 1947.

PL *The Place of the Lion.* 1931. London: Faber and Faber, 1952.

GT *The Greater Trumps.* London: Faber and Faber, 1932. New edition with Preface by William Lindsay Gresham and Tarot illustrations, Pellegrini & Cudahy, 1950. New York: Noonday Press, a Division of Farrar, Straus and Cudahy, 1962.

Citations in this volume are to the Noonday Press edition.

DH *Descent into Hell.* London: Faber and Faber, 1937.

SE *Shadows of Ecstasy.* 1933. New York: Pellegrini and Cudahy, 1950.

AHE *All Hallows' Eve.* London: Faber and Faber, 1945.

Foreword

Nancy-Lou Patterson (1929-2018) came to the University of Waterloo in 1962, and founded the fine arts department there in 1968. Soon after she retired in 1992, she was named "Distinguished Professor Emerita" by the University of Waterloo, and in the same year received an honorary doctor of letters degree from Wilfrid Laurier University. Patterson taught art history and was an active artist, poet, and fiction author, as well as a scholar, contributing twenty-seven articles and some 220 book reviews to *Mythlore: A Journal of J.R.R. Tolkien, C.S. Lewis, Charles Williams, and Mythopoeic Literature* and the affiliated *Tolkien Journal* alone. She also published in anthologies, including *For the Childlike: George MacDonald's Fantasies for Children* (1992) and *Modern British Essayists* (1990); and other journals, including the *Lamp-Post of the Southern California C.S. Lewis Society*, the *English Quarterly*, *Niekas*, and others. She wrote on numerous subjects, favoring C.S. Lewis's fiction, as well as the work of Dorothy L. Sayers, J.R.R. Tolkien, George MacDonald, Pauline Baynes, and, of course, Charles Williams. We have gathered many of these papers into the present series of anthologies, which so far includes

- *Ransoming the Waste Land: Papers on C.S. Lewis's Space Trilogy, Chronicles of Narnia, and Other Works Volume I*
- *Ransoming the Waste Land: Papers on C.S. Lewis's Space Trilogy, Chronicles of Narnia, and Other Works Volume II*
- *Detecting Wimsey: Papers on Dorothy L. Sayers's Detective Fiction*
- *Nancy-Lou Patterson Reviews Books By and About Dorothy L. Sayers, C.S. Lewis, J.R.R. Tolkien, Charles Williams, and Others*

In this volume of the Nancy-Lou Patterson papers, the main attraction is Patterson's lengthy and perceptive essay on Charles Williams's *The Greater Trumps,* "The Triumph of Love" (1974). This paper first appeared in *Mythcon Proceedings III*, the proceedings of the 1972 Mythopoeic Society conference at Long Beach, CA. Held in conjunction with Westercon XXV, the guest of honor was Poul Anderson, and this was the last Mythcon for which the Society published official proceedings until the joint conference with the British Tolkien Society in 1996. Patterson's paper was presented on Saturday, July 1, at 12:30, and was one of only a handful of papers strictly on the Mythcon schedule and not the Westercon schedule. The proceedings, printed in 1974, are held by perhaps two dozen libraries around the world and indexed nowhere but in the *Mythlore Index Plus*, so this work has languished in obscurity, unfindable, and as far as we can tell, cited only once, in over forty years.

"The Triumph of Love" is an essay well worth the reader's attention, providing an excellent introduction to the history of Tarot (updated with a light hand by Auger to correct some errors made by Patterson based on the information available at that time; see her Editorial Notes for details) and an explanation of the unique card arrangement Williams used in his novel. Incorporated as well are discussions of T.S. Eliot's *The Waste Land*, the history of the Roman and medieval Triumph and its Greek roots, and Williams's involvement with the Golden Dawn and its occult practices and mysticism. While it holds up extremely well as an insightful exploration of Williams's themes and aims in writing *The Greater Trumps*, it is also quite interesting as an example of what subjects and approaches concerned Inklings scholars in the early 1970s. And Patterson's writing—as always, lucid, clear, direct, and deeply considered—is a joy to read and a model of scholarly writing to which we might all aspire. My coeditor Emily E. Auger has added well-chosen reproductions of Tarot cards from a number of decks and periods to illustrate and clarify Patterson's text.

Following this we reprint "The Jewels of Messias: Images of Judaism and Anti-semitism in the Novels of Charles Williams" (1979), and "Charles Williams" from the reference work *Modern British Essayists* (1990). These three papers are presented here in the order of their original publication. However, readers not yet familiar with Williams may wish to read this book in a different order, starting with Patterson's "Charles Williams" as a succinct and still relevant introduction to the author, and then reading Auger's "Introduction" as a more detailed orientation to his involvement with occult organizations and practices and his knowledge of Tarot. "The Jewels of

Messias" (a companion paper to "Images of Judaism and Anti-Semitism in the Novels of Dorothy L. Sayers" (1978), now available in *Detecting Wimsey: Papers on Dorothy L. Sayers's Detective Fiction* by Nancy-Lou Patterson) offers a broader view of Williams's interest in Tarot as an element of his comprehensive interest in the occult, a useful perspective to have before moving on to "The Triumph of Love."

The remaining artwork throughout the collection is very appropriately reproduced from early issues of *Mythlore* with the kind permission of the illustrators. Auger has also added an annotated, illustrated, and descriptive list of Patterson's own highly eclectic personal Tarot collection. The volume closes with a selected bibliography of other essays on Williams published in *Mythlore* from 1969 through 2018.

——Janet Brennan Croft

Introduction to "The Triumph of Love"

"The Triumph of Love: Interpretations of the Tarot in Charles Williams's *The Greater Trumps*" (1974) is not only the longest of the three papers included in this anthology, it also—given the subject matter and the fact that she was, at the time of its publication, only just beginning her career as a research scholar—most clearly demonstrates the originality of Nancy-Lou Patterson's scholarship. The ongoing significance of "The Triumph of Love" is fourfold. First, it considers the implications of the Tarot illustrations included with the 1950 and 1962 editions of Charles Williams's *The Greater Trumps* (1932). Second, it details the card symbolism as Williams re-envisioned it in literary terms. Third, it shows how Williams integrated his belief that Tarot cards show a process, indicated by the card order, into the novel's plot. Fourth, Patterson presents a clear perspective on Williams's theory of Tarot as aligned with that best argued many years after his novel was published by Gertrude Moakley (1956, 1966).

Numerous authors have addressed the work of Charles Williams since Patterson published "The Triumph of Love," but I have found only one citation of her paper,[1] and few authors have even paused to consider Williams's use of Tarot in *The Greater Trumps* at any length. Given the scarcity of scholarly research on the subject of Tarot, particularly in the 1970s, this lack of citation is not surprising: Patterson seems to have suffered, as Williams apparently did, from poor timing insofar as her publication was available before there was an extensive audience for it. Now, however, fiction is more widely accepted as a means of conveying thoughts and philosophical ideas and Williams's twenty-first century readers may be interested, not only in Patterson's paper, but in the sources and materials that Patterson would no doubt have used had she researched and written her paper twenty or thirty years later than she did. The purpose of this introduction and other supplements (charts, lists, illustrations) to Patterson's text is to aid the contemporary reader, particularly the Williams scholar without a background in Tarot studies, in their understanding of Patterson's accomplishment by

a) providing additional details regarding the Tarot illustrations included with certain editions of *The Greater Trumps* and the other decks that Patterson uses for comparative purposes,

b) demonstrating the general perception of the role of Tarot in *The Greater Trumps* by some more recent scholars,

c) highlighting the reasons for the few corrections made directly to this edition of "The Triumph of Love," and

d) briefly reviewing Williams's involvement with Arthur E. Waite in relation to Tarot.

Patterson used the 1962 Noonday printing of *The Greater Trumps* as the basis of her research, a printing that conforms to the 1950 edition in appearance and contents, including Americanized English spellings. The 1950 edition publication information is as follows: "© 1950 by Pellegrini & Cudahy. Manufactured in the United States of America. Design and typography by Jos. Trautwein." The publication information for the 1962 paperback edition is given on the full title page as "The Noonday Press a division of Farrar, Straus and Cudahy New York," and on the back of that page as "Copyright © 1950 Pellegrini & Cudahy. Library of Congress catalog card number 50-6710 First Noonday Printing, 1962. Manufactured in the U.S.A." The Noonday Press was officially founded in 1951 by Cecil Hemley and Arthur A. Cohen.[2]

The 1950 and 1962 editions both include the preface written by American author William Lindsay Gresham (1909–1962) in 1949 and Tarot card illustrations printed on the front and end papers. These images are arranged in three rows across two pages in the front and two pages in the back of the book in an order that conforms with the roman numerals on the cards and provided in the novel itself. The top row of the front pages includes The Juggler, The Empress, High Priestess, and Hierophant; the second The Emperor, The Chariot, and The Lovers; and the third The Hermit, Temperance, Fortitude, and Justice. The top row of the back pages includes the Wheel of Fortune, Hanged Man, Death, and The Devil; the second the Falling Tower, The Star, and The Moon; and the third The Sun, Last Judgment, The Universe, and The Fool.

These illustrations are not in the first edition of the novel of 1932 and the executors for the literary estates of Charles Williams and for William Gresham know nothing about them.[3] Since Williams died in 1945, it seems unlikely that he is responsible for them, except by way of inspiring their inclusion. It may be that they were produced or provided by Gresham, who was the author of the famous Tarot novel *Nightmare Alley* (1946), made into the equally famous film noir of the same title in 1947, but simply escaped identification in the listing of his intellectual property. It is also possible that they were added by the original publisher, but, if so, they no longer have a record of how that came about or who actually created the drawings.[4]

Patterson assumes that Tarot is an essential part of *The Greater Trumps*—the illustrations and title being obvious clues in that regard—and proceeds to study Williams's characters and plot developments relative to Tarot as a sequence of trumps or triumphs. The seriousness with which she examines Williams's use of Tarot amplifies the attitude expressed in a few earlier articles published through the auspices of the Mythopoeic Society, such as Galen Peoples's "The Agnostic in The Whirlwind: The Seven Novels of Charles Williams" (1970) and Laura A. Ruskin's "Three Good Mothers: Galadriel, Psyche, & Sybil Coningsby" (1970).[5] Patterson goes much further than these authors, however, in acknowledging that Williams's novels are not, strictly speaking, fantasies because they are about kinds of experiences that were actually known to the author. One of the few scholars to immediately follow Patterson's lead is Charles Huttar, who acknowledged her work in the notes to his "Charles Williams's Christmas Novel: *The Greater Trumps*" (1983). In this paper, Huttar relates Williams's descriptions and references to cards in his novel to the themes of "seeking, fruition, and the theme of time itself."[6] Some unsubstantiated assignations of meaning to individual cards notwithstanding, Huttar's analysis in no way duplicates Patterson's research and is well worth locating and reading.

Otherwise, indications of scholarly regard for Williams's use of Tarot in *The Greater Trumps* seem infrequent and lacking in dedication until Gareth Knight's treatment of the subject in his *The Magical World of the Inklings* (1990). Thomas Howard (1983) writes dismissively of the hodgepodge that passes for the history of Tarot—certainly a valid critical view until Stuart Kaplan published the first volume of his *Encyclopedia of Tarot* in 1978—and concludes that Sybil is the "triumphant" character, insofar as she knows nothing of the "occult" and does understand a great deal about "love." This, he observes, places her in stark contrast with Henry who is fixated on Tarot as a key to occult knowledge and power. Howard associates Williams's thematic approach to love with his ideas about the affirmation and negation of "images." Howard believes that Sybil and Nancy represent what Williams called the affirmation of images insofar as the meaning of images is already known to them; while Aaron Lee, a character of the hermit type, represents the negation of images insofar as he believes he needs a key of some sort to decipher the meaning of the Tarot figures he possesses.[7]

Glen Cavaliero (1983) thinks that Williams used Tarot in *The Greater Trumps* "as a symbol of the creative power of God" and that the separation of the Tarot figures from the cards "symbolizes the separation between reason and knowledge [...] It is an image of the Fall."[8] He does not emphasize the connection between the cards and Sybil in his discussion, but rather that between the cards and Joanna who, believing she is Isis, "vainly searches for her dead child, craving the Tarot cards as a means of satisfying her own warped will to love, warped since it is an example of the inevitably thwarted human urge to love on one's own terms rather than to accommodate one's self-will to its predestined end."[9]

Gareth Knight (1990), like Patterson and unlike Howard and Cavaliero, has a thorough grasp of the history of Tarot apart from that narrated in Williams's novel, and realizes that Williams is drawing on first hand familiarity with ritual and magic. His conclusions about the role of Tarot in it are correspondingly more sophisticated:

> The novel is as much about the initiation of Nancy into love as it is about the Tarot cards per se, until one realizes that the Tarot, as an accurate representation of the archetypal forces of the universe, is itself centred upon the principle of incarnate love. The fact is that love needs and demands a response from whoever comes into its presence. It cannot relate to the closed heart.[10]

Only Sybil can see the figures move because she is the only one with this understanding of love; the others are more involved in a "desire for power" or the manipulation of others to their will.[11] Sybil and, through her influence, Nancy, ultimately engage in "a mighty act of redemptive magic" when Sybil saves Nigel from the storm and Nancy pulls Henry back from the brink. Knight concludes that these characters demonstrate the "coming to terms with the powers of the Tarot through their own spiritual realization [...]"[12]

Robert Peckham (1993) has also clearly given the subject a great deal of thought and believes that Tarot cards provided Williams with a "metaphorical vehicle," such that the suit images serve magic insofar as they are the images that correspond with reality. The derniers suit cards, for example, serve as the "images of the powers of earth." Peckham finds the distinction between image and reality as central not only to magic, but to Williams's "way of the affirmation of the images." Affirming "the glory of creation in the images of reality was beginning his journey to God; in the process he must be aware that the images are not the reality […]" Peckham emphasizes Nancy as the novel's heroine, rather than Sybil, and identifies her as "the Queen of Chalices, i.e. of love."[13]

Scott McLaren (2006) understands Williams's use of Tarot in terms of "Platonic correspondence[s] between the dancing figures in the wider world so tightly [sic] that Henry's explanation of the relationship between the two seems to skirt determinism: 'If you cry, it's because the measure will have it so; if you laugh, it's because some gayer step demands it […]'"[14] He observes that while Henry tries to use the cards as a magical tool by which he can exert his will over others, Sybil's understanding is based on the inherent goodness of such correspondences.[15] Henry's way is a form of black magic. Sybil's way represents a kind of "transcendent mysticism." This way is the way to the "experience of interconnectedness, the Co-inherence, of the cosmos and the goodness of being in itself."[16]

Joyce Goggin (2014) addresses the centrality of Tarot as a device used to create magic, and takes note of some of the associations Williams himself makes regarding the purported history of Tarot in his novel, such as those with Egypt, gypsies, and so forth, and the prevalence of these associations in the early twentieth century. She specifically discusses the significance of Williams's association of the Fool with zero,[17] thus acknowledging the importance of order in Tarot and its presentation in *The Greater Trumps*.

Grevel Lindop takes up the subject of Tarot in *The Greater Trumps* in the context of Williams's biography, *Charles Williams: The*

Third Inkling (2015). He confirms that Williams owned a Marseilles-style Tarot deck, as well as the *Rider-Waite Tarot,*[18] and takes note of the specialized knowledge of the cards informing their treatment in the novel, which shows

> all four suits of cards used magically to create the material elements to which they relate—most vividly when Henry attempts magical murder by using the court-cards of staves and cups (corresponding to air and water) to summon a blizzard […][19]

He also recognizes that the characters are not only identified with individual cards—Lothair as the Fool, his sister Sybil as the Empress, and so forth—but that the characters also experience the cards, as when Henry Lee "temporarily becomes the falling Tower of the tarot."[20] Williams, he writes, "could hardly have written" these and numerous other "visionary passages: meditations on the elements; or a panorama, from the tarot chamber […] all performing the endless dance which the tarot reflects" if he had not spent a great deal of time contemplating the symbolism and meaning of the deck. Of that contemplation, Lindop (rather sadly observes) only this novel remains.[21]

Patterson devotes her entire long paper to the subject of Tarot in *The Greater Trumps* and seems to be the only author to give careful consideration to Williams's redesigned Tarot. She discusses it in relation to its Marseilles template and the *Visconti-Sforza* deck, and with reference to the so-called "Gringonneur" Tarot, the *Rider-Waite* deck, and, by association, the Golden Dawn Tarot. She also mentions, in passing, the *Oswald Wirth* deck and the revised *Rider-Waite* deck associated with Paul Foster Case. Illustrations from all of these decks have been added to this current edition of Patterson's paper, as well as a few others that Williams is likely to have had access to, including some of Court de Gébelin's illustrations, some minchiate cards, and examples from the Etteilla deck, *Grand Jeu de Oracle des Dames* (1870); the *Egyptian Tarot* (1901), which is based on illustrations from Comte de Saint-Germain's *Practical Astrology* (1901); and the *Knapp-Hall Tarot* (1928) by Manly P. Hall and August Knapp.

The *Visconti-Sforza Tarrochi* is an important part of Patterson's discussion, as it is the earliest extant deck that is nearly complete: seventy-four cards from the original painted deck, also known as the Pierpont Morgan-Bergamo deck, still exist. Other decks from the mid-fifteenth century include the sixty-seven-card *Cary-Yale* deck and the forty-eight-card *Brera Gallery* deck. It is, however, the *Visconti-Sforza Tarot* that provides the basis of Moakley's thesis that Tarot cards are based on the idea of allegorical "trumps," similar to those represented in Petrarch's *I Trionfi* in which Love triumphs over all, but Chastity triumphs over Love, Death triumphs over Chastity, and so forth. Patterson summarizes Moakley's discussion of each card so that the context and significance of the imagery is already clear to her readers when she proceeds to her discussion of Tarot in Williams's novel.

The importance of the *Visconti-Sforza Tarot* as one of the earliest extant decks has been more recently addressed in volume I of Stuart Kaplan's four-volume *Encyclopedia of Tarot* (1978–2005). Moakley's thesis continues to be regarded as an essential contribution to the scholarship on Tarot history: Volume II of Kaplan's *Encyclopedia* includes an entire chapter about Petrarch's poem.[22] The *Visconti-Sforza* cards are also discussed and Moakley's thesis referenced in John Shephard's *The Tarot Trumps: Cosmos in Miniature* (1985), Michael Dummett's *The Visconti-Sforza Cards* (1986), and Helen Farley's *A Cultural History of Tarot from Entertainment to Esotericism* (2009). Robert Place elaborates on Moakley's thesis of Tarot cards as a series of allegorical "trumps" in his "Iconography and Allegory in Fifteenth to Seventeenth-Century Trumps" (2014).

Patterson mentions the "Gringonneur Tarot" for the purpose of enlarging her discussion of the images associated with the Juggler, World, Strength, Moon, Sun, Chariot, Hermit, Hanged Man, Death, and Tower cards. The descriptions of the cards she provides are accurate and useful; however, she repeats the attribution of the deck to the artist Gringonneur and to the year 1392, now known to be erroneous. The so-called Gringonneur deck was thought by some to have been made for King Charles VI of France (r. 1380–1422), and to have been among the prints and drawings left in 1711 to the King of France by Mons. de Gaignières, the governor of King Louis XIV's (r. 1643–1715) grandchildren.[23] The reason for the attribution of the deck—now just a partial deck of seventeen cards—to the early 1390s is a note purportedly written by Charles VI's treasurer that translates as follows: "Given to Jacquemin Gringonneur, painter, for three packs of cards, gilt and coloured, and variously ornamented, for the amusement of the king, fifty-six sols of Paris."[24] This sentence has been taken as a reference to the Tarot deck in question, but it more likely refers to regular playing decks. In addition, as early as 1848, William Chatto observed that the style, the rendering, and the costumes of the card figures suggest that they were made around 1425 or later, and more likely by an Italian than a French artist.[25]

This correction is further developed in *A Wicked Pack of Cards* (1996), along with new facts gathered by the authors of that volume—Ronald Decker, Michael Dummett, and Thierry Depaulis—who explain that the "Gringonneur" Tarot cards were in the collection of Roger de Gaignières no later than 1698 and that the cards themselves date somewhere between 1460 and 1490, with a strong probability that they were made around 1480 by a Ferrarese artist.[26] The costume, style, and design of two of these cards are, the authors observe, very like those of a set definitely made earlier for Ercole I d'Este, Duke of Ferrara (r. 1471–1505), or for his predecessor Borso d'Este (r. 1450–1471), of which fifteen cards remain as the property of the Museo Civico, Catania. Two cards from this earlier deck, the Hermit and the World, closely resemble the "Gringonneur" cards.[27] This resemblance supports Chatto's observation that the "Gringonneur" Tarot cards appeared to be more Italian than French and more fifteenth than fourteenth century in their appearance.

Unfortunately, the misdating of the "Gringonneur" Tarot deck to 1392 has been repeated by numerous authors from the nineteenth through the twentieth centuries, including Catherine Perry Hargrave, who, in her popular *A History of Playing Cards and a Bibliography of Cards and Gaming* (1930), identifies the 1392 account with the cards that are now kept in the Bibliotheque Nationale in Paris.[28] This error was repeated when the book was republished in exact duplicate in 1966: this is the copy Patterson used for her research and which scholars working outside the field still rely upon. Had the revised attribution of the earliest extant decks to the fifteenth century been known to her, Patterson would no doubt have adjusted her own comments regarding the origins of Tarot in the fourteenth century either by identifying the earliest extant painted decks as dating to the fifteenth century, or by contemplating the possibility of earlier printed decks. Patterson's references to the "Gringonneur" deck have therefore been corrected, with the corrections indicated in footnotes, directly in this edition of her paper.

Patterson identifies the Tarot used in the illustrations of *The Greater Trumps* as of the Marseilles type and realizes that the mismatch between the order indicated by the Roman numerals and the Hebrew letters on the cards has special significance, which she elaborates on in terms of triumphs, just as Moakley did with reference to the *Visconti-Sforza* deck. Williams gives the order of the cards on pages 14-15 of chapter one of his novel. That order conforms with the Roman numerals applied to the illustrations, and with no other known deck. The Hebrew letters indicate the order familiar to the popular Marseilles deck (Chart 13).

The Marseilles Tarot is not a single deck, but rather a type of deck showing a certain uniformity in card numbering and imagery. Among the earliest extant examples of this type is one now known as the *Jean Noblet Tarot* (c. 1650), but the Marseilles conventions may have developed as early as the second half of the fifteenth-century in either France or Italy, and became the most familiar form of Tarot by the eighteenth century, especially in France, where the game was popular.[29] The Marseilles deck on which the illustrations for Williams's novel were based and to which Hebrew letters were added for the novel illustrations appears to be the Milanese Tarot by G. Sironi (Milan, 1882).[30]

Although the original deck did not include Hebrew letters, it was the Marseilles Tarot that eighteenth and nineteenth-century occultists "rectified" to support their theories about Tarot and magic. The association of Tarot with Hebrew letters, as well as Egypt and gypsies, both of which Williams mentions in his novel, date back to the late eighteenth-century work of Antoine Court de Gébelin (1719–1784) and Le Comte de Mellet (1727–1804) published in Volume VIII of *Le Monde primitif* (1781). Subsequently, Etteilla (Jean-Baptiste Alliette 1738–1791) designed the first Tarot deck intended for divinatory and occult purposes by Egyptianizing the images, arranging them in a completely new order, and assigning the cards Hebrew letters in a continuous descending order.[31]

In the mid-nineteenth century, Éliphas Lévi (Alphonse Louis Constant 1810–1875) also associated the twenty-two Tarot trumps with the twenty-two letters of the Hebrew alphabet,[32] but he reversed the order of the assignment of the Hebrew letters, such that the order was ascending, and he placed the Fool between Judgment and the World.[33] No doubt because of its growing occult associations, Papus (Gérard Encausse 1865–1916) had his *Le Tarot des bohémiens: le plus ancien livre du monde* (1889) illustrated with both a Marseilles Tarot and Oswald Wirth's "restored" Tarot—a deck mentioned by Patterson in her discussion of Williams's literary treatment of the High Priestess. *Le Tarot des bohémiens* was translated into English (1892, 1896) and Arthur E. Waite wrote a foreword for the revised second edition.

Williams spoke of himself as belonging to the Golden Dawn, but, as Patterson notes, it seems clear that his association was not with the original Golden Dawn, but with an organization created later by Waite years after the original Golden Dawn disbanded called The Fellowship of the Rosy Cross. The Hermetic Order of the Golden Dawn was formed on March 1, 1888, by William Robert Woodman (1828–1891), William Westcott (1848–1925), and S.L. (MacGregor) Mathers (1854–1918), all of whom were members of the Christian Masonic order *Societas Rosicruciana in Anglia* (S.R.I.A.) [Rosicrucian Society of England]. Westcott was responsible for bringing to light the infamous Cypher manuscript, a document he claimed to have acquired from Reverend Adolphus F.A. Woodford (1821–1887).[34] This manuscript, which became the basis of the Golden Dawn order, includes outlines for rituals to graded levels of occult knowledge that follow those used since 1767 in Rosicrucian societies, such as the Society of the Golden and Rosy Cross. These grades include those of the "first order" from Zelator to Philosophus, plus a new introduction grade of Neophyte. It was at this level that initiates learned about Tarot, as well as astrology, geomancy, Kabbala, and so forth. The second, or "inner order," is the *Ordo Rosae Rubeae et Aureae Crucis* (RR. et A.C.) in which initiates began to practice magic, astral travel, and learn about alchemy. The name of the "third order" was known only to the initiated, but these individuals were supposed to receive directions from "Secret Chiefs" who did not exist on the physical plane.[35]

This system of advancement elaborated on Lévi's association of the twenty-two Tarot trumps with Hebrew letters, insofar as it aligned that advancement along the paths between the ten sephiroth of the kabbalistic Tree of Life.[36] The Golden Dawn system, as it was eventually presented in Knowledge Lecture Four, follows Lévi in making the letter assignments in ascending order, but it places the Fool at the beginning such that the letter Aleph is assigned to that card, rather than to the Magician as in Lévi, or the World as in De Mellet. To solve other perceived anomalies in the various astrological and kabbalistic correspondences, the places traditionally assigned to Justice and Strength in the standard Marseilles deck were reversed, so that Strength takes position eight and Justice position eleven.[37]

One of the most important documents on Tarot used by Golden Dawn initiates was an essay about Tarot known as *Book T*,[38] which had to be studied by those seeking admission to the inner order, along with a particular form of Tarot divination. While members initially used commercial decks, Mathers and his wife Moina are said to have designed a deck for initiates to copy, in which the transposition of Justice and Strength was confirmed.[39]

Arthur E. Waite became a member of the Golden Dawn in January of 1891. He found Golden Dawn beliefs and practices at least somewhat compatible with his own ideas about a secret tradition of Christianity, or Gnostic tradition, which he believed held the Holy Grail as its primary symbol,[40] as by April of the following year, he reached the highest first order grade. He then quit the group, but returned in February 1896, and finally joined the second order in March of 1899, by which time the organization was already falling apart.[41]

Ronald Decker and Michael Dummett explain in *A History of the Occult Tarot 1870–1970* (2002) that Waite's interest in occult studies was not limited to his involvement with the Golden Dawn.

> In 1886, he was the first to publish translations from Éliphas Lévi; in 1892, a translation appeared by A.P. Morton, a professional translator, of Papus' *Le Tarot des Bohémiens*, with the title mistranslated as *The Tarot of the Bohemians* (it should be *The Tarot of the Gypsies*). A second edition of this translation, lightly revised by Waite, with an extensive Preface by him, but with the title unaltered, was to come out in 1910. In 1896, Waite brought out a translation of Lévi's *Dogme et rituel de la haute magie*, with a Biographical Preface contributed by himself, under the title *Transcendental Magic: its Doctrine and Ritual*.[42]

In 1902, Waite joined the Freemasons and the *Societas Rosicruciana* (S.R.I.A.), to which the founders of the Golden Dawn had belonged.[43] In 1903, he became head of the Golden Dawn, renamed it the "Order of the Independent and Rectified Rite," and began disassociating its practices from what he called "lower occultism" or "practical magic," thereby causing some of the members to break away to form yet another group, the "Order of the Stella Matutina."[44] By 1914, Waite dissolved his renamed Order, and in 1915 founded "The Fellowship of the Rosy Cross" with ten former members of the Rectified Rite and ten recruits. This group, like the Golden Dawn, was based on advancement through grades, but Waite removed the Egyptian and explicitly pagan references from the rituals.[45]

In 1909, Waite published a new Tarot deck that he had developed with the assistance of artist Pamela Colman Smith (1878–1951), and in the following year he published a guidebook titled *The Pictorial Key to the Tarot* (1910).[46] The cards of this deck do not include Hebrew letters, but in the arrangement of the cards in *The Pictorial Key* he follows Lévi in placing the Fool, numbered 0, before the final World card, numbered 21. And, in spite of his skepticism and contradictory statements regarding the validity and value of the correspondences of Hebrew letters and Tarot trumps, Waite developed a Tree for use in the very Fellowship of the Rosy Cross to which Williams belonged, complete with Tarot assignments to the sephiroth and pathways. He also commissioned a new set of Tarot trumps, most of which were created in watercolor by artist John Brahms Trinick and dated 1921 or 1922 and later transformed by photographic means into plates; two images were completed by Wilfrid Pippet in 1923. Decker and Dummett included some black-and-white photographs from private collections of this Waite–Trinick Tarot in their *History of the Occult Tarot 1870–1970* (Plates 10, 11). They found these plates, although numbered outside the image frame as 0 and XI to XXXII and used by members of Waite's group as the "Great Symbols of the Paths," so transformed as to make comparison with the familiar forms of the deck difficult and their possible relationship with the Tree of Life obscure.[47]

The discovery of the original (and forgotten) set of images and their correspondences to the Tree of Life was only recently announced by Tali Goodwin and Marcus Katz in their publication

Abiding in the Sanctuary: The Waite–Trinick Tarot A Christian Mystical Tarot (1917–1923) (2011). Goodwin and Katz discovered that plates of the Waite–Trinick Tarot dated 1921–1923 were bequeathed by Waite's executors to the British Museum in 1973 where, according to the museum's records, they were never studied or even viewed. Goodwin and Katz believe that Waite may have intended to complete a full set of 32 images to correspond to the twenty-two paths and ten *Sephiroth* of the Tree of Life, but even the initial set of twenty-three—the standard twenty-two trumps plus an image for "Da'ath"—remained unfinished as five are incomplete. Goodwin and Katz do not believe these images were intended for use as cards, but rather "They were likely hung in the temple and a set of plates [was] created from the images, possibly for personal study by members of the FRC."[48] Even more intriguing is Katz's discovery that the assignments Waite made of the trumps to the Tree of Life paths differ from those that became standard in the Golden Dawn. While this order does not show a correspondence to that implied in the illustrations accompanying Gresham's preface to *The Greater Trumps*, the revelation of Waite's second Tarot, designed and executed for ritual purposes during the years of Williams's involvement with The Fellowship of the Rosy Cross is profound.

It was, however, the deck Waite designed with Pamela Colman Smith that became the most popular deck of the twentieth and twenty-first centuries: many authors, including Patterson, refer to it as the *Waite-Smith Tarot* and many Tarotists and artists have revised it according to their own interests and purposes. Paul Foster Case (1884–1954), for example, was a member of the Golden Dawn lodge in New York City, the Alpha et Omega, in the early 1920s. He wrote various papers and books on Tarot and set up his own school, later called the Builders of the Adytum, and Tarot course. Eventually, Jesse Burns Parke created a revised *Rider-Waite* Tarot, possibly from directions in Case's 1931 publication "Highlights of the Tarot," which was published in Case's book *The Tarot* (1947).[49] Case and Parke's deck is cited by Patterson in her discussion of the various approaches to Tarot card order.

Waite's work on Tarot was certainly known to Williams. Williams was reading Waite's books by 1912, met Waite in 1915, and in September of 1917, just a few months after he married in April, he became a neophyte in Waite's Salvator Mundi Temple of the Fellowship of the Rosy Cross.[50] As Lindop notes,

> his progress in the Fellowship was rapid. Between September 1917 and July 1919 he passed through six grades in all: those of Neophyte, Zelator, Theoreticus, Practicus, Philosophus, and Adeptus Minor. [...]
>
> Besides the Kabbala, the rituals drew on symbolism from alchemy and the tarot. The Zelator ritual, for example, involved a bowl of earth to symbolize the postulant's physical body and "body of life," which he or she was to purify. At the Theoreticus ritual, earth was again produced, this time said to be "transmuted" into "living and philosophical stones" for the building of the Temple. The Zelator ritual and those beyond it each involved the display of a large tarot card, specially painted, which symbolized the path to the next stage of attainment, and which was explained to the postulant in a lengthy speech.[51]

Williams was still involved with this Fellowship in 1927, as he participated in one of the ceremonies Waite devised for its advanced grade.[52] In 1939, Williams formed his own Order of the Co-inherence composed of members who joined of their own volition, rather than by petition as in the various Golden Dawn associations and those developed by Waite.[53] In conformity with these other secret societies, however, Williams's Order was based on advancement through grades or stages of initiation.

Through Waite, Waite's books, and Waite's Fellowship Williams would have learned about Tarot, as well as the Tetragrammaton, talismans, Grail, and the sephiroth, all images that he used in his novels and poetry. Humphrey Carpenter (1978) speculates that

> Perhaps, too, Williams's developing notions of human love as a ladder to God owed something to Waite's account of the concept of marriage in the Zohar, which pictures the nuptial union on earth as a type of, and path of approach to, the mystical union in heaven. And it was also from Waite's writings that Williams likely acquired at least some of his knowledge of black magic.[54]

Although Waite discouraged white magic (magia) and absolutely opposed black magic (goetia), it is likely that Williams studied other sources, such as the novels and stories of popular authors, as well as the work of Aleister Crowley.[55]

The Hebrew letters on the Marseilles-style Tarot illustrations accompanying the 1950 and 1962 editions of *The Greater Trumps*—as Patterson noticed—assert the traditional order of the Marseilles deck, but the roman numerals show the unique order Williams assigned to the cards in the novel. This uniqueness is evident in the cards numbered up to fifteen; the later cards, from card fifteen, the Devil, to the end, conform to both the Marseilles and Golden Dawn norms. In creating this new order, Williams followed the practice of nineteenth-century occultists, but in specifics he ignored the Golden Dawn practice followed by Waite of transposing the places of Justice and Strength. He also ignored Waite's placement of the Fool between the Judgement and World cards, and put him at the end. Even the Tarot illustrations are arranged so that it appears that he is, quite literally, departing from the novel. To Williams the Fool was outside the trump sequence and was thus appropriately assigned the Arabic numeral 0, but he just as clearly regarded the Fool as the final "word" in Tarot—outside and beyond all of the Triumphs, including the Triumph of Love—and thus just as appropriately deserving of the very last letter in the Hebrew alphabet, number twenty-two: Tav or Taw.

Notes

[1] See Charles Huttar's "Charles Williams's Christmas Novel: *The Greater Trumps*," *Seven: An Anglo-American Literary Review* 4 (1983): 80 note 5.

[2] Farrar, Straus and Company was founded in 1945 and renamed itself Farrar, Straus and Young in 1951. In 1953, it purchased the Chicago-based Pellegrini & Cudahy and later became Farrar, Straus and Cudahy. Farrar, Straus and Cudahy subsequently purchased the Noonday Press. In 1965, the company became Farrar, Straus and Giroux; the Noonday Press continues to be listed as one of its divisions. I found some information about "Farrar, Straus and Giroux Inc." in Company Histories < http://www.fundinguniverse.com/company- histories/Farrar-Straus-and-Giroux-Inc-Company-History.html>.

[3] The illustrations and preface have recently reappeared in an edition of the novel from Regent College Publishing in Vancouver. This publisher received the rights to publish the novel from the literary agency that represents Williams's literary estate (Watkins/Loomis) and gave me their contact information.

Julia Masnik of Watkins/Loomis (literary agents representing the literary estate of Charles Williams) explained "Unfortunately, I don't know anything (nor do I have anything in my files) about the Tarot illustrations in *The Greater Trumps*" (email Jan. 14, 2016). After checking with her UK counterparts, she confirmed "Unfortunately, our co-agents didn't have much more to go on. They have two copies of the book in their office, neither of which have the tarot illustrations, so those copyright notices aren't helpful. We do highly doubt that Williams would've done the drawings, given that they first appeared in a 1950 version of the book, and Williams died in 1945, but I'm afraid that's about all I know" (Email 15 Jan 2016).

Lina M. Granada of Brandt & Hochman Literary Agents, Inc., New York (literary agency representing the literary estate of William Gresham) wrote "I would suggest you contact the publisher of that edition that includes the illustrations. We have no information on the illustrator as we would not have represented him" (Email 15 Jan 2016).

Notes

[4] Farrar, Strauss and Giroux does not have any information about the artist who contributed the Tarot illustrations to *The Greater Trumps* (1950, 1962) and does not claim any control over the rights to them. They did ask that the illustrations be cited as "Courtesy of Farrar, Straus and Giroux, LLC" (Letter from Angelica Roman, Permissions Dept. Farrar, Straus & Giroux, 15 Apr 2016).

[5] Glen Peoples, "The Agnostic in the Whirlwind: The Seven Novels of Charles Williams," *Mythlore* 2.2 (#6) (1970): 10-15; and Laura A. Ruskin, "Three Good Mothers: Galadriel, Psyche, and Sybil Coningsby," *Mythcon I, Harvey Mudd College, Claremont, CA, 1970*, ed. Glen GoodKnight (Los Angeles: Mythopoeic Society, 1970) 12–14.

[6] Huttar 70.

[7] Thomas Howard, *The Novels of Charles Williams* (New York and London: Oxford UP, 1983) 130-32.

[8] Glen Cavaliero, *Charles Williams: Poet of Theology* (1983; Eugene, OR: Wipf & Stock, 2007) 76-77.

[9] Cavaliero 77.

[10] Gareth Knight, *The Magical World of the Inklings* (Shaftesbury, Dorset, UK: Element Books 1990) 183-84.

[11] Knight 184.

[12] Knight 185.

[13] Robert Peckham, "Rhetoric and the Supernatural in the Novels of Charles Williams," *Renascence* 45 (1993): 240.

[14] Scott McLaren, "Hermeticism and the Metaphysics of Goodness in the Novels of Charles Williams," *Mythlore* 93/94 (Winter/Spring 2006): 24.

[15] McLaren 24.

[16] McLaren 29.

[17] Joyce Goggin, "*The Greater Trumps*: Charles Williams and the Metaphysics of Otherness," *Tarot in Culture, Volume Two* (Clifford, ON: Valleyhome Books, 2014) 411-39.

[18] Grevel Lindop, *Charles Williams: The Third Inkling* (NY: Oxford UP, 2015) 194. Lindop details some of the rituals Williams would have known through his association with Waite and these have obviously influenced the imagery of *The Greater Trumps*. Lindop does not

Notes

detail these connections directly, but they are obvious to anyone reading Lindop's book who has already read the novel.

[19] Lindop, *Charles Williams: The Third Inkling* 195.

[20] Lindop, *Charles Williams: The Third Inkling* 195.

[21] Lindop, *Charles Williams: The Third Inkling* 195.

[22] The deck may have been made to commemorate the marriage of Francesco Sforza and Bianca Maria Visconti in 1441. Stuart Kaplan, *The Encyclopedia of Tarot*, vol. I (Stamford, CT: US Games, 1978) 106-07.

[23] William Andrew Chatto, *Facts and Speculations on the Origin and History of Playing Cards* (London: John Russell Smith, 1848) 195.

[24] Chatto 76.

[25] Chatto 197.

[26] Ronald Decker, Thierry Depaulis, and Michael Dummett, *A Wicked Pack of Cards: The Origins of the Occult Tarot* (New York: St. Martin's, 1996) 28.

[27] Decker, Depaulis, and Dummett 266 note 11.

[28] Catherine Perry Hargrave, *A History of Playing Cards and a Bibliography of Cards and Gaming* (1930; Toronto, Ontario: General Publishing Co., 1966) 31. Hargrave was not the last to repeat the error. See also Roger Tilley's *A History of Playing Cards* (1973).

[29] Stuart Kaplan, *Encyclopedia of Tarot* vol. II (Stamford, CT: US Games, 1986) 270; see also Decker, Depaulis, and Dummett 25.

[30] This deck is illustrated in Kaplan's *Encyclopedia of Tarot*, vol. I, 164. Note the word "Milano" on the Empress card, the Tower, and other design elements that match *The Greater Trumps* illustrations. This deck seems to be part of the design tradition associated with Carlo Dellarocca's "Soprafino" designs published by Gumppenberg in the 1820s or 1830s, and to various later editions from Edoardo Dotti. See Kaplan, Vol. II, pp. 360-62, 369, 370-73, especially p. 373. The Tower card, where it is reproduced, makes the easiest distinguishing comparison.

[31] See relevant date entries in Mary K. Greer's "Tarot Timeline 1750 to 1980," *Tarot in Culture, Volume One* (Clifford, ON: Valleyhome Books, 2014) 301-64; Ronald Decker and Michael Dummett, *A History of the Occult Tarot 1870–1970* (London: Duckworth, 2002) 85.

Notes

[32] Decker and Dummett 82. On the different associations of Tarot trumps and Hebrew letters, see Decker and Dummett 77-78; 82-83; 97-100. Decker and Dummett provide two charts that make the changes in the attributions explicit.

[33] Decker and Dummett 84-85.

[34] On the Cypher manuscript, see Decker and Dummett p 86-87, as well as Ellic Howe's chapter "Suspect Documents," in *The Magicians of the Golden Dawn A Documentary History of a Magical Order 1887–1923* (1972; York Beach, ME: Samuel Weiser, 1978) 1-25.

[35] On the Golden Dawn order and grades, see Decker and Dummett 78; and Israel Regardie, *The Golden Dawn: A Complete Course in Practical Ceremonial Magic*, sixth edition (St, Paul, MN: Llewellyn, 1993).

[36] Decker and Dummett 78, 82.

[37] On the "secret attribution," see Decker and Dummett 84-85 and citations in note 29 above.

[38] "Book 'T'–The Tarot," in Regardie, *The Golden Dawn* 540-65; and in Robert Wang's *An Introduction to The Golden Dawn Tarot* (York Beach, ME: Samuel Weiser, 1978) 64-102.

[39] Decker and Dummett 97. Some of Moina's original drawings are available in Moina Mathers and W.W. Westcott, *The Golden Dawn Court Cards*, second edition (Sequim, WA: Holmes Publishing Group, 2006).

[40] Humphrey Carpenter, *The Inklings: C.S. Lewis, J.R.R. Tolkien, Charles Williams, and their friends* (Boston: George Allen & Unwin, 1978) 82.

[41] Decker and Dummett 121. Westcott had been forced to resign and Mathers, having been suspended from his position in 1900 (114), eventually founded his own club, the "Order of the Alpha et Omega Temple" (A.O.) (123)

[42] Decker and Dummett 120-21.

[43] On Waite's contribution to the fragmentation of the Golden Dawn, see Decker and Dummett 121-22.

[44] Decker and Dummett 122.

[45] Decker and Dummett 143.

Notes

[46] For a full history of the *Rider-Waite* deck, see K. Frank Jensen's *The Story of the Waite-Smith Tarot* (Victoria, Aus.: Association for Tarot Studies, 2006).

[47] Decker and Dummett 157-59.

[48] Tali Goodwin and Marcus Katz, with a preface by Mary K. Greer, *Abiding in the Sanctuary: The Waite-Trinick Tarot A Christian Mystical Tarot (1917–1923)* (Keswick: Forge Press, 2011) 24. Goodwin and Katz clearly see their book as part of research-in-progress.

[49] See related entries in Greer, "Tarot Timeline 1750 to 1980."

[50] Thomas Willard, "Acts of the Companions: A.E. Waite's Fellowship and the Novels of Charles Williams," *Secret Texts: The Literature of Secret Societies*, eds. Marie Mulvey Roberts and Hugh Ormsby-Lennon (New York: AMS Press, 1995) 269-70, 272. The history of Williams's involvement with Waite's societies is summarized by Willard, as well as Huw Mordecai (1995), Gavin Ashenden (2008), and others.

[51] Lindop, *Charles Williams: The Third Inkling* 76.

[52] Willard 273.

[53] Willard 276.

[54] Carpenter 82.

[55] Carpenter 82-83.

Introduction Bibliography

Ashenden, Gavin. *Charles Williams: Alchemy and Integration*. Kent, Ohio: Kent State UP, 2008.

Auger, Emily E., ed. *Tarot in Culture, Volumes One and Two*. Clifford, ON: Valleyhome Books, 2014.

Brewer, Elisabeth. "Charles Williams and Arthur Edward Waite." *VII: An Anglo-American Literary Review* 4 (1983): 45-67.

Brodie-Innes, J. W. "The Tarot Cards." *The Occult Review* XXIX.2 (Feb. 1919). Scanned and corrected by hand and posted at Hermetic fellowship website.

Caldwell, Ross Gregory. "The Gringoneur Case." Trionfi <http://trionfi.com/0/p/15/>.

Carpenter, Humphrey. *Inklings: C.S. Lewis, J.R.R. Tolkien, Charles Williams, and their Friends*. Boston: George Allen & Unwin, 1978.

Cavaliero, Glen. *Charles Williams Poet of Theology*. 1983. Eugene, OR: Wipf & Stock, 2007.

Chatto, William Andrew. *Facts and Speculations on the Origin and History of Playing Cards*. London: John Russell Smith, 1848. [available on-line]

Decker, Ronald, and Michael Dummett. *A History of the Occult Tarot 1870–1970*. London: Duckworth, 2002.

Decker, Ronald, Thierry Depaulis, and Michael Dummett. *A Wicked Pack of Cards: The Origins of the Occult Tarot*. New York: St. Martin's, 1996.

Dummett, Michael. *The Visconti-Sforza Tarot Cards*. New York: George Braziller, 1986.

Farley, Helen. *A Cultural History of Tarot from Entertainment to Esotericism*. New York: I. B. Tauris, 2009.

Gauntlett, Edward. "Charles Williams and Magic." *Newsletter of the Charles Williams Society* 25 (2008). Available on line at: http://www.cwsociety.dreamhosters.com/?p=7

Gébelin, Court de. "The Game of Tarots." *Monde primitif.* Volume 8. Book 1 (1781). Public Domain. Trans. Donald Tyson. <http://www.donaldtyson.com/gebelin.html>.

Goggin, Joyce. "*The Greater Trumps*: Charles Williams and the Metaphysics of Otherness." *Tarot in Culture, Volume Two.* Ed. Emily E. Auger. Clifford, ON: Valleyhome Books, 2014. 411-37.

Goodwin, Tali, and Marcus Katz, with Preface by Mary K. Greer, *Abiding in the Sanctuary: The Waite-Trinick Tarot A Christian Mystical Tarot (1917–1923)*. Keswick: Forge Press, 2011.

Greer, Mary K. "The Iconographic History of the Lovers Card." *Tarot in Culture, Volume Two.* Ed. Emily E. Auger. Clifford, ON: Valleyhome Books, 2014. 559-96.

—— "Tarot Timeline 1750 to 1980." *Tarot in Culture, Volume One.* Ed. Emily E. Auger. Clifford, ON: Valleyhome Books, 2014. 301-64.

Hadfield, Alice M. Charles Williams. *An Exploration of His Life and Work*. New York: Oxford UP, 1983.

Hargrave, Catherine Perry. *A History of Playing Cards and a Bibliography of Cards and Gaming*. 1930. Toronto, Ontario: General Publishing Co., 1966.

Howard, Thomas. *The Novels of Charles Williams*. New York and London: Oxford UP, 1983.

Howe, Ellic. *The Magicians of the Golden Dawn A Documentary History of a Magical Order 1887–1923*. 1972. York Beach, ME: Samuel Weiser, 1978.

Huttar, Charles. "Charles Williams's Christmas Novel: *The Greater Trumps*," *Seven: An Anglo-American Literary Review* 4 (1983): 68-83.

Jensen, K. Frank. *The Story of the Waite-Smith Tarot*. Victoria, Aus.: Association for Tarot Studies, 2006.

Kaplan, Stuart, et al. *The Encyclopedia of Tarot*. 4 vols. U.S. Games Systems, 1978–2005. Vol. I (1978). Vol. II (1986). Vol. III (1990). Vol. IV (2005).

Knight, Gareth. *The Magical World of the Inklings*. Shaftesbury, Dorset, UK: Element Books 1990.

Lindop, Grevel. "Charles Williams and his Contemporaries." *Charles Williams and His Contemporaries*. Eds. Suzanne Bray and Richard Sturch. Newcastle upon Tyne: Cambridge Scholars Publishing, 2009.

—— *Charles Williams: The Third Inkling*. NY: Oxford UP, 2015.

Mathers, Moina and W.W. Westcott. *The Golden Dawn Court Cards*, Second edition. Sequim, WA: Holmes Publishing Group, 2006.

McLaren, Scott. "Hermeticism and the Metaphysics of Goodness in the Novels of Charles Williams." *Mythlore* 93/94 (Winter/Spring 2006): 5-33.

Moakley, Gertrude. *The Tarot Cards Painted by Bonifacio Bembo for the Visconti-Sforza Family: An Iconographic and Historical Study*. New York: The New York Public Library, 1966.

—— "The Tarot Trumps and Petrarch's *Trionfi*: Some Suggestions on their Relationship." *Bulletin of the New York Public Library* (Feb. 1956): 55-69.

Mordecai, Huw. "Charles Williams and the Occult." *Charles Williams: A Celebration*. Ed. Brian Horne. Herefordshire: Gracewing Gowler Wright Books, 1995. 265-75.

Newman, Barbara. "Charles Williams and the Companions of the Coinherence." *Spiritus: A Journal of Christian Spirituality* 9.1 (Spring 2009): 1-26.

Peckham, Robert. "Rhetoric and the Supernatural in the Novels of Charles Williams." *Renascence* 45 (1993): 337-246.

Peoples, Galen. "The Agnostic in the Whirlwind: The Seven Novels of Charles Williams." *Mythlore* 2.2 (#6) (1970): 10-15.

Place, Robert. "Iconography and Allegory in Fifteenth to Seventeenth-Century Trumps." *Tarot in Culture, Volume Two*. Ed. Emily E. Auger. Clifford, ON: Valleyhome Books, 2014. 17-55.

Regardie, Israel. *The Golden Dawn: A Complete Course in Practical Ceremonial Magic*. 1971. Sixth edition. St. Paul, MN: Llewellyn, 1993.

Ridler, Anne. *The Image of the City and Other Essays by Charles Willliams*. London: Oxford UP, 1958.

Ruskin, Laura A. "Three Good Mothers: Galadriel, Psyche, and Sybil Coningsby." *Mythcon I, Harvey Mudd College, Claremont, CA, 1970*. Ed. Glen GoodKnight. Los Angeles: Mythopoeic Society, 1970. 12–14.

Shephard, John. *The Tarot Trumps: Cosmos in Miniature: The Structure and Symbolism of the Twenty-Two Tarot Trump Cards*. Wellingborough, Northamptonshire: Aquarian Press, 1985.

Spencer, Kathleen. "Naturalizing the Fantastic: Narrative Techniques in the Novels of Charles Williams." *Extrapolation* 28.1 (1987): 62-74.

Tilley, Roger. *A History of Playing Cards*. New York: Clarkson N. Potter, 1973.

—— *Playing Cards*. © 1967. London: Octopus Books, 1973.

Tolkien, J.R.R. "On Fairy-stories." *The Tolkien Reader*. New York: Ballantine Books, 1966. 33-99.

Wang, Robert. *An Introduction to The Golden Dawn Tarot*. York Beach, ME: Samuel Weiser, 1978.

Willard, Thomas. "Acts of the Companions: A.E. Waite's Fellowship and the Novels of Charles Williams." *Secret Texts: The Literature of Secret Societies*. Eds. Marie Mulvey Roberts and Hugh Ormsby-Lennon. New York: AMS Press, 1995. 269-302. Available on-line at <http://arizona.academia.edu/ThomasWillard/Papers/143381/_Acts_of_the_Companions_A._E._Waites_Fellowship_and_the_Novels_of_Charles_Williams_>.

Editorial Notes

This anthology includes all of Nancy-Lou Patterson's papers on Charles Williams that we have been able to locate. Unfortunately, several conference papers that she presented on his work seem to have disappeared entirely. Her numerous reviews of books about and relating to Williams and his work have been gathered and are available under a separate cover. Many of these books were published after Patterson wrote the papers gathered here; the original publication information for these reviews has been added to her bibliography citations in this volume.

Abstracts and credit paragraphs have been added to the published papers gathered here: "The Triumph of Love: Interpretations of the Tarot in Charles Williams's *The Greater Trumps*" (1974), "Jewels of Messias: Images of Judaism and Anti-semitism in the Novels of Charles Williams" (1979), and "Charles Williams" (1990). Where possible, quotations and sources have been checked and corrected as needed. References to bibles and dictionaries have been left as Patterson gave them with her notes regarding the versions and editions used. "Charles Williams" included a bibliography but it lacked specific notes, so all of those included in this version are editorial additions. Only those sources in the "Charles Williams" bibliography that Patterson cites specifically have been included in the general bibliography of this volume.

I corrected a few errors of fact in "The Triumph of Love" that do not impact Patterson's thesis, indicated these corrections in the notes, and explained them in "Introduction to 'The Triumph of Love.'" The sources for the "editor's notes" in the paper are given in the Introduction's bibliography, so as to preserve the original bibliography created by Patterson.

In addition, I added several charts and lists to clarify and amplify a number of Patterson's points and, in one or two places, matters of debate in Tarot scholarship. These charts include the triumphal arrangements proposed by Moakley for the *Visconti-Sforza Tarot* and by Williams in his novel:

Artists Patrick H. Wynne (cover), Sarah Beach, and Bonnie Callahan very generously contributed drawings that visualize some of the Tarot scenes. I added a number of Tarot card illustrations, some of which are mentioned in Patterson's text, and others from decks that were available and possibly known to Williams at the time he wrote his novel. These images are reproduced here courtesy of their publishers: U.S. Games and Lo Scarabeo.

By way of acknowledgements, I want to thank my co-editor Janet Brennan Croft, editor of *Mythlore*: without her interest in Patterson's work and generous contributions (research, source checking, indexing) this collection would simply never have come to publication. Mary K. Greer provided invaluable pointers for the Introduction. E Palmer Patterson and his daughters Fanny, Melanie, and Samantha have also been very supportive and generous with their time and interest.

In addition, I am grateful to Laura Schmidt, the archivist at the Marion E. Wade Center (Wheaton College, Wheaton, IL 60187), who quickly resolved several points regarding the publication history of *The Greater Trumps*. The Special Collections Library of the University of Waterloo (Waterloo, Ontario, Canada), which holds fonds relating to Nancy-Lou Patterson's research, provided me with copies of a number of letters relating to the paper at hand. Anita Streicher, the project archivist of the Special Collections section, was particularly helpful. All of the librarians with whom I came in contact at the Universities of Guelph, Waterloo, and Sir Wilfrid Laurier were extraordinarily helpful and interested in supporting this project. I also made extensive use of the library resources of the University of Regina and the University of Saskatchewan.

1. The Triumph of Love: Interpretations of the Tarot in Charles Williams's *The Greater Trumps*

Nancy-Lou Patterson's "The Triumph of Love" is a study of Tarot in The Greater Trumps *(1932) by Charles Williams. Patterson considers the views of critics and supporters of the novel and the interest in Tarot Williams shared with some of his contemporaries. She also gives much attention to arguments and sources, particularly those presented by Gertrude Moakley (1956, 1966), that show how the original Renaissance Tarot derived from a preoccupation with aspects of the past, notably the Roman triumph and its allegorization in Petrarch's poem* I Trionfi. *Her goal is not only to show the particular Tarot Williams describes in his novel, but to demonstrate that Williams's novel presents an understanding of Tarot cards as a sequence of triumphs, lending special attention to the triumph of Love and the appearance of the Fool.*

"The Triumph of Love: Interpretations of the Tarot in Charles Williams's The Greater Trumps*" was first presented at the Mythcon III conference held at Regency Hyatt House, Long Beach, Ca., 1972, and published in the proceedings of that conference, edited by Glen Goodknight (Los Angeles: The Mythopoeic Society, 1974) 12-32.*

I. The Greater Trumps

Illus. 1 "Nancy and the Trumps." Sarah Beach. First pub. *Mythlore* (#40) 11.2 (Autumn 1984): 32. Reproduced by permission of the artist. Further reproduction prohibited.

The Age of Aquarius has been prefigured repeatedly, and just as scholars now find the Renaissance in the twelfth century, and before that in Charlemagne's time, and so on back to the Hellenistic world from which it was born, so the contemporary fascination with the occult has enjoyed periodic rebirth. C.S. Lewis (1954) documents the attention to magic in the sixteenth century. It was, he writes, "a vigorous efflorescence of forbidden and phantasmal arts"[1] of "high magic: not concealed but avowed,"[2] for which the term "medieval survival" is inadequate. "We might reasonably call eighteenth-century magic, if there is any, a 'survival' from the seventeenth century."[3] The nineteenth century inherited this passion for the occult as part of Romanticism; and the cold bath of mid-nineteenth-century realism gave way to the arts and letters of the *fin-de-siècle* Symbolist movement, until, in the days of Charles Williams's (1886–1945) (and C.S. Lewis's) youth, a fascination with the occult was again in style.

Today, Charles Williams's novels are found on the shelves of occult bookshops, which have sprung up like mushrooms (Amanita muscaria, of course) in the past few years. Each of his seven novels deals with a specific occult motif, and in the present atmosphere their excitement is more easily understood than at any time perhaps, since they began to be written.[4] Each of the themes has been enriched by Williams's use of it, and perhaps none so greatly as that of the Tarot in *The Greater Trumps*, first published in 1932. William Lindsay Gresham (1949), who was the first husband of Joy Davidman, C.S. Lewis's wife, and who used the Tarot theme in his own writings, says of *The Greater Trumps* that "it has transformed the Tarot for the modern student."[5] Edmund Fuller (1962) explains:

> He [Williams] makes a brilliantly original contribution to an old cryptic tradition in his treatment of the Tarots. They have fascinated innumerable writers who have tried to take something out of them. Williams instead has brought something to them. Few of his inventions are more stunningly fine than the table of the little golden, dancing figures, the moving center, of which the cards are but illustrations and talismans.[6]

Richard Cavendish, a British journalist who has played a significant role in popularizing the occult, pays further tribute to the wide-ranging influence of *The Greater Trumps* in his book *The Black*

Arts (1968) where he writes of the Tarot in terms that are based directly on Williams's own invention:

> There is something extraordinarily fascinating about the Tarot. It opens strange windows into a world in which things are never quite what they seem, can never quite be grasped, a sunlit medieval landscape of tiny figures moving like marvelous toys—the Fool with cap and bells, the Emperor and Empress with a glittering cavalcade, Death at his reaping, the Hermit with staff and lamp, the Hanged Man swinging from his gibbet, the pale Tower falling. If they could be fully understood, occultists believe that these figures would reveal the secret of the inner mechanism of the universe, the hidden rhythms of the Dance of Life.[7]

There could scarcely be a better précis of the novel's theme, and the whole idea of the "tiny figures moving like marvelous toys" is Williams's own. How accurate his intuition is in the matter is the theme of the present essay.

The Greater Trumps is a typical Charles Williams novel. It begins in a banal family setting, introduces the occult theme, escalates the events to a supra-normal level that Carlos Castaneda would call a state of "non-ordinary reality," and finally relieves the tension, most of which has been created not only by the confrontation of good and evil but by the strain upon the original "ordinary" reality, through a eucatastrophic resolution.[8] It is typical, that is to say, of his first five novels. *Descent into Hell* (1937) and *All Hallows' Eve* (1945) are more deeply dramatic because the confrontation between good and evil, the sense of "real" danger is much more deeply felt, and because there is damnation as well as salvation for the characters in them.

In the earlier books, as Gunnar Urang (1971) says, "the focus is not only on the energy of the human imagination but also on certain objects, creatures and rituals which become centers of power."[9] Urang finds that "The novels of Charles Williams raise in us higher hopes than do those of C.S. Lewis, but they disappoint us more."[10] This is so, he states, because "the power of fantasy claims attention in its own right."[11] Williams, Urang says, lifts our visionary apprehension that "existence itself may be Christian" entirely "beyond our grasp by incorporating all these things in a supratemporal, suprapersonal vision of the whole. About to demonstrate the proposition that the power of being itself is the energy of Love, he instead projects a vision of power such as to inhibit the freedom, temporality, and concrete individuality without which love is merely empty form."[12] But love on a supratemporal and suprapersonal level is not merely empty form," it is the exact nature of the Holy Trinity which is, as C.S. Lewis has said, "Beyond personality." The vision of power as Williams evokes it in novel after novel, resembles that exhibited by God in his answer to Job. Urang concludes his criticism with the somewhat wistful statement that "When the fantasy leaves us incredulous, we discover that what we have found unbelievable is not […] the world of gracious possibility as such, but what has now become for us the other world of the *Consolation of Philosophy* or the *Summa*."[13]

What Urang implies is true, as Fuller attests: "Thus Williams brings the Tarots into what is in fact, though he deliberately chooses not to name it, a Christian symbolism."[14] As Gresham says, "In *The Greater Trumps* we have the Tarot of a Christian mystic, gifted with uncanny insight."[15] This is the root of his interpretation, and one of the very traits that disturb Urang. Alice Mary Hadfield (1969) explains Williams's method:

> In his experience, the extraordinary always used the commonplace, and once the extraordinary was recognized in the situation one's sights were raised and all extraordinary developments could be accepted and assimilated in the manner of the commonplace.[16]

In another study, she quotes a letter from Williams to Thelma Shuttleworth: "Once Love is believed to be actual and present […] powers entirely beyond our own are at work."[17] If the Tarot cards are used, then, "they are not brought in as trimmings or make-weights, but because C.W. grasped their particular point and glory, and saw what a remarkable tale could arise from it."[18] Hadfield states categorically of the novels, "They are not fantasies."[19] T.S. Eliot likewise explains, "Williams is telling us about a world of experience known to him,"[20] and "for him there was no frontier between the material and the spiritual world."[21] This is the point which is the most important to understand, and which so often confuses Williams's critics.

The story of *The Greater Trumps* is that of two ways of using power. On the one hand "the evil attempts at unlimited power center on possession of a power-giving object"[22]—"Aaron and Henry desire by the possession of a magical thing, the pack of Tarot cards, union with the power which creates and controls the matter of life."[23] As George Winship (1969) describes their function:

> In *The Greater Trumps* there is the same Tarot pack which fascinated Eliot when he wrote *The Waste Land*, the cards that reflect or direct the Great Dance of all that is. These are the true Cards, not the truncated pack of our bridge, poker, and gin, not the greasy cardboards of a fortune-teller, but the originals, with a cunningly-wrought automaton to correspond: the whole device, cards and machine, is powerful not in mere divination but in control of wind and weather, life and death.[24]

The climax of the novel comes when Henry Lee, the betrothed lover of Nancy Coningsby, tries to kill his future father-in-law, Lothair, because he will not give up the Tarot pack he owns so that it can be matched with the automata, owned by Henry's uncle, Aaron Lee. Henry plans to murder Lothair with a magical snow storm produced by manipulating the Tarot deck, and specifically by the suits controlling wind and water. It is at this point that goodness wields power:

> Sacrifice is the act by which evil is turned into good; he who, under God, performs the act is sacrificed. Williams' clearest illustration of this has [...] been described in terms of the conversion of energy: Nancy's confrontation with the storm in *The Greater Trumps*, where she draws upon herself the supernatural energy of the storm, and transmutes its magical power into natural energy.[25]

As theologian Mary McDermott Shideler (1962) observes, "Evil was converted into good by Nancy's passionate love, as simply as the direction of a bell is changed by impact with a surface."[26]

The secondary theme of the book, that of Aaron's mad sister Joanna's obsession that she is Isis, is resolved when she finds her lost child, Horus, to be Nancy. When Nancy's father Lothair protests that Horus is a boy, Nancy's aunt Sybil explains, on the very last page of the book:

> "No," Sybil said, "I mean Nancy. I don't think it much matters about girl or boy. She thought her child was Messias."
> "Oh!" Mr Coningsby said, "And is Nancy Messias?"
> "Near enough," Sybil answered. (GT 268; ch. 16)

This conflation of girl and savior would offend R.J. Reilly (1971) as much as does Williams's interpretation of the role of Beatrice for Dante in *The Divine Comedy*: "he loved both woman and God at the same time in seemingly the same way. Eros and agape merge: a single human affection may encompass both God and man."[27] Reilly finds this to be bad theology, because "Even if we distinguish as carefully as the Athanasian Creed does between substance and person, the identification of Beatrice and God seems hardly avoidable."[28] I make this comparison because Reilly mentions the Athanasian Creed, which Williams makes the second major symbol of his novel after the Tarot itself. Reilly objects that Williams's novels do not "clarify romantic theology," though "the girl in *The Greater Trumps* who created matter did so because she was really in love."[29] Here, Reilly is referring to Nancy, who, before meeting the storm with her own body, cooperated with Henry in creating earth by means of the Tarots. Reilly is distressed because "where one might hope to find some sort of explication of the particular duties of the romantic lover acting in accord with the Beatrician vision, one finds generally that the union of thought and feeling with a particular vision has produced, not the good life arrived at in a new way, but sheer power."[30] He seems to agree with Urang: "the 'occultism' of the novels prevents their being taken seriously as examples of romantic theology or of theologized true love."[31] But this is precisely the point: in Shideler's words: "love is like that figure among the Greater Trumps of the Tarot which 'is called the Fool, because mankind finds it folly till it is known. It is sovereign or it is nothing, and if it is nothing then man was born dead' [GT 227; ch. 14]. It may be that man was and is born dead. Or it may be that Williams is right when he declares that love is sovereign [...]"[32]

II. Occult and Unconscious

Illus. 2 "The Shuffling of the Cards." Sarah Beach. First pub. *Mythlore* (#40) 11.2 (Autumn 1984): 31. Reproduced by permission of the artist. Further reproduction prohibited.

Williams was most of all a great Christian mystic, one of the greatest of twentieth-century Anglican writers. His early experience of the occult only served to prepare him for this later role, for, as T.S. Eliot says of him, "His is a mysticism, not of curiosity, or of the lust for power, but of Love."[33] His theology has been discussed extensively by a number of writers, including Shideler, and it is not my intention to add to these studies. I only propose to explore his use of occult imagery in the novels, in particular the Tarot of *The Greater Trumps*.

I do not want to promote the use of the occult or other romantic materials for religious purposes as such, for as Williams so feelingly put it,

> It will—generally speaking—be an unfortunate day for Romantic Theology if it ever gets into the hands of the official ministers of the Church. The "stupor" [or sense of astonishment at the Beatrician vision, the unbidden epiphany of the godhead in direct experience] will, with the best intentions, be hideously organized and encouraged. The covenanted mercies are their concern. This, uncovenanted, rides in our very nature—within and without the Church; say, rather, this is that ancient covenant which reveals what all the others support. "My covenant shall be in your flesh."[34]

What was the experience of Williams with the "uncovenanted" mercies? Anne Ridler (1958) thinks that he belonged to the "new Rite"[35] by which in 1914, A.E. Waite had replaced the Isis-Urania Temple of London, itself taken over by Waite from W.B. Yeats—who had headed it as a dissident form derived from the Order of the Golden Dawn. Williams's wife was sure that he did not make contact with the order until after their marriage in 1917, which means that he could not have been a member of the Isis-Urania Temple version of the order of the Golden Dawn, so, "it would seem (according to the date given by Mrs. Williams) that it must have been to this later unnamed Order that Charles Williams belonged. Yet he always spoke of himself as having belonged to the Golden Dawn."[36] In any event, all of the abovementioned Orders derived from nineteenth-century studies of Rosicrucianism. His secretary, Alice Mary Hadfield (1959), says,

> He had learnt something of one of the great approaches to such a contemplation in his study of the Rosicrucian Order and the writings of A.E. Waite. He had touched the fringe of knowledge of occult sciences, of centres of hidden knowledge or mysteries, and the discipline and practice required of learners.[37]

Ridler reports that Williams "took pleasure in memorizing what had to be said [in the ceremonies of the Order] so that he could celebrate with dignity."[38]

Williams made several close friends in the Order, including a Church of England clergyman named, interesting enough, since the name appears in *The Greater Trumps*, Henry Lee.[39] Williams did not see Waite in later years, but continued to be influenced by him, especially by *The Secret Doctrine in Israel* (1913), which examines the *Zohar* and shows the Sephirotic Tree as a frontispiece.[40] Ridler thinks the book was the foundation of "his lifelong attempt to develop an adequate theology of marriage—and in this last, the influence of Waite can be distinguished from that of the Golden Dawn in its original form, for the subject of sex played no part in its teachings."[41] The influence of the entire experience—of his acquaintance with and study of A.E. Waite, and his actual membership in a magical Order—was, Ridler concludes, "considerable—witness the symbolism used in his novels (for instance the Tarot cards, the angelic hierarchies, the talisman, all of which were important to the Golden Dawn cosmology) [...].[42]

Williams has obviously not been the only twentieth-century writer to deal with the Tarot. The most famous, and certainly the most widely influential use of it is in *The Waste Land* (1922) by T.S. Eliot. The poem predates *The Greater Trumps* (1932) by ten years, and some examination of it is in order, to establish whatever influence it may have had upon Williams. The famous passage is as follows:

Madam Sosostris, famous clairvoyante,
Had a bad cold, nevertheless
Is known to be the wisest woman in Europe,
With a wicked pack of cards. Here, said she,
Is your card, the drowned Phoenician Sailor,
(Those are pearls that were his eyes. Look!)
Here is Belladonna, the Lady of the Rocks,
The lady of situations.
Here is the man with three staves, and here the Wheel
And here is the one-eyed merchant, and this card,
Which is blank, is something he carries on his back,
Which I am forbidden to see. I do not find
The Hanged Man. Fear death by water.
I see crowds of people, walking round in a ring.
Thank you. If you see dear Mrs. Equitone,
Tell her I bring the horoscope myself:
One must be so careful these days.[43]

—From T.S. Eliot's *The Waste Land* (1922)

Illus. 3 Madame Sosostris's Reading. From Catherine Waitinas, "Tarot as 'Secret Tradition' in T.S. Eliot's *The Waste Land*: 'These fragments I have shored against my ruins.'" *Tarot in Culture Volume Two*. Ed. Emily E. Auger. Clifford, ON: Valleyhome Books, 2014. 367-410. Illus. reproduced by permission of Catherine Waitinas. Further reproduction prohibited.

All card illustrations: Pamela Smith (artist) and Arthur Waite. *Rider-Waite Tarot®*. 1909. © 1971 U.S. Games Systems. Illus. reproduced by permission of U.S. Games Systems. Further reproduction prohibited.

Eliot's note on the symbolism of this passage—the footnotes are really part of the poem—details his interpretation:

> I am not familiar with the exact constitution of the Tarot pack of cards, from which I have obviously departed to suit my own convenience. The Hanged Man, a member of the traditional pack, fits my purpose in two ways; because he is associated in my mind with the Hanged God of Frazier, and because I associate him with the hooded figure in the passage of the disciples to Emmaus in Part V [...] The Man with Three Staves (an authentic member of the Tarot pack) I associate, quite arbitrarily, with the Fisher King himself.[44]

Reams of paper have been devoted to commentary on these few lines,[45] but the following is a very recent and evocative interpretation by Anthony Burgess (1972) who reports that he read the poem at the age of fifteen and promptly memorized it:

> We now have to meet Madame Sosotris, famous clairvoyant. An age that has rejected fertility has naturally rejected religion, which has its roots in ancient vegetation magic, and has to make do with such feeble substitutes as cartomancy. Madame Sosostris (her name seems to come from Flaubert's *Temptation of Saint Anthony*) tells fortunes with the old tarot pack. This, with its strange pictures of the Hanged Man and the Day of Judgment and the Tower Struck by Lightning, is of very venerable origin, being tied up with the grail legend and the myths of death and purification and rebirth that underlie it. Now the cards have been debased to serve a superstitious end, a forbidden prying into the future. Madame Sosostris is herself a debased seer—she has a bad cold and cannot speak very clearly—but she sees certain truths: the crowd of people walking around in a ring, making their own hell; the beautiful woman who is reduced to ruling over barren rocks and managing empty social situations. She does not find the Hanged Man among the cards she deals, for the Hanged Man is Christ, or the sacrificed seer-king who will restore water to the parched land. She is very direct in telling her client to "fear death by water."[46]

One of the pioneer critics of the Oxford school of mythopoeic writings is Charles Moorman (1960). His comments on Eliot's Tarot may be compared with those of Burgess:

> In Eliot's presentation of Madame Sosostris, the fortuneteller (ll. 43-59), the Tarot deck of cards, which once played a part in ancient fertility rituals, is here seen as a mere fortunetelling device used, significantly, by a society fortuneteller who has a "cold," which is generally in Eliot a sterility symbol. The characters as they appear on the cards also become symbols connected with the basic fertility-sterility image pattern that dominates the poem. The "drowned Phoenician sailor" is later connected with the Phoenician merchant who suffers "death by water" and so becomes, as Brooks suggests a "type of the fertility god whose image was thrown into the sea annually ... [sic]" "Belladonna [symbolically a modern poisoning of the image of the Blessed Virgin] [sic] the Lady of the Rocks" is a denial of the Divine Motherhood, hence motherhood itself, in terms of the waste land. She has become simply the "lady of situations," a phrase that would seem to carry connotations of illicit sexual relationships. The "man with three staves" is associated by Eliot himself with the maimed Fisher King; the one-eyed merchant later becomes associated with the homosexual Mr. Eugenides, who represents another kind of sexual sterility; the Hanged Man of the Tarot deck is associated by Eliot with Frazer's Hanged God and so directly with Christ and indirectly with the Grail. Thus again, the emphasis of the scene is directed to the principal themes and symbols of the Fisher King myth—sexual sterility and the saving power of the Grail.[47]

Jessie L. Weston, whose *From Ritual to Romance* (1920) formed one of the basic influences upon T.S. Eliot's *The Waste Land*, offers "evidence that these four objects [cup, dish, lance, and sword: the 'Hallows' of the Grail] do, in fact, form a special group entirely independent of any appearance in Folk-lore or Romance. They exist today as the four suits of the Tarot."[48] She documents A.E. Waite in support of this thesis, and lists the following correspondences, as they appear in Waite's *The Holy Grail*: the Cup (Chalice, or Goblet), which equals the modern Hearts; the Lance (Wand or Scepter), which equals Diamonds; the Sword which equals Spades, and the Dish (circles, "Pentangles"), which equals Clubs.[49] She cites a number of sources for the Tarot including Egypt, China, and the Gypsies—because of supposed Eastern orthodox images in the clothing of the Trump figures—and refers to "Sanskrit, or Hindustani" influence,[50] and to a private letter from W.B. Yeats:

> (1) Cup, Lance, Dish, Sword, in slightly varying forms, have never lost their mystic significance, and are today a part of magical operations. (2) The memory kept by the four suits of the Tarot, Cup, Lance, Sword, Pentacle (Dish), is an esoterical notation for fortune-telling purposes.[51]

She concludes that there is no evidence of contact between the Grail Legend and the Tarot, and suggests that

> while the Lance and Cup, in their associated form, are primarily symbols of Human Life energy, in conjunction with others they formed a group of "Fertility" symbols, connected with a very ancient ritual of which fragmentary survivals alone have been preserved to us.[52]

This is exactly how Eliot has used the Tarot, as both Burgess and Moorman demonstrate.

A final commentary on Eliot's use of the Tarot is provided by Gertrude Moakley in her introduction to a new edition of A.E. Waite's *The Pictorial Key to the Tarot* (1959), first published in 1910. She says that *The Pictorial Key*

> will be useful to anyone who is curious about the imagery of T.S. Eliot's great poem, *The Waste Land* and who refuses to let his curiosity be inhibited by Eliot's recent disparaging remarks about "wild-goose chases after Tarot cards." The "traditional Tarot" which plays so great a part in this poem must have been Waite's and it is all to Eliot's credit that his imagination was kindled by it in the second decade of the twentieth century. One of the cards Eliot mentions in the poem is "the Man with Three Staves," a very good title for the Three of Wands in Waite's Tarot, and a very poor title for that card in any other Tarot. And it is only in this Tarot that the Hanged Man is a

> noble figure, capable of reminding anyone of the Hanged God in Frazer's *Golden Bough*, as Eliot says this card did.[53]

The foregoing series of quotations from critical writing about Eliot shows something of the range of images that appear in, or can be applied to, the Tarot. Also relevant here is William Lindsay Gresham's novel *Nightmare Alley* (1946), where the Tarot is used in a carnival setting and emphasis is placed upon the Hanged Man as a menacing image.[54] Williams's *The Greater Trumps* differs from both Eliot and Gresham in making the Tarot the true subject of his novel, not merely a symbol, whether one of many, as in *The Waste Land*, or the central motif, as in *Nightmare Alley*. The Tarot and its members become characters in Williams's story, most particularly the Fool. In *The Greater Trumps*, mention of the Tarot or one of its components occurs on some 145 out of its 268 pages: more than fifty per cent.

But what exactly are these cards called the Tarot? Williams calls them "the magical leaves" (GT 160; ch. 10), which are "the symbols of our origins" (GT 207; ch. 13) containing "up to seventy-eight degrees of knowledge" (GT 177; ch. 11), especially "the one and twenty revelations of the Greater Trumps" (GT 262; ch. 16). His characters wonder "if the strange and half-mystical signs and names of the Greater Trumps had meaning and life" (GT 163; ch. 10), or "if indeed the Tarots and the images had no power in themselves and were but passive reflections of more universal things" (GT 175; ch. 11). He suggests "But if the Tarots hold, as had been dreamed, the message which all things in all places and times have also been dreamed to hold, then perhaps there was meaning in the order as in the paintings" (GT 226; ch. 14), and states most pregnantly, "It isn't the time behind them, but the process in them that's important" (GT 46-47; ch. 3).

In referring to the cards, which, because they are the dreamed-of original deck, are "pieces of painted papyrus" (GT 163; ch. 10), he frequently calls them leaves: "the translucent painted leaves" (GT 178; ch. 11), or "the leaves of the presentation" (GT 178; ch. 11). In one visionary passage, when Nancy handles the cards, he writes of them:

> They were huge things now, as if the great leaves of some aboriginal tree, the sacred bodhi-tree under which our Lord

> Gautama achieved Nirvana or that Northern dream of Igdrasil or the olives of Gethsemane, were drifting downward from the cluster round which her hands were clasped. (GT 89; ch. 5)

This passage demonstrates the influence of Waite on Williams's interpretation, for the tree is the sephiroth or Tree of God, of kabbalist lore. In the *Zohar*, which, according to Gershom Scholem (1941), represents "a Jewish form of theosophy,"[55] the world of the divinity, the Gnostic *pleroma,* is expressed in the "spheres" or "regions" of the sephiroth.[56] While the "Hidden God, the innermost Being of Divinity [...] has neither qualities nor attributes," this Being is often called *En-Sof*, or the Infinite, by Kabbalists and in the Zohar.[57] The sephiroth consists of ten attributes, variously conceived as the crowns, faces, garments, or stages of descent of God, which form the "mystical Tree of God or tree of divine power."[58] In Kabbalism the sephiroth are equally often seen as forming "the symbolic figure of *Adam Kadmon*, the primordial man,"[59] but the image of the tree is the one usually used by occultists in finding Kabbalist content in the Tarot. Williams alludes not only to the Kabbalist motif, but to two other common attributions of the Tarot's origins, to the Egyptians on the one hand, and the Gypsies on the other.

The search for the origins of the Tarot, which led to its association with Egyptians and Gypsies, referred to by both Waite and Weston, found numerous contributors, among them scholars as diverse as Steven Runciman and C.G. Jung. Runciman (1961) writes, "The only occultist product of Christian Dualism may lie [...] in the symbolism of the Tarot Pack."[60] He points out that "generations of fortune-tellers have handed down the doctrine that the Devil betokens the direction of affairs in this world and have seen in Pope Joan, the High Priestess, the token of the Gnosis. But other of the Tarot interpretations are clearly begotten of a different tradition."[61] Enlarging on this theme, he adds in an Appendix,

> There seems to me to be a trace of Dualism in the pack, but it has since been overlaid with debased Kabalistic lore. It shows in the antithesis of the *Emperor* and the *Empress* on the one hand and the *Pope* and the *Priestess* or *Pope Joan* on the other, in the traditional interpretation of the *Devil* as betokening natural forces—he is represented holding a naked man and

> woman in chains—and in the card betokening disaster, the *Tower Struck by Lightning* or *Maison Dieu*, which suggests the heretics' view of a Catholic church. The *Priestess* is also reminiscent of the Gnosis-Goddess of the Gnostics. But the evidence is far too slight to allow of any definite pronouncement.[62]

Jung's mention of Tarot occurs in a discussion of the archetypal symbolism of transformation and his remarks show his characteristic approach:

> If one wants to form a picture of the symbolic process, the series of pictures found in alchemy are good examples, though the symbols they contain are for the most part traditional despite their often obscure origin and significance. An excellent Eastern example is the Tantric *chakra* system, or the mystical nerve system of Chinese yoga. It also seems as if the set of pictures in the Tarot cards were distantly descended from the archetypes of transformation [...][63]

Of such symbols, Jung offers the following combined definition and caution:

> [...] the process itself involves another class of *archetypes of transformation.* They are not personalities [...] Like the personalities, these archetypes are true and genuine symbols that cannot be exhaustively interpreted, either as signs or allegories. They are genuine symbols precisely because they are ambiguous, full of half-glimpsed meanings, and in the end inexhaustible.[64]

A.E. Waite's (1910) definition of the Tarot lies close to Jungian thought: "The Tarot embodies symbolical presentations of universal ideas behind which lie all the implicits of the human mind, and it is in this sense that they contain secret doctrine, which is the realization by the few of the truths imbedded in the consciousness of all [...]"[65]

III. Origins of the Tarot

Illus. 4 "Triumph of Love." Petrarch's *I Trionfi.* Trieste. 1508. Public Domain.

With these analyses in mind, we will survey the history of the Tarot. Catherine Perry Hargrave, to whose *History of Playing Cards* (1930, 1966) every student of cards in North America resorts, states that playing cards and all other games of chance derived from divination.[66] Various original sources (previous to their appearance in Europe) have been suggested. Proponents of a Chinese origin for the cards relate the four Chinese suits of coins, strings of coins, myriads of strings of coins, and tens of myriads of strings of coins to the four suits of earlier Italian cards. Proponents of Indian origin point out that the composite Siva/Devi holds in his/her hands, among other things, a cup, wand, sword, and ring, and that Hanuman (the monkey—god son of a nymph and the wine god) holds a cup, sword, ring, and scepter; but Indian cards have eight or ten suits.[67] Needless to say, considerably more evidence is marshaled to defend these various sources, along with more to support a near eastern source (see below), but in concluding the arguments, Roger Tilley (1967) says, "It seems possible; even probable, that they are the product of European genius."[68] He gives the following time-table of the appearance of cards in Europe: the first cards, 1370 (a 52-card pack; a more precise date is given below); the Tarots, 1470 (as "a distinct entity"); and a marriage of the two in the games of *Tarocchi* of Venice (78 cards), *Tarocchino* of Bologna (62 cards), and the *Minchiate* of Florence (97 cards).[69]

Support for this chronology is readily available. In 1377 a German monk, Johannes, living in a Swiss monastery, wrote a Latin account of which the following passage is especially intriguing:

> Hence it is that a certain game called the game of cards (*ludus cartorum*) has come to us in this year, viz the year of our Lord M.CCC.LXXVIJ. In which game the state of the world as it now is excellently described and figured.[70]

The description of the game as given by the "holy friar" makes no mention of the Greater Trumps. Playing cards are not mentioned in descriptions of dice or other games of chance in 1363, nor against gaming in 1369, and most significantly, perhaps, they are not mentioned by Petrarch (1304–1374), the author of *I Trionfi*.[71]

A history written in 1480 suggests that numeral cards first appeared in Italy in 1379. In his *Istoria della citta di Viterbo*, Covelluzo states "in this year of such great tribulations the game of cards was introduced into Viterbo, which came from the Saracens and was called Naib."[72] Hargrave states "that the Hebrew word for sorcery is *Naibi*."[73] In 1393, the Florentine Jean Morelli recommended as a game for young men (instead of dice) "games which are for children [...] les naibis."[74]

St. Bernardine of Sienna preached a sermon at Bologna in 1423, and made no mention of anything except the four suits and the court cards.[75] In c. 1450–70, however, a Franciscan Friar of northern Italy denounced among other "instruments of gambling" the four-suited pack and "the twenty-two variously called tarots or *tarocchi* or *attuti* or *trionfi* in Italy and *atouts* in France on the grounds that they triumph over all other cards."[76] This reference to Tarot cards as triumphing over the others is most interesting for an understanding of Moakley's interpretation of the Tarot deck sequence, as is a 1450 sermon quoted by Tilley: "Concerning the third class of games, that is 'triumphs.' There is nothing in the world of gaming so hateful to God as the game of 'triumphs.' For everything that is base in the eyes of the Christian faith is seen in 'triumphs.'"[77] The preacher rages on:

> In it not only are God, the angels, the planets, and the cardinal virtues represented and named, but also the world's luminaries, I mean the Pope and the Emperor, are forced, a thing which is ridiculous and degrading to Christians, to enter the game.[78]

Douglas McMurtrie (1962) reports records of bans on playing cards in Germany in 1377, at Nurenberg in 1380, at Ulm and Paris in 1397, at Augsburg in 1400, and—for clergy—at the Synod of Langres in 1404. These bans, may, however, have been related to taxation and duties rather than the matters cited by preachers: by 1441 the blockprinting of cards had become a sufficiently powerful industry for an embargo on importation to be enacted.[79]

The denunciation, rather than the mere banning, of cards seems to coincide with their increased availability in printed form. Woodcuts were first printed in Europe in the early fifteenth century and the earliest extant examples are religious prints, protective prayers against the plague, and New Year's greetings. The very earliest preserved is the St. Christopher woodcut of 1423, but playing cards may have antedated it. [80] The earliest date of precise record for woodblock-printed cards is 1430: in that year, an artist told the Florence tax office that he had many wood blocks which he used to make playing cards and images of saints.[81] The printing process made holy pictures and playing cards available to everybody, and at the same time. Marshall McLuhan thinks that the introduction of printing produced a revolution in European thought; apparently the Tarot was involved in this development. It may be that the relative stasis of the Tarot deck, with its quite minimal changes in structure or appearance, are due to their being fixed so early by the printing process.[82]

Illus. 5 Lovers and Illus. 6 Strength. *Golden Tarot of the Renaissance* (Estensi Tarot). Seventeen cards based on originals of the "Charles VI" or "Gringonneur" Tarot, Italy, late 1400s. © 2004 Lo Scarabeo. Illus. reproduced by permission of Lo Scarabeo. Further reproduction prohibited.

However, the earliest extant and nearly complete Tarot decks are painted, not printed, and include the seventy-four-card *Visconti-Sforza* (Pierpont Morgan-Bergamo) deck analyzed at length by Moakley. The so-called "Tarot of Charles VI," once dated to 1392 and credited to Jacquemin Gringonneur, is now thought to be the work of an Italian artist of the later fifteenth century.[83] This latter deck, also called the "Gringonneur" Tarot, is widely and erroneously believed to be the earliest extant Tarot. Its cards include a Juggler with a string of balls and numerous children playing at his feet. Three pairs of lovers are the prey of two cupids in a cloud above them. The World, with scepter and orb, stands astride a globe with a landscape inside. The three Virtues are women; Strength breaks a column. Two astronomer/astrologists point to the Moon, and a woman spins (?) on the Sun card. A knight stands on the Chariot and the Hermit (Time) holds an hourglass. The Hanged Man holds a bag of gold in each dependent hand. Death rides a horse (as he is not to do again until the *Rider-Waite* pack) and strikes down many with his scythe. The Tower is falling in ruin on one side, and many people are resurrected beneath a pair of trumpeting angels.[84]

It was certainly in their popular and widely-disseminated printed form that the Tarot pack made its impact upon occult thought in the eighteenth century. Just before the French Revolution, Court de Gébelin, an anthropologist-Mason, published *Monde primitif* in which he declared that the Tarot was "the remnants of an Egyptian book."[85] His conclusion was drawn in the context of his period, when "the Nile was beginning to loom largely in the preoccupation of learned thought."[86] It was de Gébelin who saw Isis in the High Priestess, the Moon, and the Star, which he identified with Sirius,[87] and he called Tarot the *Book of Thoth.* Waite demolishes the thesis of its Egyptian origins effectively, although there may be an element of Egyptian imagery in the Tarot, via the Renaissance. Erwin Panofsky (1955) points out that Petrarch's *Africa*, written in 1338, contains passages describing Egyptian art and symbolism, based upon the poet's reading of the *Saturnalia* of Macrobius (c. 399–422).[88] As Panofsky describes it, "the dark and remote sphere of the Egyptian or pseudo-Egyptian mystery religions—a sphere which had vanished from sight in the Christian Middle Ages, dimly emerged above the horizon with the beginning of Renaissance humanism toward the middle of the fourteenth century, and became the object of passionate interest after the discovery of Horapollo's *Hieroglyphica* in 1419."[89] He continues, "this discovery not only gave rise to an enormous enthusiasm for everything Egyptian or would-be Egyptian but also produced—or, at least, immeasurably promoted that 'emblematic' spirit which is so characteristic of the sixteenth and seventeenth centuries."[90]

The passion for things Egyptian developed in Roman times with the increased interest in mystery religions: the religion of Isis, which Williams makes a motif in *The Greater Trumps*, is most vividly preserved from the past in *The Golden Ass of Apuleius*, where her worship is wonderfully evoked, especially in the description of the triumphal procession of the goddess and her devotees. This atmosphere favored and accompanied the early dissemination of Christianity.

During the Renaissance, there was a renewal of this genuine preoccupation of classical times. Vincent Cronin (1971) makes the context of this renewal clear—he emphasizes that "the early humanists were Christians,"[91] and states:

> The humanists formulated the view that such men [virtuous men born before Christ] had attained salvation because they "foresaw" the truths of Christianity. They put great emphasis on the elements they believed to be common to both paganism and Christianity: vestal virgins foreshadowing nuns; Mercury, the angel Gabriel; Jupiter, Neptune, and Pluto, the Trinity. Much of the painting of the period, culminating in Raphael's *School of Athens*, is a statement of the view that there exists a body of truth common to both pre-Christian religions and to Christianity. Indeed, it was held that this common body of truth had been adumbrated in Egypt, then passed to the Hebrews and Greeks, and finally to the Christians.[92]

It is exactly this catholic view that is symbolized by Williams in his novel when he relates his Tarots to a fictional set of golden images, stating that "this hidden secret of the gypsies had been borne about the world." Aaron, the old adept, muses that

> one band of all those restless companies possessed the mystery which long since some wise adept of philosophical truths had made in the lands of the east or in the secret houses of Europe: Egyptian or Jew or Christian heretic—Paulician, Bogophil [sic], or Nestorian—or perhaps still further off in the desert-circled empire or Abyssinia, for there were hints of all in the strange medley of sign-bearing images [...] (GT 176-77; ch. 11)

Illus. 7 High Priestess, Illus. 8 Star, Illus. 9 Moon from Court de Gébelin, "The Game of Tarots" in *Monde primitif* Volume 8, Book 1 (1781). Public Domain. Quotations from Translation by Donald Tyson. http://www.donaldtyson.com/gebelin.html

The High Priestess
[...] she has a double crown with two horns like that of Isis [...]

The Moon
Pausanias teaches us in his description of Phocide, that according to the Egyptians it was the tears of Isis which flooded each year the waters of the Nile and which thus rendered fertile the fields of Egypt. The historians of that country also speak about a drop or tear, which falls from the Moon at the time when the water of the Nile must grow bigger. [...] Between the two columns are two dogs which seem to bark against the Moon and to guard it: perfectly Egyptian ideas. [...] Clement, himself Egyptian, since he was of Alexandria, and who consequently knew what he was talking about, assures us in his Tapestries [or Stromates, Liv. V.] that the Egyptians represented the Tropics under the figure of two dogs, which similar to gatekeepers or faithful guards, kept the Sun and the Moon from going to the Poles.

The Star
The lady [...] is the Queen of Heaven, Isis, to the benevolence of whom were attributed the floods of the Nile, which start with the rising of the Dog Star; thus this rising was the signal of the inundation. The reason the Dog Star was consecrated to Isis, is that it was her perfect symbol. [...] Lastly, the flower and the butterfly which it supports, represent the symbols of regeneration and resurrection: they signify at the same time the blessing of the benefits of Isis, and the rising of the Dog Star, when the lands of Egypt, which were absolutely naked, cover themselves with new crops.

A.E. Waite, having disposed of any direct relation between Egypt and the Tarots, discusses the association of the cards with the Gypsies and with their origin as nomads in India. He thinks these connections were first formulated by Boiteau in 1854.[93] Perhaps in part due to a long-standing notion that the Gypsies themselves were Egyptian—hence the name by which they are called—the Egyptian origin stuck. As Waite describes it, Éliphas Lévi, the greatest of nineteenth-century occultists, and one who "openly regarded charlatanry as a great means to an end,"[94] took the Tarot, and with it "de Gébelin's hypothesis [...] into his heart of hearts, and all occult France and all esoteric Britain, Martinists, half-instructed Kabalists, schools of *soi-disant* theosophy—there, here, and everywhere—have accepted his judgment about it."[95]

Waite says of the relation between Gypsies and the Tarot, "not that they brought them into Europe but found them there already and added them to their stock-in-trade."[96] He cites the first report of Gypsy cartomancy with Tarots as 1854 and concludes his discussion by dating the cards, whether as a game or as "Secret Doctrine," from the fourteenth century.[97] Jean-Paul Clébert (1963), a recent writer on the Gypsies, cites the observation of Gérard Encausse (Papus) that the "Gypsies alone have the primitive game intact."[98] Clébert documents Gypsy use of the Tarot in some detail. He says that since there is a record (discussed above) of the cards (called "Naib"—"the game of cards") for Viterbos in 1379, and the Gypsies are not mentioned in Italy until 1422, this probably shows that they did not introduce the cards.[99] He continues:

> In any case, the Gypsies have used tarots for a very long time as support for their divination. It is difficult to say which pack of cards was first used. Between the Egyptian Tarot, in which Solomon, Moses and Judas reigned [Clébert is describing a very corrupt occult version of the eighteenth century] and the Marseilles Tarot, whose symbols are occidental, the Gypsies have been able to make their own choice in accordance with the routes of their migrations. However, it does not look as though they had an original pack of cards of their own.[100]

Illus. 10, Illus. 11, Illus. 12 *Egyptian Tarot*. Based on illustrations from Comte de Saint-Germain's *Practical Astrology*, 1901. Comte de Saint-Germain's illustrations were derived from the work of Paul Christian (Jean-Baptiste Pitois 1811-1877). © 1978 U.S. Games Systems. Illus. reproduced by permission of U.S. Games Systems. Further reproduction prohibited.

Gresham writes from his youthful experiences in the carnival world that the Gypsies "know the archetypes of humanities fears, desires and dreams,"[101] and thinks that they combined this knowledge with their cards to do what is called "cold reading"—that is, the application of basic psychology, empathy, and intuition, to the fact that most people have the same problems and desires, and will pour these out in perfect confidence to anyone who will listen.[102]

We may conclude that the Tarots originated in the very late fourteenth or early fifteenth century.[103] The cards continue to show a preoccupation with this period, as the figures are usually in medieval dress or in a Renaissance version of Roman or Greek dress. In addition, they appear, as Moakley demonstrates, to be based on the Roman triumph as allegorized in Petrarch's poem *I Trionfi* and as expressed in actual Renaissance triumphs, both on historic occasions and as part of the Lenten (or other seasonal) carnival processions. This thesis regarding the origins of the Tarot is of special relevance to my interpretation of Williams's novel and thus requires a thorough explanation.

IV. *The Visconti-Sforza Tarot*

Illus. 13 Lovers. *Visconti-Sforza Tarocchi*.
Facsimile and reconstructed edition created from hand-painted original produced in Milan c. 1450. © 1985 U.S. Games Systems.
Illus. reproduced by permission of U.S. Games Systems.
Further reproduction prohibited.

Gertrude Moakley presented her research and conclusions about Tarot, based largely on her study of the *Visconti-Sforza* deck, in "The Tarot Trumps and Petrarch's *Trionfi*" (1956) and her book *The Tarot Cards Painted by Bonifacio Bembo for the Visconti-Sforza Family* (1966). The *Visconti-Sforza* deck, not the only one preserved from the period, is the work of Bonifacio Bembo, painted some time after the betrothal of Francesco Sforza and Bianca Maria Visconti, perhaps in the year 1450.[104] The magnificently illuminated cards, executed in colours and gold on heavy cardboard, are lacking four of their original cards, and contain six by a hand other than Bembo's. The Trumps are neither numbered nor titled.

The order of the Trumps is known from two fifteenth-century sermons and a verse series describing the tarocchi of the same period. Hargrave gives the list from one of the sermons;[105] that in the other sermon, one against gambling, is very similar to it.[106] The list Moakley gives contains titles from "a set of versified tarocchi [...] written in honour of the ladies of Ferrara." She uses this list in her discussion because the names "are more like modern Italian."[107]

Moakley says that "in modern packs the Car follows the card of L'Amore, but in all the fifteenth-century lists it precedes it."[108] The order given in Hargrave is as I cite it, however; I cannot account for this anomaly and presume that Moakley was able to examine the original manuscripts.[109]

Moakley interpolates the four suits into her list according to her theory of their meaning. She believes that the cards are based upon the tradition of the Triumph—hence, Trumps—that is, the triumphal procession, and in particular upon, first, the allegorical use of the Triumph theme in Petrarch's *I Trionfi*, and, second, the pre-Lenten procession which is also based upon the Triumph tradition. This latter concept enables her to identify the card *Il Bagatino*—Williams's "Juggler"—with the Carnival King, being led to his death as "The Dying God" of Sir. James G. Frazer's *The Golden Bough*,[110] and *Il Matto*—Williams's "Fool"—with "the personification of Lent" who "is on the point of claiming his seven-week kingship."[111] William Willeford (1969), whose ideas concerning the Fool contribute much to the study of Tarot, cautions, a "mental adjustment must be made by anyone who for any reason reads earlier anthropological literature in the hope of gaining something."[112]

Chart 1. Tarot Titles and Order

	Moakley		Hargrave
I	Il Bagatino	1.	El Bagatella
	Le Coppe		
II	L'Imperatrice	2.	Imperatrice
III	L'Imperadore	3.	Imperator
IV	La Papessa	4.	La papessa (note referring to those who deny the Christian faith)
V	Il Papa	5.	El Papa
VI	La Temperanza	6.	La Tempentia
VII	Il Carro	7.	L'amore
VIII	L'Amore	8.	La Caro Triumphale
IX	La Fortezza	9.	La Fortez
	I Bastoni		
X	La Ruota	10.	La Rotta
	I Danari		
XI	Il Gobbo	11.	El Gobbo
XII	Il Traditore	12.	Lo impichato (the hanged)
XIII	La Morte	13.	La morte
XIV	Il Diavolo	14.	El Diavolo
XV	La Casa del Diavolo	15.	La Sagitta (in place of la maison Dieu)
	Le Spade		
XVI	La Stella	16.	La stella (L'étoile)
XVII	La Luna	17.	La lune
XVIII	Il Sole	18.	El sole
XIX	L'Agnolo	19.	Lo angelo
XX	La Justicia	20.	La justicia
XXI	Il Mondo	21.	El Mondo ave dio padre
	Il Matto	22.	El mato

The reader should be aware that this part of Moakley's thesis, for which she admits, "I have no direct authority,"[113] may have been given excessive emphasis, perhaps due to an undue faith in Frazer which, coupled with an equal emphasis on Freud, gives Moakley's book a certain flavor, or at least a very definite bias; not, as we shall see, without what is a sound intuition.

She proves the association of the Tarot with the allegorical use of the Triumph theme most conclusively, and it may be the ancient Dionysian element—Dionysus was a "Dying God"—in that theme which makes her think of Frazer and the phallic element in that cult which makes her think of Freud. She suggests the charming simile of "the cards given away with bubble-gum"[114]—implying that the Tarot set was a pictorial version of a Triumph. If that is so, then the cards are another example of the Triumph as a motif, influenced by the allegorical tradition, and also by the actual Triumphs, including the Carnival Triumphs as such. The game itself is an example of the motif, one of many forms taken by it, not necessarily a one-for-one record of a particular procession, although the Bembo deck does seem to have particular application to the specific family for which it was painted.

The other aspect of Moakley's theory is her identification of the suit cards with the four Virtues: The Cups of Temperance, the Staves of Fortitude, the Coins of Prudence, and the Swords of Justice. She places the suits as attendants of the virtues within the trump sequence to support her notion of them as recording a carnival procession. The cards themselves never seem to have been placed in such an order, and her "original order" (listed above) thus contains some imaginative expansion. Moakley quotes Giorgio Vasari's opinion that "it was the Florentine painter, Giorgio di Cosimo, who first adopted Carnival maskings to the character of a triumph [...] by introducing the long trains of men all dressed to suit the character of a particular triumph."[115] This is her reason for placing the suits within the context of the Trumps. Again, there is a sound intuition here regarding the importance of the Virtues as controlling or reinforcing the structure of the Trumps, and this matter will be discussed below. I will only say here that the three virtues in the early deck are not in the same order they later take. As Moakley observes, in the Bembo deck they do seem to be placed in association with the particular car or triumph most appropriate to them: Temperance and Fortitude escort the Car of Love, Justice follows the Last Judgement, and Prudence is absent.

The final element in Moakley's thesis is the one she has most effectively proven: its relationship to the allegorical Triumph and the influence upon it of Petrarch's poem, "The main outline of which supplied themes for a decorative art and triumphal processions and finally for the game of triumphs played with the tarocchi."[116] In the poem, *I Trionfi*, there are six Triumphs, each of which, as it were, triumphs over the one it follows. First Cupid triumphs over men and gods alike, including Jove himself (he is the prototype of the "Hierophant" and retains his identity, which is not merely a euphemism for Pope or Priest, in some decks), and over Petrarch, who is in love with Laura. The four high personages in the beginning of the Tarot are thus Love's captives, both sacred and secular. Then Chastity (Laura's) triumphs over Petrarch's Love. Chastity does not appear in the Tarot, but one of her captives (along with Love) was Fortune, who is central or significant in her own right in the fifteenth-century deck. Fortune is given added emphasis by Moakley who lets the company of Coins escort her. Third is the Triumph of Death, because Laura died in the Black Death. In the poem, the Love of Petrarch (Cupid) is a captive of this triumphator, along with the Chastity of his lost Laura. Nevertheless, Death himself becomes a captive of Laura's Fame, who forms the next Triumph; Moakley finds the trumpet of Fame at the lips of the Angel of the Last Judgement in the Tarot. The fifth Triumph is that of Time, who overcomes even Fame, and Time appears as himself in early Tarots, as Il Gobbo with an hourglass, and as the Hermit with a lantern in later decks. The sixth and final Triumph in Petrarch's poem is that of Eternity, wherein Petrarch and Laura are united. This is the car drawn by the Tetramorphs, depicted in the Tarot as the World, with the agents of Time—Star, Moon, and Sun—as her captives.[117]

A number of different games of Triumphs existed, related to these motifs, including several that are still used today. The most elaborate is the minchiate with its ninety-seven cards, representing all of Petrarch's six Triumphs and following his themes more directly than the tarocchi do. Of note is the association of the three usual Tarot virtues with Chastity, whose absence from the Tarot frees them to find various positions of their own. Interestingly, Williams, who loved and understood Chastity, reunites them in his Tarot in a position something like the original, giving them Fortune (Chastity's captive) as a companion, just as she is in the minchiate deck. In the minchiate also, Fame has Prudence, usually absent in the Tarot, and the three theological virtues of Faith, Hope, and Charity as well: of these not a shred or feather is seen in the tarocchi.

Chart 2. The Trumps of the 97-Card Minchiate Deck

I	The Juggler or Mountebank	XXI	Water
		XXII	Earth
II	The Grand Duke	XXIII	Air
III	The Western Emperor	XXIII	Libra, The Balance or The Scales
IIII	The Eastern Emperor		
V	The Lovers	XXV	Virgo, The Virgin
VI	Temperance	XXVI	Scorpion, The Scorpio
VII	Force or Fortitude	XXVII	Aries, The Ram
VIII	Justice	XXVIII	Capricornus, The Goat
VIIII	The Wheel of Fortune	XXVIIII	Sagittarius, The Archer
X	The Chariot	XXX	Cancer, The Crab
XI	Time or The Hermit	XXXI	Pisces, The Fishes
VII	The Traitor or Hanged Man	XXXI	Aquarius, The Water Carrier
		XXXIII	Leo, The Lion
XIII	Death	XXXIIII	Taurus, The Bull
XIIII	The Devil	XXXV	Gemini, The Twins
XV	The Tower		The Star
XVI	Hope		The Moon
XVII	Prudence		The Sun
XVIII	Faith		The World
XVIIII	Charity		The Last Judgment or Fame
XX	Fire		The Fool

The conventionalized minchiate deck consists of forty-one trumps and fifty-six suit cards, but some decks included up to 120 cards. Eighteen of the trumps are the same as those in the Tarot deck. Stuart Kaplan. The Encyclopedia of Tarot, Volume I *(Stamford, CT: U.S. Games Systems, 1978) 49, 53; and Volume II (1986) 256.*

Sample minchiate cards. Top row: Illus. 14 Temperance, Illus. 15 Strength or Fortitude, Illus. 16 Justice, and Illus. 17 Hope. Bottom: Illus. 18 Prudence, Illus. 19 Faith, Illus. 20 Charity, and Illus. 21 Chastity. Reproduced from Catherine Perry Hargrave's *A History of Playing Cards* (1930; New York: Dover Publications, Inc, 1966) 228-30.

Chastity is not typically included in lists of minchiate cards (see opposite page). Moakley cites the "Italian Minchiate Cards" illustrated in Hargrave (228-30) as the basis for including it in her discussion. Hargrave indicates that the deck shown has forty-two, rather than the more common forty-one, trumps. The last two atouts are on the upper left corner of the last page of the set of illustrations. The card in the upper left corner, with the Fool to her right, is shown here (Illus. 21). With her crescent moon crown and leash holding a dog, she can only be Diana, goddess of Chastity. The dimensions of this card seem to be the same as that for the sample court and pip cards and these all differ from the trumps. However, it appears the illustrations are sketches so the renderings may simply be off scale. The book is illustrated with decks from the United States Playing Card Company in Cincinnati, but this particular deck is not given any more specific identification.

The Tarot, then, contains an abbreviated version of Petrarch's Triumphs. Petrarch's Triumphs include Love, Chastity, Death, Fame, Time, and Eternity. In Tarot some of these are absent or suppressed, as indicated here by parentheses: Love, (Chastity), Death, (Fame), (Time), Eternity. Tarot preserves the prominence of the three most powerful motifs, and gives a remnant of position to Time, while allowing one of the captives thus freed—Fortune, captive of the absent Chastity—to assume a position central to the structure of the deck. This essential order is retained in all subsequent decks, though the surviving Virtues move about, perhaps to lend a more aesthetic balance. There is, however one glaring problem with this interpretation and that is the relevance of the Juggler and Fool.

Moakley seeks an explanation for the Juggler and Fool in the pre-Lenten procession, a version of the Triumph contemporary with the milieu within which the tarocchi was produced. These cards certainly have a carnival air, and the Fool is very closely linked to the Saturnalian Carnival which comes at the Winter Solstice. Il Bagatino or El Bagatello—the name means "Quarterpenny"—is perhaps ancestral to the little Juggler of the *commedia dell'arte*, which derives from the carnival: he is a clown named Bagatino.[118] The Fool becomes the Harlequin of the *commedia dell'arte*.

In later decks, Il Bagatino, looking much the same but with varying equipment on his table, becomes "The Juggler" and "The Cobbler," because bagatt means both "chatterbox" and "cobbler" in Milanese dialect. The card so designated shows a shoe and even a complete cobbler's bench in some modern Milanese tarocchi cards, including the ones illustrating *The Greater Trumps*. It also becomes "The Magician" or "The Conjuror." Moakley tries to prove that the full deck is thus an actual Carnival procession: one need only think of modern parades with their free-running clowns, or modern carnivals with their shell games to recognize the emotional pull of her argument and the context of its appeal. Perhaps she is right. The Roman Triumph also had free-running (and phallic/scatological) clown or fools who made fun of the triumphator. Moakley identifies Il Bagatino as the Carnival King because of his scepter, which he bears in the *Visconti-Sforza* deck. He appears in the minchiate as well, and I really do not think that the secret of his identity has yet been solved. Perhaps it is just as well.

Chart 3. Moakley's Triumphal Cars

Triumph of Love — The Juggler
The Cups
Empress, Emperor, Popess, Pope
Love
Temperance, Love's Car, Fortitude
(all of the above in a single car)

Triumph of Death — *The Staves*
Fortune
The Coins
The Hanged Man
Time, Death, the Devil
Hell-Mouth
(all of the above in a single car)

Triumph of Eternity — *The Swords*
Star
Moon
Sun
Justice, The Universe, the Last Judgement
(all of the above in a single car)

The Fool
(who has been running about)[119]

The minchiate cards include some wonderful images, such as the lamb in the burning bush (he is the element "Fire"); Prudence with her snake and mirror; the boat of "Water"; the landscape of "Earth," the stars, birds, clouds, and mysterious beast of what I take to be "Air"; and Diana with her crescent moon and hunting dog. One wonders why fortune-tellers did not take up this deck with the same enthusiasm as Tarot. The minchiate includes, along with the "usual atouts" and the four suits, the full complement of Virtues, the four elements, and the twelve signs of the Zodiac.[120] The presence of the elements probably accounts for their association with the four suits in the common occult interpretation of the Tarot, used to such great effect by Williams.

The following analysis of the *Visconti-Sforza* Tarot painted by Bembo will help to show the changes that occurred in the development of the conventional exoteric Tarot of the Marseilles type, and help prepare the reader for an analysis of Williams's Tarot as he develops it in *The Greater Trumps*.

Car One

Il Bagatino (Quarterpenny, the Juggler)[121]

Moakley says he is the King of Carnival on his way to be killed and replaced by the King of Lent, which she identifies with the Fool. In support of this theory, besides the appearance of Il Bagatino as a clown in the *commedia dell'arte*, which is probably descended from the Carnival triumphal procession, she cites the association of playing cards with Carnival (being forbidden otherwise), and the fact that the *Visconti-Sforza* set shows him with a scepter in his hand. He has a table before him with a handle-less cup, two small disks (like coins) and a large "covered dish."[122] He has no crown, and is rather plainly dressed. I have already discussed other versions of this card above; in the *Waite-Smith* deck he has become a magician with a table of marvels that seem to symbolize the four suits.

Le Coppe (Cups)[123]

This is the first of the four suits, which Moakley places in the context of the Trumps to show their presumed relationship to the Carnival triumph. The Cups in her interpretation heralds Cupid's Triumph and refer to the "Love and drunkenness" of which the Carnival King is the "exponent." Cups are associated with Temperance elsewhere[124] and Temperance does follow in the set a little further on as attendant (with Fortitude) of Love's Chariot. Moakley makes I Bastoni (Staves) follow this car, with all its other cards.

The cups have a crowned King and Queen, a mounted Knight and standing Page, all bearing extremely elaborate cups. The Ace is placed after the Page because Cups is a feminine suit and in the early Tarots this was the consequent order. The Ace is a splendid fountain surmounted by a bird. The numbered cards of Cups are golden chalices.

In the first-known card games the suits alone are known, with the twenty-two Trumps joining them as a separate suit later. The relationship of the Virtues with the Tarot and the possibility of their association with the armed companies of the suits is in accord both with the origin of the Virtues and with the custom of placing them in triumphal processions. Emile Mâle (1958) discusses their origins: "From primitive Christian times the Virtues took concrete and living form, and were conceived as heroic maidens, beautiful and simple. As early as the *Shepherd* of Hermas they appeared as female figures, a little later we see them as armed maidens"[125] Later, the *Psychomachia* of the Roman Christian poet Prudentius (348–c. 413) gave "concrete embodiment" to the "idea of an inner battle."[126] Prudentius's structure was developed by others into its most complete visual Gothic form at Chartres, where "Prudence is opposed to Folly, Justice to Injustice, Fortitude to Cowardice, Temperance to Intemperance."[127] The additional Virtues and Vices (Faith/Infidelity, Hope/Despair, and Charity/Avarice) are extended to include Humility/Pride. In the thirteenth century, the Virtues "are seated women, serious, tranquil, majestic, who bear on their shields a heraldic animal in sign of their nobility."[128]

L'Imperatrice (The Empress)[129]

The second Trump is the Empress: in later Tarots, the Popess/Priestess takes this position. She is crowned and seated confronting us, bearing upon her knee a jousting shield. In the *Visconti-Sforza* set her gown is adorned with devices associated with Milan. Some of the above motifs survive in the conventional deck.

L'Imperadore (The Emperor)[130]

He is shown as Frederick III, according to Moakley. He sits looking to the viewer's right. He is robed to match the Empress, he wears the huge flared hat under his crown that appears in many other playing cards, and he holds an orb and scepter.

La Papess (The Popess)[131]

This title, remember, is modern, chosen by Moakley from a 1917 Italian deck. There are no names or numbers on the *Visconti-Sforza* deck. Moakley calls this card a "Ghibelline gibe" at the corrupt

Papacy.[132] In this deck she is clothed in the habit of the Umiliata order: there was a Sister Manfreda, distantly related to the Visconti family, who had herself declared Pope. According to Runciman, this sort of male–female equality appeared fairly frequently in Christian dualist and otherwise heretical sects. Although robed in a habit, the lady wears the triple crown and bears a cross on a tall staff and a book. The developed deck has no such topical references and the figure wears ecclesiastical garb to match that of her hieratic companion.

Il Papa (The Pope)[133]

The hierophant has a triple crown, a splendid robe, and a cross-tipped staff. He is blessing us. The foregoing pairs of Empress and Emperor and Papess/Priestess and Pope are captives of Love, and each pair is opposed to the other. (Guelphs and Ghibellines were groups siding with the opposing forces.) There was an alternative fourteenth-century deck with Jupiter and Juno in the positions of the Papess/Priestess and Pope, positions that they still occupy in the *1JJ Swiss Tarot*. In his guise as a planet, Jupiter wore ecclesiastical robes in a painting of c. 1420,[134] and Moakley implies that the Papal image arose from this concept. The triumphator of the Roman Triumph also assumed the robes of Jupiter during his ride, returning them to the temple of the god's image afterwards.

La Temperanza (Temperance)[135]

The cards of Temperance and Fortitude in the *Visconti-Sforza* deck were not painted by Bembo but by a distinctly different hand. Temperance is a lady with two urns, from which she pours a stream of water back and forth: this is the traditional presentation of the Virtue. Moakley sees her as riding the Chariot of Love (with Fortitude) as a feminine symbol. The association of the Virtues with triumphal cars can be seen in the Car of Beatrice in *The Divine Comedy* (to be discussed below), and in many drawings of imaginary—usually allegorical—Triumphs. Designs by Albrecht Durer for the triumphal car of Emperor Maximillian include the Virtues standing on pedestals bearing wreaths.[136]

Illus. 22 Papess and Illus. 23 Pope. *Visconti-Sforza Tarocchi*. Facsimile and reconstructed edition created from hand-painted original produced in Milan c. 1450. © 1985 U.S. Games Systems. Illus. reproduced by permission of U.S. Games Systems. Further reproduction prohibited.

Il Carro (The Car)[137]

Moakley says that fifteenth-century packs have the Chariot ahead of its passenger, Love, and that modern packs place it after the Lovers. The *Visconti-Sforza* set shows a beautiful queen with an orb, driving two white, winged horses. Moakley thinks this lady is the same one who is seen as one of the lovers in the next Trump; they both have gowns with the same motif on them, but the lady lover has neither crown nor orb. The later conventional deck replaces the lady with a male driver.

L'Amore (Love, the Lovers)[138]

Cupid is blindfolded on a pedestal and before him are two happy lovers clasping their right hands. Cupid appears in the later conventional deck, in flight and often in a cloud, taking aim at varying numbers of lovers.

La Fortezza (Fortitude, Force, Strength)[139]

This card is by the same artist that painted Temperance and not by Bembo. It is masculine, showing the Virtue in one of its three usual forms; the other versions are feminine. Fortitude is usually shown as a lady, with a column (as in the "Tarot of Charles VI"), or with a lion, as in the 1415 minchiate cards associated with Marziano da Tortona. Mâle describes her traditional appearance in the cathedral setting as a mailed and helmeted warrior-lady in a long robe, "seated in an attitude full of repose and dignity,"[140] bearing a shield with a lion, which, to the medieval symbolists, "was one of the types of courage."[141] The male version shows Hercules, usually wearing a lion skin, with his club. The column of the lady is a reference to the strength of Samson. Moakley thinks the male Fortitude is deliberately of that sex so that it will match the suit of Staves, which is a masculine suit with the Ace low. The fact that the two Virtues are by an artist other than Bembo makes it difficult to prove what the original intention may have been. The sexual dualism of the suits is described below, in a discussion of the game played with these cards.

Car Two

I Bastoni (Staves)[142]

Moakley puts Staves here to associate them with Fortitude and as heralds of Fortune. She erects an elaborate proof upon it for the ribald element, including the crossed legs of the King of Staves and Coins as signs of Chrysos (gold)—X is "chi" and a hard "C" sound in Greek—implying that they relate gold to faeces. This would make Temperance's cups hold urine, if the Latin maxim that birth occurs "between urine and faeces" can be applied here. The court card figures of the Staves bear long batons with large complex gold bulbs at the top (as well as scepters for the King and Queen) and the numbered cards of Staves show similar batons with bulbs at both ends. As a masculine suit, Staves has the Ace low, as the very last card in the series.

Top: Illus. 24 Temperance and Illus. 25 Strength. Bottom: Illus. 26 King of Staves and Illus. 27 King of Coins. *Visconti-Sforza Tarocchi*. Facsimile and reconstructed edition created from hand-painted original produced in Milan c. 1450. © 1985 U.S. Games Systems. Illus. reproduced by permission of U.S. Games Systems. Further reproduction prohibited.

La Ruota (The Wheel of Fortune)[143]

Fortune is a splendidly gowned, winged, blindfolded lady in the center of a wheel that bears four people being first raised and then lowered in worldly position. The highest, who proclaims "I reign," has ass's ears, like Pinocchio. All the conventional Tarot decks have some similar arrangement of the wheel but Fortune herself is frequently absent. The Wheel of Fortune is another medieval symbol that was often carved on the outside of cathedrals around the same circular form that, from the inside, contained the rose window. Mâle quotes from *Somme le Roi*, a medieval work: "In these cathedral churches and royal abbeys is Dame Fortune who turns topsy-turvy faster than a windmill."[144] The idea also appears in Boethius' *Consolation of Philosophy*: "I cause a rapid wheel to turn; I love to raise the fallen and to abase the proud."[145]

The arrangement suggested by Moakley puts Fortune exactly in the center, as the pivotal image. Thus, as she says, Love and Death are equated and related. Fortune is the enemy of Chastity. (Chastity is left out of the Tarot, though in this deck the Moon is borne by Diana, who also appears in the *minchiate*, and she is the goddess of a rather fierce chastity who sometimes rode in Renaissance processions.)[146] She thus becomes a major figure instead of an attribute. Her position is reversed from that of the later Tarot, which puts the Hermit (Time) ahead of her.

I Danari (Coins)[147]

Moakley's placement of Coins right after Fortune further reinforces Fortune's pivotal position. She relates them to the gold of the traitor (the Hanged Man holds bags of gold in some later decks) and to the mirror of Prudence, who in some decks replaces him. Moakley states that the motifs on the Queen's robe in this suit match those of Fortune but this is not apparent from the photographs. Fortune's motifs are like those of the Pope. The Queen of Coins faces the viewer's left and the Queen of Swords faces the viewer's right. The coin the Queen bears—depicted as a very large disk of gold—does have a motif like those on Fortune's dress: so does the gown of the lady on the Chariot, as does that of the lady Lover. As a feminine suit, the ace is high, and follows the Page. It shows an enormous disk. The name of this suit shows considerable variation, from Coins (Deniers) to Pentacles; the association of it with Prudence, who is not usually in the deck, requires the Coins to be interpreted as mirrors; while Waite's association of them with the Dish of the Grail Hallows requires them to become dishes. The conversion of the dish into the suit of Diamonds is problematical too, though Waite's suggestion that it became Clubs is even more forced. There may be no absolute relation between the Italian suits and the French ones from which our English suits derives.[148] This ambivalent suit inserts a note of doubt into most interpretations, and it is interesting that this is the one of which Williams makes the most use: it is mentioned twice as often as the others, by a rough count (seven times, to only three each for the other three suits). Williams makes it the means for creating earth, from which gold comes.

Illus. 28 Queen of Swords and Illus. 29 Queen of Coins.
Visconti-Sforza Tarocchi.
Facsimile and reconstructed edition created from hand-painted original produced in Milan c. 1450. © 1985 U.S. Games Systems.
Illus. reproduced by permission of U.S. Games Systems.
Further reproduction prohibited.

Il Traditore (The Hanged Man)[149]

Traitors have broken the medieval allegiance based on land and military service, and mutual fealty between the levels of hierarchy. During the Renaissance these things could be bought for gold. The customary punishment of the traitor was to be hung upside-down and beaten; or, if not caught, to be painted in this ignoble attitude.

Prudence is a dancing man in some packs (he does a balancing act) and the card is sometimes called "The Acrobat." Hargrave shows such a card, in an early eighteenth-century French Tarot: he is a handsome youth in slashed sleeves and shapely stockings, standing on one foot with the other raised, arms akimbo as he balances. He is, as it were, the Hanged Man right side up.[150] Moakley thinks that only the *Waite-Smith* deck has a truly noble Hanged Man, and he does have the golden look of Balder upon his face, as he hangs from a single pole as from a cross, while all the others hang from a pair of posts with a lintel, suggesting the doorway, or the gibbet, or the swing. Moakley thinks "the hanged knight" may have been an acrobat who did tricks in the Carnival procession.[151]

The association of the traitor with an inverted position is fully supported by Moakley. I would add that in the *Hell* of Dante's *Divine Comedy*, the devil has fallen from Heaven and plunged head down into the center of the earth, where he sticks fast in a sea of ice, forever gnawing the heads of three traitors, right-side-up only from Hell's point of view. Satan is, of course, the ultimate traitor. The position of the Hanged Man (XII) next to Death (XIII) is the same in every deck: he is the most ambivalent card of all and it is typical of Williams to move him from position twelve to position thirteen, which in every real Tarot is occupied by the nameless Death. Williams, like Eliot, associates the Hanged Man with Christ: I will discuss below the effect the change of position has on the overall structure of the deck.

Il Gobbo (The Hunchback, Time, The Hermit)[152]

He is an old hunchback who carries an hourglass. This later becomes a lantern and he becomes a hermit, but he continues to bear his staff. Time had his own triumph in Petrarch's poem and in the *minchiate* deck still has his signs of the Zodiac and the four Elements. Williams is in line with both Petrarch and occult tradition in making the four suits represent the four Elements, though his order is not the same as the one given in occult books. The Hermit is sometimes seen in depictions of the Triumph of Death, as Moakley says. In later decks he no longer accompanies Death, but escorts Fortune instead. Williams associates him with the Lovers, as a type of the Way of Negation.

Illus. 30 Time (Hermit). *Visconti-Sforza Tarocchi.* Facsimile and reconstructed edition created from hand-painted original produced in Milan c. 1450. © 1985 U.S. Games Systems. Illus. reproduced by permission of U.S. Games Systems. Further reproduction prohibited.

La Morte (Death)[153]

Moakley quotes Vasari in support of the assertion that Death was not associated with the Carnival until the sixteenth century, but here he is, and he is central to the Triumphs of Petrarch. Death is always XIII except in Williams. He is a semi-skeleton, with a bow in his hand and no dead but himself. He certainly resembles the Death of the medieval Dance of Death. Later decks give him a scythe and let him reap heads and limbs. Here he is crowned in a scrap of gravecloth and grins macabrely. This whole section is his Triumph, and Moakley conceives him as sharing his car with the Tower and the

Devil, the Hanged Man serving as his captive whom the Devil carries off to Hell.

Il Diavolo (The Devil)[154]

This card and the next are missing from the *Visconti-Sforza* set so we shall never know what they looked like as Bembo portrayed them. The Devil is part of Death's Triumph, bearing away damned souls; Moakley says that the conventional Tarot's winged Temperance (who became XIV) represents the Angel come for the souls of the saved. She suggests that the developed placement of the Virtues was arranged just to keep Death in position thirteen, but it is more symmetrical and elegant an arrangement than that. Moakley supports her identification of the suits with the Virtues by citing Saint Bernardine's famous sermon: "Consider the avarice of money, the stupidity or doggish ferocity of clubs, the goblets or cups of drunkenness and gluttony, the swords of hatred and war."[155] The fifteenth-century card chosen by Moakley to illustrate this position shows a horned, bearded, winged, bird-footed being with a second face over his genitals and a pitchfork on his shoulder. He has no captives.

La Casa de Diavolo (The Devil's House, the Tower)[156]

Moakley says it is the Hellmouth of the medieval mystery plays. I wish I could find a Tarot card of any period where it possesses the fierce animal mask of open maw that the Hellmouth implies. The fifteenth-century card she shows here to substitute for the lost Bembo original is a burning tower just as it is in the conventional decks. It may be a gate of Hell but it is no Hellmouth, for it lacks a gaping bestial orifice. The famous setting for the Valenciennes Passion Play of 1547 shows the "mansions" that formed the scenery arranged in a straight line, and has, next to *L'enfer* (Hell), with its elaborate display of devils and the proper open jaws of a Hellmouth, a second flaming building. This building is labeled "*Le Limbo des peres*"—The Limbo of the Fathers—depicted as a tower which burns vigorously and is just as conveniently located beside "*La mer*," as Moakley says Hell should be. This tower looks more like the Falling Tower than the Hellmouth does, but of course the date allows the influence to be from the Tarot card to the play, rather than the other way around.[157] In the Chester Cycle, one of the pageant wagons (an alternative to the stationary "mansion") showed the Tower of Babel, a playlet put on by the carpenter's guild and featuring a comic dialogue by the carpenters.[158] This Cycle is of course of another country, so it cannot be used as proof either, but the case for equating the Tower with Hell as such is not perfectly proven.

Car Three

Le Spade (Swords)[159]

These figures are all in armor. Moakley puts them here because Justice is included in the following group, which is the Triumph of Eternity. As a masculine suit, Ten is highest, and the Ace comes at the end of the sequence. The King and Queen are crowned as well as armored, and all bear swords.

La Stella (The Star)[160]

This beautiful lady, by the same hand as Fortitude and Temperance, supports a gleaming star. The Star, Sun, and Moon are captives of Eternity, being carried away from their former allegiance to Time. The conventional deck puts the star in the sky without the aid of the lady, who kneels and pours streams of water from two cups.

La Luna (The Moon)[161]

Since the moon looks larger than a star, it is placed next in order in all Tarots: the *Visconti-Sforza* deck shows Diana holding a crescent moon. Her bow is broken because she is a captive of Eternity. Later versions of the card associate the moon with madness by including a mysterious pair of howling dogs, and a reference to the sea in the form of a menacing lobster or whatever creature of the deep it is. The Moon card of the "Tarot of Charles VI" shows a pair of astronomer/astrologists as attendants: maybe a modern card should show a pair of astronauts.

Il Sole (The Sun)[162]

Here, a winged putto holds up a red sun-face triumphing over the Moon by his size, but he is himself a captive of Eternity. Perhaps the fat putto gave rise to the playing children of the conventional deck, though in some of the decks they appear as a pair of adults.

L'Agnolo (The Angel, The Day of Judgment)[163]

God the Father with crown and orb looks down over two angels with trumpets: perhaps Williams intends the word Trumps in his novel's title to be a pun addressing not only the atout-trumps but the Trump of Judgement as well? The three dead arise from a common tomb. The conventional deck shows only the angel and the rising dead.

La Justicia (Justice)[164]

I wonder if perhaps Justice is here in the early decks because so many medieval Last Judgements show St. Michael with his scales dividing the damned from the saved. In the *Visconti-Sforza* deck a knight in armour with a sword rides across the top of the card, and the feminine Virtue sits crowned, with a sword in one hand and a scales in the other; but she is not blindfolded as is modern Justice in representations of her on public buildings. The presence of the knight seems to offer special corroboration of Moakley's thesis that the suits represent the Virtues, for the suit of Swords shows all its court figures in armour.

Il Mondo (The World)[165]

This card, according to Moakley, shows the Car of Eternity. In the *Visconti-Sforza* deck it includes a globe with the New Jerusalem depicted as a splendid mandala-castle, held aloft by two putti. Moakley explains that in late Renaissance triumphal processions the Car of Eternity was supported, like the throne of God, with the tetramorphs, the four evangelical beasts of Lion, Ox, Eagle, and Man, and these appear around the garland mandorla of "the World" in modern cards. (The soul of Carnival went to Heaven in a balloon in a procession of 1891, in latter-day support of the thesis that the King of Carnival died to give way to Lent.)

The appearance of the mandala form—it is constant in the cards, being a lovely globe with a city or a landscape inside it the early cards and a dancing nude figure inside a wreath in later forms—suggests a truly universal application. This card is the symbol of completion in every sense: it completes the deck, it ends the procession, it reveals the triumphator of Petrarch's poem (Eternity), it exhibits a mandala which in C.G. Jung's thought is the spontaneous image of completion in all cultures and in the dreams of moderns as well. Williams lays emphasis on the singleness of the dancing figure, so that he too sees this card as an image of the One.

Jung writes concerning the mandala:

> [...] it could even be called the *archetype of wholeness*. Because of this significance, the "quaternity of the One" is the schema for all images of God, as depicted in the visions of Ezekiel, Daniel, and Enoch, and as the representation of Horus with his four sons also shows. The latter suggests an interesting differentiation, inasmuch as there are occasionally representations in which three of the sons have animals' heads and only one human head, in keeping with the Old Testament visions as well as with the emblems of the seraphim which were transferred to the evangelists [...][166]

The early Tarot card for "the World" or "the Universe" is suggested in this passage:

> The Heavenly Jerusalem of Revelation is known to everybody. Coming to the Indian world of ideas, we find the city of Brahma on the world mountain, Meru. We read in the *Golden Flower* "[...] In the purple hall of the city of Jade dwells the God of Utmost Emptiness and life."[167]

Other mandala symbols are the wheel, sun, star, and circular formations:[168] the captives of Eternity include sun, star, and moon, while the wheel appears earlier in the deck. Jung is precise about the psychological meaning of this symbol:

> As I have said, mandala means "circle." There are innumerable variants of the motif [...] but they are all based on the squaring of a circle. Their basic motif is a premonition of a centre of personality, a kind of central point within the psyche, to which everything is related, by which everything is arranged, and which is itself a source of energy.[169]

He explains, "[t]his centre is not felt or thought of as the ego but, if one may so express it, as the *self*."[170]

Chart 4. Moakley's Triumph of Love

The Juggler
The Cups
Empress, Emperor, Popess, Pope
Love
Temperance, Love's Car, Fortitude
(all of the above in a single car)

Visconti-Sforza Tarot
Facsimile and reconstructed edition created from hand-painted original produced in Milan c. 1450. © 1985 U.S. Games Systems.

Chart 5. Moakley's Triumph of Death

The Staves
Fortune
The Coins
The Hanged Man
Time, Death, the Devil
Hell-Mouth
(all of the above in a single car)

Visconti-Sforza Tarot
Facsimile and reconstructed edition created from hand-painted original produced in Milan c. 1450.

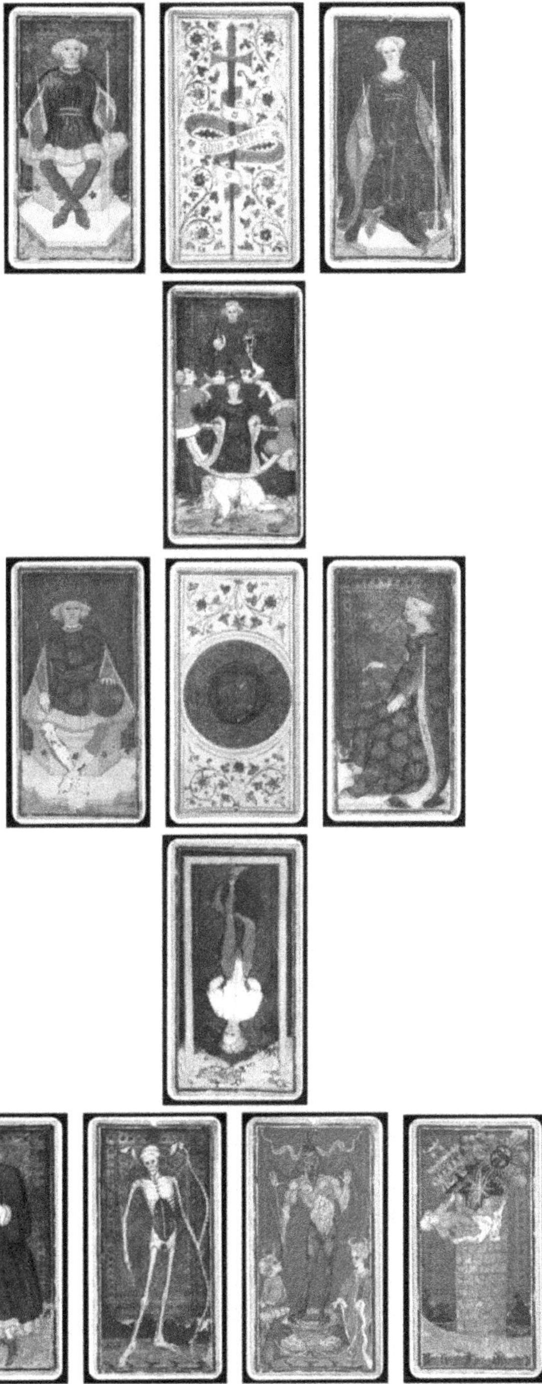

Chart 6. Moakley's Triumph of Eternity

The Swords

Star

Moon

Sun

Justice, The Universe, the Last Judgement

(all of the above in a single car)

Visconti-Sforza Tarot
Facsimile and reconstructed edition created from hand-painted original produced in Milan c. 1450. © 1985 U.S. Games Systems.

Il Matto (the Fool)[171]

He has no number and Moakley has him roaming about amongst the Trumps just as Williams does. He is dressed in the *Visconti-Sforza* deck as Folly, with feathers and torn clothes, and lacks his modern dog, though he has his club. In the developed Carnival, as in the medieval Feast of Fools, he was the Carnival King, for his associations go back to the Roman Saturnalia. E.O. James (1961) describes the mock-religious festival held on or about January first from the twelfth century onward, especially in France, which "was an occasion of excessive buffoonery and extravagance incorporating New Year and Saturnalian customs, some of which were borrowed from the folk plays."[172] He goes on to explain the function of the "Lord of Misrule:"

> At Beverley, Vienne, Noyon and Besançon such a burlesque figure was actually called, and treated as, Mock King. In this context the Christmas Mummers' play is true to type. The leader of the mighty forces of evil there becomes a farcical figure [...]. The reanimation of the slain or wounded hero is performed by a burlesque Doctor [...] and the masked personifications of the gods are now merely clowns with bladders, blackened faces and calves' tails. The all-important ritual marriage is performed in conjunction with the functionless Man-Woman or Boy-Girl character.[173]

This description is of a folk survival in another part of Europe than the one where Tarot cards were actively produced and actively preserved, but the association of the motifs will be seen below to have perfect conformity to Moakley's thesis, or at least to the factors which lead to her interpretations. She describes an Italian figure of "Lent" as having feathers placed like legs, to be pulled out week by week, and she says that the Fool is dressed as a penitent in baggy clothes which are fore-runners of the modern clowns.[174] She mentions the figure of Folly in Giotto's Arena Chapel, who also has feathers.

Mâle describes the Folly who opposes Prudence at the Cathedrals of Paris, Amiens, and Auzerre, as

> a scantily-clad man armed with a club, who walks among stones and at times receives one thrown at his head. He almost invariably has some shapeless object in his mouth. It is obvi-

ously the picture of an idiot at whom invisible boys throw stones. This realistic figure which seems to be taken direct from everyday life, has in fact a popular origin. Following an old tradition, mediaeval representations of idiots showed them carrying a club—later to become a fool's bauble—and eating a cheese.[175]

Left: Illus. 31 Fool. *Visconti-Sforza Tarocchi*. Facsimile and reconstructed edition created from hand-painted original produced in Milan c. 1450. © 1985 U.S. Games Systems. Illus. reproduced by permission of U.S. Games Systems.
Further reproduction prohibited.

Right: Illus. 32 Line drawing of Fresco of Folly or Foolishness.
Giotto. Arena Chapel, Padua. 1306.

This particular personification of the Fool (as an idiot) is perhaps associated with the popular notion that the idiot's penis is unusually large, in compensation for his lack of brains. Willeford quotes John Cleland's *Memoirs of a Woman of Pleasure* (1963) to this effect. The Fool's bauble, the club, the clown's bladder or slapstick, all represent both phallus and scepter:[176] the triumphator of Rome carried a red-painted phallus as well as a scepter.[177] The profoundly Dionysian symbolism of all of this will be discussed in detail below. Mâle's suggestion of the medieval idiot pursued by children helps suggest the origin of the pursuing dog in the conventional Tarot:

> Hark, hark, the dogs do bark,
> Beggars are coming to town;
> Some in jags, and some in rags,
> And some in velvet gowns.[178]

Moakley makes "the ragged tramp"[179] move freely as modern parade clowns do in fact move freely along outside the regular procession of automobiles, marching bands, and floats. The Fool gradually acquired more and more elegant and royal clothes (one thinks of the "velvet gowns"). Apparently the court jester, the circus clown, and the playing card Joker are all related to this image. *The Little Tramp* of Charlie Chaplin, the two tramps of *Waiting for Godot*, the Lenten penitent, the clowns of the *commedia dell'arte*, and the temporary saturnalian King—the Lord of Misrule—are all united in it. In the mockery of Christ, his crowning with thorns, the royal cloak placed over his scourge-striped back, and the reed-scepter in bound hands, we see a Saturnalian practice carried out by Roman soldiers. In that case, Williams's equation of this card with the One who unites all the others—Christ the Fool—is very close to the mark indeed. *Ecce Homo*: in the Fool we do indeed behold the Man, despised and rejected of men, the eternal outsider who makes all things new.

I conclude this annotated review of Gertrude Moakley's profoundly significant work with her description of the early game of Tarots, from "Notes on the Tarot as a Game" in the 1959 edition of A.E. Waite's *Pictorial Key to the Tarot*. The oldest form of the game, she tells us, is played by three players (a fourth player becomes a dealer only). Each player receives twenty-four cards, the remaining six being set aside or traded in by the dealer for six of his own. The game proceeds with declarations of melds, playing for tricks (the Fool may be played as a Joker usually is). The game continues until the player scores 100 points. The structure of the scoring is especially interesting for the interpretation of the Tarot.

> The five Greater Trumps (XVII-XXI, the cards which represent the triumph of Eternity): count 5 points for three of these, 10 points for four, 15 points if a player has all five.

The five Lesser Trumps (I-V, the cards which represent the captives of Cupid): count the same as the Greater Trumps.
The seven "Tarot Trumps," (I, XXI, Fool, and the Kings of the four suits): count 15 points for any three of these.[180]

Moakley gives the following explanation of the masculine-feminine dualism of the suits: "The masculine suits of Swords and Staves rank from king high to ace low. The feminine suits of Cups and Coins rank the same as the masculine from king down to page, but from there on the order is reversed: ace is highest, then two, and so on down to ten."[181]

For the aid of the reader in visualizing the concept of Greater and Lesser Trumps in the early deck, I give the following lists: I think she means them to be applied to a conventional deck of the sort developed in the eighteenth century so I give both the fifteenth century order and the modern:

Chart 7. Greater and Lesser Trumps

Greater Trumps: "triumph of Eternity"

(15th C)	Moon	XVII	Star	(18th C)
	Sun	XVIII	Moon	
	Judgement	XIX	Sun	
	Justice	XX	Judgement	
	World	XXI	World	

Lesser Trumps: "captives of Cupid"

	Juggler	I	Juggler	
	Empress	II	Popess	
	Emperor	III	Empress	
	Popess	IV	Emperor	
	Pope	V	Pope	

The "Tarot Trumps" are set up in a combination of three and four: three from the arcana and four representing the four suits. The arcana are represented by their first and last card (alpha and omega, as it were), and by the one that can play the part of any of them: the Fool. It is as Williams says: "till the confusion of substance be abolished and the unity of person be proclaimed" (GT 179; ch. 11).

V. The Traditional Tarot

Top left: Illus. 33. *Visconti-Sforza Tarocchi*. Facsimile and reconstructed edition created from hand-painted original produced in Milan c. 1450. © 1985 U.S. Games Systems. Top right: Illus. 34 Marseilles Tarot. B.P. Grimaud. No date. Bottom left: Illus. 35 *Egyptian Tarot*, Based on illus. from Comte de Saint-Germain's *Practical Astrology* (1901), derived from Paul Christian (Jean-Baptiste Pitois 1811-1877). © 1978 U.S. Games Systems. Bottom right: Illus. 36 *Rider-Waite Tarot*®. Pamela Smith (artist) and Arthur Waite. 1909. © 1971 U.S. Games Systems. Illustrations reproduced by permission of U.S. Games Systems. Further reproduction prohibited.

Before going on to discuss Charles Williams's own version of the Tarot, I will outline the conventional deck, to bring out its traditional structure. It differs from the fifteenth-century pattern in small ways, but not more than might be expected of five hundred years: in fact its relative fixedness is remarkable. It has followed the general rule of becoming more coherent, more rational and symmetrical in its form as it passed through various anonymous hands. The attempts of various occultists in the past two hundred years to improve upon this received order are not really very successful, and have a rather forced quality to an artist's eye.

Following the suggestion of Williams that the meaning of the cards lies in their order—"it isn't the time behind them, but the process in them, that's important" (GT 46-47; ch. 3)—and "perhaps there was meaning in the order as in the paintings" (GT 226; ch. 14)—I have set them out in both linear and circular form. Gershom Scholem (1965) says of the world of the Kabbalah, "in the chain of being, everything is magically contained in everything else," because, as a Kabbalist has written, "where you stand, there stand all the worlds."[182]

The linear order derives from the Tarot as a triumphal procession. It is an especially medieval sort of order, with its roots in deepest antiquity. Wylie Sypher (1955) says in discussing the Gothic style:

> All these images from actuality [are] presented in a simple linear succession, like the story unfolded in the medallions of stained glass or in the statues arranged side by side within a cathedral porch or along a façade.[183]

He continues:

> [T]his simple linear arrangement of episodes, as in the mystery play, presented on pageant wagons—wagon following wagon past the same spot until the cycle of playlets is complete. This one-dimensional form of the theatric movement has been called "processional" [...][184]

Chart 8. The Linear Order

	Juggler	1.	
		2.	Popess
		3.	Empress
LOVE		4.	Emperor
		5.	Pope
	Lovers	6.	
	Chariot	7.	
			8. Justice
	Hermit	9.	
	Fortune	10.	
DEATH			11. Fortitude
	Hanged Man	12.	
	Death	13.	
			14. Temperance
	Devil	15.	
	Tower	16.	
		17.	Star
ETERNITY		18.	Moon
		19.	Sun
		20.	Judgement
	World	21.	
	Fool	22.	

He concludes:

> In contrast to this Renaissance unified time-space perspective, the medieval time-space perspective seems linear and non-Euclidian, having a one-dimensional extension, unrolling like the episodes on a film.[185]

The circular form is suggested by Moakley's statement that sometimes a procession moved around a palace courtyard while the spectators watched from the windows. "It was then called a carrousel. Today our amusement park merry-go-rounds still have triumphal 'cars' and horses for the 'knights'—and are often called 'carrousels.'"[186]

I find that each arrangement is suggestive of meanings without contradicting the other, but in the circular form the Fool goes best in the center, as Williams has him. Those who have used the Tarot cards for divination will note that the following arrangements are not "spreads" to be used to receive the random fall of the cards that have been shuffled or otherwise ordered to induce the action of synchronicity. Rather, they are the orders used for contemplation, to make the inner relationships of the cards apparent.

The Virtues seem to perform a structural task in the deck. They are present as attendants, and hence do not have any specific symbolic function in their placement as such (so that elaborate mental acrobatics about their meaning in any specific position are unnecessary). Rather, they serve in the developed Tarot to set various parts of the deck apart. I cannot account for there being only three of them except to say that when an odd number—twenty-one—is being divided into four parts, it is helpful to do this with an odd number of dividers. None of the traditional Vices associated with Virtues is present except that of the missing Virtue (Prudence)—that is Folly, or the Fool, who plays quite a different role here. I am postulating that the Fool does not form part of the sequence.

In the standard Tarot, there are seven cards in the first sequence (Love), followed by the Virtue Justice (moved from its early position near the very end of the deck as an attribute of the Last Judgment). There follow two cards, then Fortitude, then two more cards, followed by Temperance. The latter two Virtues, which were originally attendants of Love, according to Moakley, have moved over to complete the balance of the deck. In the deck designed by A.E. Waite and Pamela Colman Smith, these positions are the same but their order is changed to Fortitude/Justice/Temperance in an attempt to make them mean something in particular. Another occult deck, that of Paul Foster Case and Jesse Burns Park, changes the order to Fortitude/Justice/Temperance for the same reason. These efforts suggest that the conventional order really *is* meaningless except for its structuring purpose, and that various attempts to place the Virtues in a more meaningful position are unnecessary.

Chart 9. The Circular Order

ETERNITY World 21. I. Juggler LOVE

Judgement 20. 2. Popess

Sun 19. 3. Empress

Moon 18. 4. Emperor

Star 17. 0. 5. Pope

Tower 16. Fool 6. Lovers

Devil 15. 7. Chariot

Temperance 14. 8. Justice

Death 13. 9. Hermit

Hanged Man 12. 10. Fortune

11.

Fortitude

DEATH

If the Virtues are designated by a "V" and the other cards by the number thus separated, the sequence is 7–V–2–V–2–V–7, or, as becomes obvious, 7–7–7. The central set of seven cards includes the Virtues along with four profoundly ambivalent cards the Hermit and the Wheel of Fortune in one part and the Hanged Man and Death in the other. In the first seven cards, Love is the triumphator; in the second seven, Death triumphs; and in the last seven, it is Eternity who triumphs. The shift of the Virtues has only served to emphasize this structure more clearly. Furthermore, there is a nice relationship between the placement of Love and his Chariot, at the end of the first sequence, and the Devil and his Tower at the beginning of the final sequence. They become Love versus Anti-Love. They are exactly balanced and when the cards are arranged in a circle this becomes especially clear. Moreover, the Juggler at the beginning balances with the Universe (or World) at the end, suggesting very strongly the relationship of Creator/Creation which Williams uses in *The Greater Trumps*. Between the Juggler and Love are the four captives of love, made up of two pairs, one sacred and one secular, comprising the whole power structure of *this world*. Between the Devil and the Universe (Eternity) are the three celestial cards and the Last Judgement, all attributes of the *other world*. The central sequence is one of transition, or as Jung himself would put it, *transformation*, culminating in the pivotal thirteenth card, Death, whether the Hermit is Time or a contemplative as he accompanies Fortune, and whether the Hanged Man is a condemned traitor, or the acrobat of sudden reversals, or an image of Death's ultimate conqueror, as he accompanies Death.

Placing the Fool outside the deck, or central to it when the deck is made into a circle, enables him to relate to all of the cards in turn, since "everything is magically contained in everything else." There is in the Fool tradition a special relationship between the Fool and the King, the Lover, the Saint, the Penitent, Fortune, Death, and the Devil, as well as with the primal One. Williams suggests that he is really identical with the Juggler-Magician-Creator as well.

As Moakley argues, the Tarot represents a Triumph, or series of allegorical Triumphs, based upon the Roman Triumph. The word "trump" is a corruption of the original name, "Game of Triumphs." The word "Triumph" itself, however, is even more significant. It was the special cheer—*triumpe*—with which the triumphator was hailed. The Latin word, *triumphus*, from which "triumph" comes, was equated by the oldest explanation of its meaning (that of the Roman writer Varro) with the Greek θρι'αμβος: t(h)riambe.[187] According to H.S. Versnel, whose book *Triumphus* (1970) examines the matter in detail, the Greek word *triumphos* appeared "as an epiclesis [invocation] and as the name of a song developed from an exclamation θρι'αμβος."[188] As a song, a dithyramb, in honor of Dionysus, and an exclamation invoking his epiphany, the word *triumpe* came from Greece, both directly in Dionysian cult and by way of Etruscan processions from which the Roman triumph was derived. And before its arrival in Greece it came even earlier from Asia Minor, where Dionysus himself originated. Versnel says, "the cheer *triumpe*, which gave the triumph its name, was originally an exclamation by which a god of the 'dying and rising' type was summoned to epiphany."[189] Linguistically, this "exclamation derived from a pre-Greek language has in Greek developed into θρι'αμβος, in Latin into *triumpe*. In both cases its function is that of invoking a god or gods and inviting them to manifest themselves. Etruria is the link connecting θρι'αμβος and *triumpe*, it being possible that a pre-Greek word was taken over by Etruscan and, independently, by Greek."[190]

Versnel states that "the triumph developed after the example of a New Year festival in which the appearance of the reborn or returning god was accompanied with, sometimes identical with the annual investiture of the King."[191] There was in Rome the *ludi Romani* (New Year Festival), which took place in September.[192] The *ludi* had a procession, games (competitions), and a banquet (similar to the Babylonian *atiku*: see below).[193] Versnel says of these activities, "the New Year festival was, as we know, characterized by a renewal of the kingship by means of a re-investiture of the king, and at the same time by the epiphany of the great god in the shape of the king!"[194] This Roman festival, which the Triumph resembled, through its two elements: the Dionysiac call to epiphany *triumpe* (via Etruria) and the identification of the triumphator with the God Jupiter, came from Etruria. The Etruscans brought this New Year festival with them from Asia Minor, along with its centre, a god called *Dionysos* in Greece: he was "a figure of the 'dying and rising' type,"[195] who invoked by a cry which became *triompe* in Greek, was represented on New Year's Day by the King. Dionysus himself came to Rome from Greece directly, but he was known earlier in Etruria as well and was called *Tinia*, where he was associated with the sun and depicted as a "beardless, sometimes ivy-wreathed youth."[196] Versnel notes that Zeus and Dionysus were to the Cretans different aspects of the same god: Dionysus may mean "Zeus-son" or "child Zeus."[197] The Triumph itself identified the triumphator with Jupiter (who is the Roman Zeus) and hailed him with the cry of greeting derived from Dionysian worship.

In the *pompa triumphalis*, the Triumph of the victorious general, upon which the allegorical and actual Triumphs of the Renaissance are based, the procession came into the city of Rome ahead of the triumphator's chariot, bearing the spoils of war, pictures of battles and of conquered cities and peoples, gifts from the conquered ones (laurel wreaths), white oxen to be sacrificed to Jupiter, and trumpeters. Then came the prisoners in chains (sometimes to be executed privately) directly before the *currus triumphalis*. The lectors in "red war dress" carried the *fasces*, a bundle of rods bound together with an axe. Then came the triumphator.[198] His face was painted with red lead[199] as was the statue of Jupiter in his temple.[200] Over his head was lifted aloft the *corona triumphalis* of gold oak leaves.[201] The chariot upon which he stood was tall and two-wheeled, pulled by four white horses. It was decorated with laurel leaves and had a phallus fastened beneath it. Possibly bells and whips were attached as well. His splendid costume consisted of the special garments of the god Jupiter, the *vesta triumphalis*: these were the *tunica palmata* which had palm-leaves embroidered upon it in gold, and the toga *picta* which bore gold stars. Both garments were dyed purple. He wore a crown of laurel on his head, and carried a laurel branch in his right hand and an eagle-surmounted ivory scepter in his left.[202] The slave who bore up the crown of golden oak leaves over his head said to him again and again, "*Respice post te, hominem te esse memento*,"[203] which is translated, "O Conqueror, look behind you, and remember you are mortal."[204] Versnel says that various elements of the chariot, including the phallus, flails and bells, and the iron ring which the slave wore, were all "apotropaeic means of warding off *invidia*."[205] Apotropaeic objects "turn away" evil. Willeford adds that the chariot of the conqueror was "surrounded by dancing gold-crowned clowns and satyrs, who made obscene gestures and course jokes," and that the conqueror himself held "a dried cockerel's comb as an amulet against the evil eye."[206]

The triumphator was a bearer of good fortune to the city of Rome, Versnel says. He had "dynamism," that quality frequently called *mana*, a term which is under controversy, but which conveys the sense of numinous power.[207] "The victor has a power he can impart to others."[208] When he comes into the city, he brings with him a period of "prosperity, peace and welfare."[209] Here we see the relationship which Versnel postulates between the Triumph and the New Year's festival, and we will now see how he explains the significance of the relationship.

In Egypt there was "a sacred mystery play" in which the old king was given a funeral and resurrected "in the person of the new King."[210] He was invested, installed, and banqueted. The new king (who was of course still the old king who had undergone a symbolic ceremony) was regarded as Horus, and the old king as Osiris (who had been killed by Set). There was a ritual fight between Horus and Set in the ceremonial drama.[211] Horus was in fact the old god of the Nile Valley, and Set the god of Upper Egypt; the union of these two divisions of the Nile had formed the Kingdom of Egypt. In his person as Osiris the king carried the crook, the flail, and the scepter.[212] The Heb Sed, as this drama was called, was a periodic rite, in which the death and "resurrection in death" of Osiris was enacted, on New Year's Eve, followed by the rejuvenation and ritual re-identification of the king with Horus.[213]

In Mesopotamia, the "New Year Festival" was called the *atiku*, celebrated at the Vernal Equinox, in which the divine marriage was re-enacted.[214] The king enacted the part of the god, while the role of the goddess was played by a priestess. New Year's Day in Rome occurred both at the Ides of March (the Vernal Equinox) and at the Saturnalia (January 1) from which our own New Year's comes.[215]

The Greek *Anthesterion* was also a spring festival of Dionysus. It consisted of three days: the first featured the opening of the wine casks, the second a drinking feast, and the third, the entertainment of the dead.[216] It was on the second day that Dionysus entered the city,[217] riding upon a *carrus navilis* (a boat-shaped car) accompanied by a sacrificial bull and an entourage of revellers. Versnel remarks that Shrove Tuesday is "the New Year's Eve of the Christians"[218] and that its carnival customs have an origin in Dionysian rite, including the use of masks, phalloi, and street fighters.

All of these "New Years" are thus spring (or pre-spring) festivals of new life, whether they renew the king's power by resurrecting him as a god, as in Egypt; by causing him to consummate the divine marriage of a god, as in Mesopotamia; or by hailing him in the wine, as in the Greek Dionysian *Anthesterion* procession, or in the Etruscan procession the *ludi Romani*, and finally in the Triumph of Rome. The echo of these motifs in the various cards of the Tarot will be apparent.

In *The Roman Triumph* (1962) Robert Payne gives a history of the many Triumphs of Rome, describing their various forms, both those of conquering generals and those of the Emperors. He describes the Triumphs of Christian Emperors and shows how the Triumph became associated with the Church as well, in peaceful processions over the centuries, especially in the Corpus Christi procession, where the Host—the Body of Christ—was borne along in honour. Renaissance paintings show this being done, and the practise continues to the present day. Payne also details the resurgence of the Triumph in the early Renaissance. According to his account, in AD 1037, Heribert, Archbishop of Milan, had made a battle-car with the city's patron saint and the banner of the commune, to serve as a "symbol to represent the unity of the people fighting for communal liberty."[219] We have already seen that the triumphator of Roman times brought his dynamism as a victor, and the captured dynamism of his enemies, sealed in their blood and enshrined in their captured war apparel, which was brought to the Capitoline Hill to remain there in honour of Jupiter the All-Powerful. Heribert himself identified his battle-car with the Ark of the Covenant, which after the destruction of the Temple came to be represented as travelling on wheels—it appears in that form at the early Synagogue in Capernaum and in the paintings in the Synagogue of Dura Europos on the Euphrates, both of which draw their symbolism from Hellenistic sources. The vehicle continued to serve as a rolling rallying point, and took on the significance of a triumphal car. The procession that accompanied the *carrocio*, as the battle-wagon was called, became known as a *trionfi*. The importance of the vehicle itself may account for the presence in the Tarot of a "Chariot" card, which has its own identity.

As Payne says, Dante saw Beatrice rising in a griffin-drawn chariot in a divine pageant. First came "Four living creatures with green foliage crowned; / Each with six wings was plumed, their plumage lined / All full of eyes;"[220]—these are the Tetramorphs which usually appear on the Tarot card "The World," as we have seen—Dante writes, "But read Ezekiel, who's depicted them / Even as he saw them [...]"[221]

> And in the space betwixt the four came on
> A triumph-car, on two wheels travelling,
> And at the shoulders of a Gryphon drawn;[222]

Besides this magnificent steed, "golden of limb," and "all dappled red-and-white," (who represents the "twy-natured" Christ, in Charles Williams's interpretations, The Figure of Beatrice), there are three dancing ladies, one of red, one of green, and one of white, representing the theological Virtues of Faith, Hope, and Charity, and:

> Four by the left wheel, clad in purple guise,
> Made festival; and she who led the ball
> Among them, in her forehead had three eyes.[223]

These are the four cardinal Virtues that are so frequently associated with Triumphs in Renaissance art, three of which appear in the Tarot: she who bore three eyes was Prudence.[224] Dorothy Sayers (1955) points out that "in the Corpus Christi procession, the Holy Host would normally be carried under a canopy; but for the canopy, Dante has substituted a *carroccio*, or war chariot, such as then belonged to every Italian city."[225]

The Corpus Christi procession, the Papal processions, and the *carroccio*, were examples of Triumph tradition in a medieval context. Frederick II captured the Milanese *carroccio* and brought it to Rome as a spoil.[226] This marked a renewal of the older tradition, and the condottiere and emperors copied the Roman forms in this as in other ways. Petrarch wrote *I Trionfi* as an allegory based upon this revival of Roman tradition. The Triumph was more and more frequently enacted, with Christian elements where pagan motifs no longer served, and the Triumphs of the past were depicted in art. In the sixteenth century the masque of the Triumph (as had been described in Dante) became popular, often designed by contemporary artists. The procession became more and more abstract and symbolic, and the depiction of imaginary processions continued as well. An eighteenth-century example of the Triumph can be seen in the sculptured relief of Pierre Prud'hon, "Le Triomphe de la Revolution," in which Revolution rides on a four-wheeled car with her Phyrgian cap and staff, holding a level; she is drawn by Justice with her scales, Fortitude with a column, and a figure which, being nude, is identified as Truth, holding a mirror aloft. Ahead of them all is Fraternity with an up-rearing *fasces*, driving the forces of reaction (these include a figure holding a mask) before the triumphant Revolution. Temperance is conspicuously absent.[227]

Many of the conventions of the Triumph passed into the theater, and the public procession continued, still enshrined in its carnival form in North America, for instance, in the Mardi Gras parades of

New Orleans, as well as in many other public events. The persistent association of the triumphal procession with Carnival, and with Dionysus in particular, brings us to the final element in our preparation for Williams's Tarot: an examination of the "dying and rising" god himself. On this subject, I will use Walter Otto's *Dionysus, Myth and Cult* (1965) as a source. Seeking to understand the god's role, Otto says, "Plutarch gives us the answer that Dionysus, according to Greek belief, was the lord and bearer of all moist nature."[228] Associated with him are ivy, trees (especially fruit trees), the vine (hence wine), the myrtle (associated with the dead), flowers (especially the flowers of the vine), roses, violets, the fig tree, and the pine. The *thyrsus* which his devotees carried was a tall staff wreathed in ivy and crowned with a pine cone, and the phalluses associated with him were made of fig wood because of the shape of the fruit.[229] Of these associations,

> the sovereignty of Dionysus was not only to be recognized in the juice of fruits whose crowning glory was wine but also in the sperms of living creatures. From this sphere of the god's activity [can be] traced the origin of the custom in which a phallus was crowned with wreaths and carried around in the god's cult.[230]

In further emphasis upon the god's "moist" associations, Otto points out, "Dionysus comes out of the water and returns to it."[231] He emerges out of the sea, out of lakes, out of the damp forest, out of grottoes.[232]

The chief animals associated with Dionysus are those whose sexual traits are highly regarded by man: the bull,[233] which was sacrificed even in Rome, and the goat,[234] which we still see as an incarnation of Satan—he appears so in the Tarot. Also associated with Dionysus in a lesser position was the ass,[235] who is often associated in medieval times with the Fool, who was sometimes depicted as wearing an ass's ears, a motif which also appears in the Tarot.

Otto declares that Dionysus is "a god who is mad!"[236] As he says, "the visage of every true god is the visage of a world. There can be a god who is mad only if there is a mad world which reveals itself through him."[237] Dionysus is the god both of noise—pandaemonium—and of silence, a "deathly silence."[238] A mask representing his face as a brooding bearded visage with an ivy crown (looking not unlike the Holy Face of Lucca) was hung upon a wooden column, and the wine was mixed before it and offered to it. The bearded face was enhanced by a long robe draped about the column,[239] and twined with ivy and flowers: one thinks of the effigy or the scarecrow. He is thus "the god of confrontation."[240] Otto says "it is his nature to appear suddenly and with overwhelming might before mankind;"[241] thus he is the god of "all moist nature," the "god who is mad," and especially importantly for the present paper, "the god who appears."[242]

As Otto says:

> The name Θρι'αμβος which was applied to a Dionysiac hymn and to the god himself (perhaps it is basically identical with Διθυ'ραμβος) is perpetuated, as we know, in the Etrusco-Latin word *triump(h)us*; and in the Roman triumphal procession, which has become historical, it is no accident that the *triumphator*, who took over not only the costume of the image of Jupiter but also its red make-up, reminds us of Dionysus.[243]

Otto's definitive study of Dionysus is introduced with the following extraordinarily apt statement:

> In the center of everything significant, in the center of every final intention stands the image of man himself—the form in which he wishes to see himself. It is asinine to say that he lent this image to the Almighty, and thus the forms of men's god came into being. It was in the godhead that this image first appeared to him. Before man was in the position to see himself, God manifested Himself to him. His image preceded the human image. What the form and nature of man could or should be, man learned from the appearance of the Divine.[244]

I have quoted above Versnel's designation of the word *triumphus* "as an epiclesis," which "developed from the exclamation θρι'αμβος (Triompe)," and Otto's statement that "the name Θρι'αμβος was applied [...] to the god himself." Versnel is borrowing a technical term from the vocabulary of the Christian Liturgy: epiclesis, which means "invocation." It is usually applied to that part of Eucharist called the Prayer of Consecration where the Holy Spirit is invoked, and the bread and wine are transformed into the Body and Blood of Christ in the Name of the Father.

In his classic study of the Christian liturgy, *The Shape of the Liturgy* (1945), Dom Gregory Dix refers to "that passage of Theodotus which relates the 'transformation of the Bread into spiritual power' to the 'hallowing by the power of *the Name*,'" He continues,

> A similar notion lies behind the phrase of Irenaeus that "the bread receiving the invocation (or 'naming', epiclesis) of God is no more common bread but eucharist," It seems, indeed, likely that the whole primitive usage of the word epiclesis in connection with the eucharist is intimately connected with this Jewish "blessing of the Name" in all food benedictions, obligatory on Jews and primitive Christians alike in their table-blessings.[245]

In early Judaic Christianity, Christ was sometimes called "the Name of the Father." Fr. Jean Daniélou (1964) says that "the Name, which in the Old Testament signified the manifestation of God in the world, alongside but independently of God's Word, was for the primitive Christian community a designation of Christ as Word of God incarnate."[246] He quotes a second-century homily, the Gospel of Truth: "Now the Name of the Father is the Son."[247] The Name of God and the invocation which bring about his epiphany are thus the same thing: and the epiclesis is present in the Christian Liturgy, in the Dionysian rite, and in the name of the Roman procession. This name is ultimately present, then, in the name of the deck of cards, the Game of Triumphs, the Tarot.

VI. The Charles Williams Tarot

Illus. 37 Ace of Cups, Illus. 38 Ace of Coins, Illus. 39 Ace of Clubs, Illus. 40 Ace of Swords. Marseilles Tarot. B.P. Grimaud. No date.

We are now ready to turn to *The Greater Trumps* for a study of the Tarot of Charles Williams. We know already that it is a Christian Tarot and that it embodies a process. The purpose of the uses to which the cards are put, Williams shows us, determines the end result and their effects not only upon the user but upon others as well. The fifteenth-century Italian Franciscan friar who declared that "the game of 'triumphs'" was "hateful to God" and "base in the eyes of the Christian faith" was only an early example of the long tradition of condemning the Tarot.

An English clergyman, writing on the occult (1971), warns,

> [...] there is a special danger for those who are serious practitioners of the Tarot. The devotee is called upon to pass through a mystical identification with each of the pleasant and unpleasant pictures on the cards. Even the dabbler suffers, and a student told me how he had to change his rooms because of the sense of evil that was released when his fellow students continually consulted the Tarot for guidance. Moreover, in constantly living by the Tarot, these students caused their proper capacities for decision-making to atrophy.[248]

Williams is not unaware that the Tarot is a double-edged weapon. This is especially true of his interpretation of the four suits. The crisis of the novel is brought about by a misuse of their power, for "there is in these suits a great relation to the four compacted elements of the created earth" (GT 47; ch. 3). When they are manipulated, they become "innumerable shapes, continuously shifting, sliding over and between each other. They were in masses of color—black, mostly, she seemed to see, but with ripples of grey and silver and fiery-red passing over them. Dark pillars of earth stood in the walls, and through them burning swords pierced, and huge old cups of pouring water were emptied, and grey clubs were beaten" (GT 257-58; ch. 16).

These colors correspond to the "outlandish dress of four striped colors, black and grey and silver and red" (GT 18; ch. 1) worn by the Fool in Williams's deck. Williams relates "Earth, water, air, and fire," to "Deniers, cups, scepters, swords" (GT 53; ch. 3). He thus sets up the following correspondence:

Clubs	=	grey	=	"grey clubs"
Deniers	=	black	=	"dark earth"
Swords	=	red	=	"burning swords"
Cups	=	silver	=	"cups of pouring water"

The entire deck, of which the suits are a part, are part of a dance, and "'the Dance is [...] everything' he answered. 'You'll see. Earth, air, fire, water—and the Greater Trumps'" (GT 54; ch. 3). The Trumps themselves "are the truths—the facts—call them what you will—principles of thought, actualities of corporate existence, Death and Love and certain Virtues and Meditation and the Benign Sun of Wisdom, and so on. You must see them—there aren't any words to tell you" (GT 110; ch. 7).

The suits of the Knapp-Hall deck are assigned colors: red for cups, yellow for coins, orange-bronze for wands, and blue for swords.

Illus. 41 Ace of Cups, Illus. 42 Ace of Coins, Illus. 43 Ace of Wands, Illus. 44 Ace of Swords. *Knapp-Hall Tarot.* Manly P. Hall and August Knapp. 1928. © 1985 U.S. Games Systems. Illus. reproduced by permission of U.S. Games Systems. Further reproduction prohibited.

Left: Illus. 45 Country Gentleman. Right: Illus. 46 A Stranger.
Grand Etteilla Egyptian Gypsies Tarot.
Based on an eighteenth-century Etteilla deck. B.P. Grimaud. No date.

Williams's attempt to make us "see them" occupies a goodly portion of his novel, and I will now show how he envisages the cards. Of the suits we are given only occasional glimpses. The King of Swords is called "The crowned chieftain of fire" (GT 263-64; ch. 16), "whose weapon quivered and glowed as if in a flame" (GT 250; ch. 15). The Queen of Chalices is seen "holding her cup against her heart" (GT 90; ch. 5): she is a "crowned and robed woman bearing the crimson cup" (GT 189; ch. 12). The Knight of Scepters is invoked in the figure of Aaron, Henry's uncle and Nancy's future father-in-law: "the old man's walking stick was the raised scepter; the old man was young again, and yet the same. The skull-cap was a heavy medieval head-dress [...]" (GT 89; ch. 5). Because the suit of Deniers is most frequently mentioned, we are allowed to see two of them, first the King: "a hatted figure, with a four-forked beard, holding a coin—or whatever it was—in a gloved hand" (GT 50; ch. 3). Second, "the black and purple of the Esquire of Deniers showed for a moment before it was swallowed up in the cloud as a negro youth in an outlandish garment holding aloft a shining bronze coin" (GT 189; ch. 12).[249]

We turn now to Williams's unique version of the order of the Greater Trumps themselves. I give them below as Williams gives them together with the approximate number of times they are mentioned in the text, which I think reflects their importance for Williams.

Chart 10. The Tarot Trumps, Triumphal Cars, and the Number of Times Each Trump is Mentioned in *The Greater Trumps*

Triumph of Love	1.	Juggler	14
	2.	Empress	10
	3.	Priestess	10
	4.	Priest	8
	5.	Emperor	12
	6.	Chariot	7
	7.	**Lovers**	**10**
	8.	Hermit	5
	9.	Temperance	3
	10.	Fortitude	3
	11.	Justice	3
Triumph of Death	12.	Wheel	8
	13.	Hanged Man	11
	14.	**Death**	**16**
	15.	Devil	9
	16.	Tower	10
Triumph of Eternity	17.	Star	3
	18.	Moon	4
	19.	**Sun**	**8**
	20.	Judgement	4
	21.	World	3
	22.	Fool	40

Chart 11. Williams's Triumph of Love

Chart 11 & 12. Illus. from Charles Williams, *The Triumph of Love* (New York: Noonday Press, 1962) front and end pages. Courtesy of Farrar, Straus and Giroux, LLC.

Chart 12. Williams's Triumphs of Death and Eternity

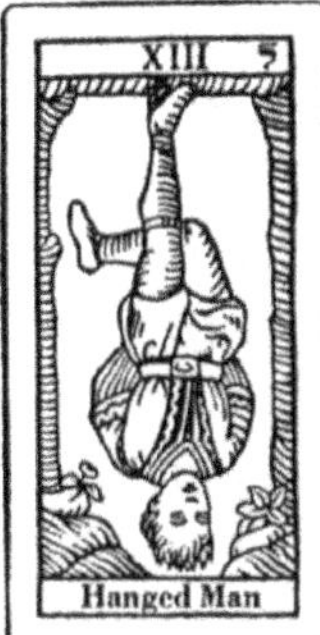

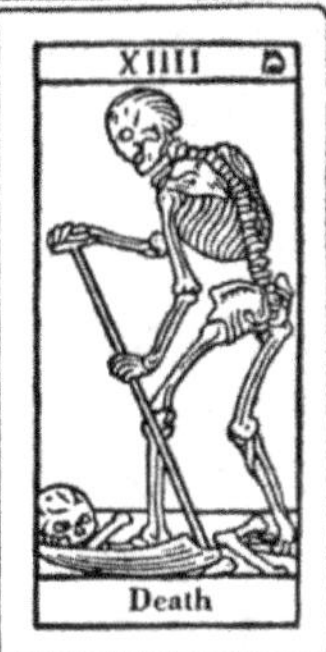

Some things spring out instantly from this arrangement. First, the Virtues are classed together and accorded only moderate importance. Second, the cards of Eternity are of secondary importance for Williams, except for the Sun. Third, Death, who is displaced to fourteenth position, is nonetheless very important, having the second greatest number of mentions in the whole deck. Between Death and the cards of low importance are a series of cards of about equal significance: the Empress, Priestess, Priest, Emperor, Chariot, Lovers, Wheel, Hanged Man, Devil, Tower, and the aforementioned Sun. Leading these a little, and only just less frequently mentioned than Death, is the Juggler. A huge majority of mentions is accorded to the Fool, who is obviously by far the most important figure in the deck.

In Williams's structure, the Juggler leads, followed by the Triumph of Love with a series of equally important cards. These are followed by the Hermit and the Virtues in the train of the rather significant Wheel, which, in the twelfth place, introduces a series of important cards of which Death is most frequently mentioned: this is the Triumph of Death. There follows the Triumph of Eternity to which only moderate attention is given, followed by the Fool, who is altogether the most important. The deck thus has two halves: first we see this world, where Love is dominant, and the Virtues are attendants of his car. The first eleven cards are thus devoted to this Triumph, led by the Juggler who created this world. The second half of the deck is the other world—subdivided into two parts. First is the Triumph of Death which has five cards, of which Death is the central one: Wheel, Hanged Man, Death, Devil, and Tower. Second is the Triumph of Eternity, which also comprises five cards and gives preponderance of mention to the central card, the Sun. The sequence is Star, Moon, Sun, Judgement, World. The Fool dominates the entire deck. Williams regards all luck as good, as he has shown in a lengthy passage in *The Figure of Beatrice* and in many of his plays, and in *Thomas Cranmer* he makes Death ("the Skeleton") a Christ-figure who identifies himself as "Christ's back." This series of Shiva-like figures who are both creator and destroyer, but always divine, will be discussed below. The shifting of Death to a less "unlucky" place demonstrates Williams's idea, and also gives that position—thirteenth—to the Hanged Man, in line with modern fascination with that card, which has come a long way from being merely an ignoble traitor.

The Noonday Press edition of *The Greater Trumps* has a set of illustrations of the Tarot cards in which the order of titles and numbers corresponds to that given by Williams in the text,[250] where he first names and numbers the cards. Closer examination of these illustrations shows them to include Hebrew letters that do not accord, in their presented order, with the true order of the Hebrew alphabet. When they are placed in the order of the letters they bear, they revert to the order of the fully developed—and numbered—cards of the exoteric Tarot. Thus the drawings and their Hebrew letters came from a traditional deck (Italian and Milanese) which have been re-ordered, re-titled, and re-numbered to accord with Williams's construction of the deck. This seems to me to prove finally that Williams invented his order and did so deliberately.

Illus. 47. Cover of the Paperback 1962 Noonday Press Edition of *The Greater Trumps*

Chart 13. Card Order in *The Greater Trump* Illustrations

Williams Roman Numerals		**Williams Hebrew Letters**		**Milanese Tarot by G. Sironi, Milan, 1882**	
I	The Juggler	Alef	The Juggler	I	Il Bagattel
II	The Empress	Beth	High Priestess	II	La Papessa
III	High Priestess	Gimel	The Empress	III	L'Imperatrice
IIII	Hierophant	Daleth	The Emperor	IIII	L'Imperatore
V	Emperor	He	Hierophant	V	Il Papa
VI	The Chariot	Vau	The Lovers	VI	Gli Amanti
VII	The Lovers	Zayin	The Chariot	VII	Il Carro
VIII	The Hermit	Cheth	Justice	VIII	La Giustizia
IX	Temperance	Teth	The Hermit	VIIII	L'Eremita
X	Fortitude	Yod	Wheel of Fortune	X	Ruota della For [?]
XI	Justice	Kaph	Fortitude	XI	La Forza
XII	Wheel of Fortune	Lamed	Hanged Man	XII	L'Appeso
XIII	Hanged Man	Mem	Death	XIII	La Morte
XIV	Death	Nun	Temperance	XIIII	La Temperan[za]
XV	The Devil	Samekh	The Devil	XV	Il Diavolo
XVI	Falling Tower	Ayin	Falling Tower	XVI	La Torre
XVII	The Star	Pe	The Star	XVII	La Stelle
XVIII	The Moon	Tzaddi	The Moon	XVIII	La Luna
XIX	The Sun	Qoph	The Sun	XIX	Il Sole
XX	Last Judgment	Resh	Last Judgment	XX	Il Giudizio
XXI	The Universe	Shin	The Universe	XXI	Milano
0	The Fool	Tav	The Fool		Il Matto

Note: This chart has been added to emphasize Patterson's point about the relationship between the Tarot illustrations in the Noonday Press edition of The Greater Trumps, *the "traditional" Tarot, and the order Williams gave the cards in his novel.*

The Greater Trumps contains a description, ranging from brief to lengthy, of every one of the Trumps. I have brought together the various descriptions and mentions of the cards (and in some cases of the figures of gold which match them in Williams's novel) in order to examine the full deck as Williams conceived it. The cards, in Williams's order, are as follows.

Juggler

The most characteristic trait of the Juggler is the set of golden balls he tosses: "the first [...] showed a Juggler casting little balls into the air" (GT 112; ch. 7). He is continually in movement: "the Juggler who danced continuously round the edge of the circle, tossing little balls and catching them again" (GT 28; ch. 2); "He seemed to her to run swiftly, while still he kept a score or so of balls spinning over him in the air" (GT 113; ch. 7), and "about him [the Fool] in a circle the juggler ran, forever tossing his balls" (GT 116; ch. 7).

When first seen as a card, he demonstrates Williams's conception of the deck as a whole:

> It was a man in a white tunic, but the face, tilted back, was foreshortened and darkened by the brim of some black cap that he wore, a cap so black that something of night itself seemed to have been used in the painting. The heavy shadow and the short pointed beard hid the face from the observer. On the breast of the tunic were three embroidered circles, the first made of swords and staffs and cups and coins, balanced one on the other from the coin at the bottom to the apex of two pointing swords at the top. Within this was a circle, so far as Nancy could see, made up of rounded representations of twenty of the superior cards each in its own round; and within that was a circle containing one figure, but that was so small she couldn't make out what it was. The man was apparently supposed to be juggling; one hand was up in the air, one hand was low and open towards the ground, and betwe en them, in an arch, as if tossed and caught and tossed again, were innumerable shining balls. (GT 16; ch. 1)

The suits are peripheral here, represented only by their symbols. There are only twenty Trumps (because the Juggler is present in his own form, wearing images of the rest of his companions), and the central figure is presumably the Fool. The Juggler has neither table nor scepter. Williams adds, "at the top left-hand corner of the card was a complex device of curiously interwoven lines." This device is mentioned once again, on the third of Williams's cards, the Priestess. Perhaps this "device" derives from the elaborate interlaced initials which the artist Pamela Colman Smith put on the deck she drew for A.E. Waite. Later, Williams explains, "'The cards were made with the images,' he answered, 'the marks in the corner of each of them is the seal of the bottom of each golden shape: seventy-eight figures, and as many seals on as many cards'" (GT 109; ch. 7).

Williams makes his interpretation of the Juggler perfectly clear:

> "The Juggler—if it is a juggler?" she asked.
>
> "It is the beginning of all things—a show, a dexterity of balance, a flight, and a falling. It's the only way he—whoever he was—could form the beginning and the continuation of the dance itself."
>
> "Is it God then?" Nancy asked, herself yet more hushed.
>
> Henry moved impatiently. "What do we know?" he answered. "This isn't a question of words. God or gods or no gods, these things are, and they're meant and manifested thus. Call it God if you like, but it's better to call it the Juggler and mean neither God nor no God." (GT 110-11; ch. 7)

The role of the Juggler as Creator (Yahweh? demiurge?) is made yet clearer:

> She saw—but this more in her own mind—the remote figure of the Juggler, standing in the void before creation was, and flinging up the glowing balls which came into being as they left his hands, and became planets and stars, and they remained some of them poised in the air, but others fell almost at once and dropped down below and soared again, until the creating form was lost behind the flight and the maze of the worlds. (GT 162; ch. 10)

Left: Illus. 48 Magician. Marseilles Tarot. B.P. Grimaud. No date.

Middle: Illus. 49 Magician. *Grand Jeu de Oracle des Dames*. Etteilla. France, 1870. Published as *The Book of Thoth*, © 2003 Lo Scarabeo. Illus. reproduced by permission of Lo Scarabeo. Further reproduction prohibited.

Right: Illus. 50 Magician. *Rider-Waite Tarot®*. Pamela Smith (artist) and Arthur Waite. 1909. © 1971 U.S. Games Systems. Illus. reproduced by permission of U.S. Games Systems. Further reproduction prohibited.

Even more explicit is this passage:

> Strain and stress were everywhere; the very arch held itself together by extreme force; the latest name for matter was Force, wasn't it? Electrical nuclei or something of that sort. If this antique beauty was all made of electrical nuclei, there might be—there must be—a dance going on somewhere in which even that running figure with the balls flying over it in curves would be outpaced. (GT 121; ch. 8)

Clearly Williams relates the balls to the conventional diagram of the atom with its nucleus surrounded by spinning particles, which in its turn owes much to the conventional diagram of the solar system. He states his meaning most succinctly of all: "the hand of the Juggler has been stretched to cast and catch the tossed balls of existence" (GT 265; ch. 16). These motifs are repeated when the Juggler and the Fool are united, but that will be examined below.

The Empress

Though he places the Empress second in the deck, she is clearly related by Williams to the Emperor. In putting her second he follows the fifteenth-century order of the deck, but he departs from that order in placing the Priestess in position three. The variant orders of Love's captives are:

15th Century (Moakley)		18th Century (traditional)	
II.	L'imperatrice	II.	La Papessa
III.	L'Imperadore	III.	L'Imperatrice
IV.	La Papessa	IV.	L'Imperatore
V.	Il Papa	V.	Il Papa

A.E. Waite		Charles Williams	
II.	High Priestess	II.	Empress
III.	Empress	III.	Woman Pope–High Priestess
IV.	Emperor	IV.	Pope–Hierophant
V.	Hierophant	V.	Emperor

Clearly, Williams is following the tradition of separating the sexes, but he reverses the order in each case: the primitive deck put the lovers in mixed couples—"the royal shapes of the Emperor with the Empress" (GT 74; ch. 5).[251] In discussing the couples, Williams follows this earlier pattern. He describes the Empress:

> [...] ceremonial robes; imperial head-dress, cloak falling like folded wings, proud, austere face lifted towards where in the arch of the gate, so that the light just caught it, was a heraldic carving of some flying creature. (GT 61; ch. 4)

This is actually his description of a large public effigy of a nurse which Nancy sees during her visionary ride in an automobile in Chapter Four, "The Chariot," and which she identifies with the Empress. The face is the diagnostic trait: "the clear cold face of the Empress" (GT 62; ch. 4).

Top left Illus. 51 Empress. Bottom left Illus. 54 Emperor.
Marseilles Tarot. B.P. Grimaud. No date.

Top middle: Illus. 52 Empress. *Oswald Wirth Tarot*. Oswald Wirth. Trumps 1889, revised 1926, redrawn by Michael Simeon 1966 (see U.S. Games edition). © 1976 U.S. Games Systems. Illus. reproduced by permission of U.S. Games Systems. Further reproduction prohibited.

Top right: Illus. 53 Empress. Bottom right: Illus. 55 Emperor. *Rider-Waite Tarot®*. Pamela Smith (artist) and Arthur Waite. 1909. © 1971 U.S. Games Systems. Illus. reproduced by permission of U.S. Games Systems. Further reproduction prohibited.

The High Priestess, the Woman Pope

The High Priestess is placed after the Empress, as in the fifteenth-century deck, but the order retains the sexual division of two women preceding two men of the traditional deck. Williams calls her "the hierophantic woman" (GT 16; ch. 1), and compares her to Sybil Coningsby, the mystical co-heroine of the novel: "She's like the Woman on the cards, but she doesn't know it—hierophantic, maid and matron at once" (GT 96; ch. 6) Williams gives a complete description of this card:

> It had been drawn sitting on an ancient throne between two heavy pillars; a cloud of smoke rolled high above the priestly head-dress and solemn veil that she wore, and under her feet were rivers pouring out in falling cataracts. One hand was stretched out as if directing the flow of those waters, the other lay on a heavy open volume, with great clasps undone, that rested on her knees. This card was stamped in the top left-hand corner with an involved figure of intermingled lines. (GT 16-17; ch. 1)

This lady owes much to the A.E. Waite and Oswald Wirth esoteric versions of the card, though the book she carries goes back to the earliest forms. The stream of water may have developed from the flowing hem of her robe as Pamela Colman Smith drew it. There is probably an element of this card in Joanna as well: her name parallels that of "Pope Joan" as this card is sometimes called, and in her final terrible wounding encounter with Nancy she seems to function as a hierophant. Sibyl's name, of course, means sibyl, or prophetess.

The High Priest, the Pope

Early and late decks put the Pope in position five, fourth of Love's captives, but Williams does not. He placed him next to his companion: "the mitred hierophant with the woman who equaled him" (GT 116; ch. 7). For description, he says only, "the hierophant, the Pope of the Tarots, took ritual steps" (GT 115; ch. 7). I would suggest that Williams equates Aaron (which was the name of the first High Priest of Israel to minister in the Tabernacle: he was the brother of Moses) with this card.

Top: Illus. 56 Pope. Illus. 57 High Priestess. Marseilles Tarot. B.P. Grimaud. No date.

Bottom left: Illus. 58 Popess. *Oswald Wirth Tarot*. Oswald Wirth. Trumps 1889, revised 1926, redrawn by Michael Simeon 1966 (see U.S. Games edition). © 1976 U.S. Games Systems. Illus. reproduced by permission of U.S. Games Systems. Further reproduction prohibited.

Bottom right: Illus. 59 High Priestess. *Rider-Waite Tarot®*. Pamela Smith (artist) and Arthur Waite. 1909. © 1971 U.S. Games Systems. Illus. reproduced by permission of U.S. Games Systems. Further reproduction prohibited.

The Emperor

This card is described directly by reference to "the white cloak of the Emperor" (GT 62; ch. 4), and "the crown of the Emperor" (GT 262; ch. 16): he is depicted as "a man in a great white cloak and a golden helmet with a crown round it" (GT 258; ch. 16). But he appears in the most quoted vision of Nancy's "Chariot" ride, as the policeman:

> [...] the Emperor of the Trumps, helmed, in a white cloak, stretching out one sceptred arm, as if Charlemagne, or one like him, stretched out his controlling sword over the tribes of Europe pouring from the forests and bade them pause or march as he would. (GT 60; ch. 4)

C.S. Lewis (1952) sees this vision of the world as "Order, envisaged not as restraint nor even as a convenience but as a beauty and splendour." Lewis continues wryly, "Perhaps no element in Williams's imagination separates him so widely as this from other writers. The modern world has planners and orderers in plenty, but they are not often poets: it has poets not a few, but they seldom see beauty in policemen."[252]

It is possible that Williams echoes the importance of the male lover in the character of Henry, whose name means "Ruler," or "Ruler in the home." The placement of the above-listed four cards emerges as that of the hierophantic couple (side-by-side) flanked and escorted by the Imperial couple whose function lies within the world, as below:

Empress	Priestess	Priest	Emperor
/ Nancy	/ Sybil	/ Aaron	/ Henry

The above and very tentative identification of Nancy with the Empress is based on her role as deflector of the magical storm: "She stretched out her arms, instinctively passionate to control the storm" (GT 224; ch. 14). The name Nancy derives from Anne, which means "Grace" (from the Hebrew Hannah, the mother of Samuel). She becomes a vehicle of Grace in this act, and to her lover Henry as well: "the warm hands of humanity in hers met the invasion and turned it" (GT 225; ch. 14). Williams's own explanation of this group is as follows:

She saw, as the girl's excited voice rushed on, the four great figures between whom the earth itself hovered—the double manifestation of a single fact, the body and soul of human existence, the Emperor and the Empress, and diagonally opposite them, the hierophants male and female, the quadruple security of knowledge and process upon earth. (GT 162; ch. 10)

The Chariot

Left: Illus. 60. *Grand Jeu de Oracle des Dames*. Etteilla. France, 1870. Published as *The Book of Thoth*, © 2003 Lo Scarabeo. Illus. reproduced by permission of Lo Scarabeo. Further reproduction prohibited.

Middle: Illus. 61. Chariot. *Oswald Wirth Tarot*. Oswald Wirth. Trumps 1889, revised 1926, redrawn by Michael Simeon 1966 (see U.S. Games edition). © 1976 U.S. Games Systems. Illus. reproduced by permission of U.S. Games Systems. Further reproduction prohibited.

Right: Illus. 62. Chariot. *Rider-Waite Tarot*®. Pamela Smith (artist) and Arthur Waite. 1909. © 1971 U.S. Games Systems. Illus. reproduced by permission of U.S. Games Systems. Further reproduction prohibited.

The appearance of this card as Williams describes it is clearly based upon the tradition of A.E. Waite and Oswald Wirth, for the emphasis is upon the sphinxes which draw it, and these do not appear in the traditional deck, which uses the conventional horses of the ancient Triumph. It is described as "the sphinx-drawn Chariot" (GT 29; ch. 2 and 262; ch. 16), which is "driven by some semi-Greek figure scourging on two sphinxes who drew that car" (GT 62; ch. 4). The Chariot itself is not only, for Williams, the Car of Love, but becomes "the rushing chariot of the world" (GT 162; ch. 10) for as Williams writes, "'Listen, among *them* is not the Chariot an Egyptian car, devised with two sphinxes, driven by a Greek, and having on it paintings of cities and islands?'" (GT 26; ch. 2). This is my source for relating the first half of Williams's deck to "this world." This is "the earth itself" which "hovered" between "the four great figures" of Empress, Priestess, Priest, and Emperor," just as the "other world" (which the World—Eternity—become) hovers between the four great supernatural figures of the Tetramorphs in the traditional Tarot. In Williams's interpretation, then, the four lovers are not the captives, but rather the attendants or escorts of the Chariot. The "Greek" driver may be derived from his traditional garb, which in both esoteric and exoteric deck is shown as Roman armor.

The Lovers

This Lovers card shows for Williams "the soul in its delighted society of terrestrial love" (GT 162; ch. 10). As he describes it,

> [...] and she saw the two lovers, each aureoled, each with hands stretched out, each clad in some wild beast's skin, dancing side by side down a long road that ran from a far-off point right down to the foreground. (GT 20; ch. 1)

Together they form "that joined beauty of the two lovers" (GT 115; ch. 7). Obviously this card is closely related to Nancy and Henry themselves. But beyond that (or rather an extension of that) they make clear the whole emphasis of the deck's first section: it represents the world of mankind, including the primeval pair, Adam and Eve, who outside of the Garden have turned from leaves to garments of "wild beast's skins"—or as Williams put it, "the Incarnation of Love," who is sovereign over the entire deck. It is time to quote what may be the most significant passage in the entire novel:

> "And what," Mr. Coningsby said, as if this riddle were entirely unanswerable, "what do you call the hypothesis of Christianity?"
>
> "The Deity of Love and the incarnation of Love?" Sybil suggested, adding "Of course, whether you agree with it is another thing." (GT 120; ch. 8)

Left: Illus. 63 Marseilles Tarot. B.P. Grimaud. No date.

Middle: Illus. 64 Lovers. *The Golden Dawn Tarot.* Robert Wang. 1977. © 1982 U.S. Games Systems. Illus. reproduced by permission of U.S. Games Systems. Further reproduction prohibited.

Right: Illus. 65 Lovers. *Rider-Waite Tarot®*. Pamela Smith (artist) and Arthur Waite. 1909. © 1971 U.S. Games Systems. Illus. reproduced by permission of U.S. Games Systems. Further reproduction prohibited.

"[A] major iconographical change and the most radical of all versions occurred around 1890 as part of the creation of the secret 'Inner Order' Tarot for the Hermetic Order of the Golden Dawn (founded in 1888). The deck did not become public until the 1970s when Robert Wang produced his version of The Golden Dawn Tarot. *Two founders of the Golden Dawn, Wynn Westcott (1848-1925) and S.L. MacGregor Mathers (1854-1918), despite earlier works by each in which the more usual Marseille-style Lovers were used, chose to depict Perseus freeing a chained Andromeda from a rock before she could be devoured by a threatening sea monster."*

Mary Greer, "An Iconographic History of the Lover's Card," Tarot in Culture Volume Two *(Clifford, ON: Valleyhome Books, 2014) 568.*

The Lovers card in Wang's deck conforms closely to the drawing published by Westcott in the 1890s. Waite's version contrasts sharply from it in its emphasis on Christian, rather than classical, symbolism.

The deck is divided into the Triumph of Love incarnate (God in man made manifest) and the Triumph of Love as Deity ("God is love"). These twin Triumphs demonstrate, in other words, (those of St. Athanasius) that "God and man is one Christ." The novel takes place during the days surrounding the Feast of the Incarnation—Christmas—and the church-going scene of Christmas Eve is not a mere nod at conventional Christianity but the precise presentation of the central theme of the novel:

> The mingled voices of men and boys were proclaiming the nature of Christ—"God and man is one Christ"; then the boys fell silent, and the men went on, "One, not by conversion of the Godhead into flesh, but by taking of the manhood into God." On the assertion they ceased, and the boys rushed joyously in, "One altogether, not"—they looked at the idea and tossed it airily away—"*not* by confusion of substance, but by unity"—they rose, they danced, they triumphed—"by unity, by unity"—they were silent, all but one, and that one fresh perfection proclaimed the full consummation, each syllable rounded, prolonged, exact—""by unity of person." (GT 125; ch. 8)

"They triumphed"—of course. The symbol of this doctrine is the embrace of Juggler and Fool, but that will be discussed below.

The Hermit

For Williams the Lovers demonstrate the form of Love incarnate which had been most meaningful in his life: that of marriage. He is the great theologian of married love, and of romantic love in general. But he recognized and wrote also of the other kind of love, that of the contemplative, for whom God does not appear in the flesh of the beloved (as in the Way of Affirmation), but through the Way of Negation. This is why he pairs the Hermit, "the old anchorite" (GT 29; ch. 2) with the Lovers, both in his list of cards and in the following passage, which I quote here in full: "On one side went the Hermit, the soul in its delighted solitude of contemplation, and on the other the Lovers, the soul in its delighted society of terrestrial love" (GT 162; ch. 10).

Illus. 66 Lovers. Illus. 67 Hermit. *Knapp-Hall Tarot.* Manly P. Hall and August Knapp. 1928. © 1985 U.S. Games Systems. Illus. reproduced by permission of U.S. Games Systems. Further reproduction prohibited.

The Knapp-Hall Tarot *incorporates a long road that comes right to the immediate foreground of the card, although the lovers do not dance, as Williams suggests. The Hermit from this same deck also seems to be walking a path, rather than standing in a stationary position.*

Temperance, Fortitude, Justice

Apparently the order of the Virtues is not important to Williams: he gives the one just quoted in his first listing of the deck, and another in the following passage, which is his only description of them: they are "an image closing the mouth of a lion, and another bearing a cup closed by its hand, and another with scales but with unbandaged eyes—which had been numbered in the paintings under the titles of Strength and Temperance and Justice" (GT 29; ch. 2). It will be noted that he gives Fortitude her common alternative name of "Strength" here, having used "Fortitude" previously. They are not mentioned again except in the summary (quoted above) in which Williams identified the Trumps with "the truths—the facts [...] principles of thought"—where he refers to "certain Virtues" (GT 110; ch. 7).

Clearly he thinks of them as a group and places them in association with "Love and certain Virtues and Meditation."

The Virtues complete the part of the deck representing Man, and especially Deity incarnate in Man, the human nature of Christ. Mankind is represented as composed of body and soul, each of which has a masculine and feminine form, and as seeking unity with God in Himself and within Mankind, in the union of male and female. We now turn to the second part of the deck. Before doing so, and in order to understand perfectly Williams's brilliant invention, we will examine the portion of the Creed of St. Athanasius bearing upon the Incarnation:

> Now the right Faith is that we believe and confess / that Our Lord Jesus Christ, the Son of God, is both God and man.
> He is God of the Substance of the Father, begotten before the worlds; / and he is Man, of the Substance of his Mother, born in the world;
> Perfect God; / perfect man, of reasoning soul and human flesh subsisting;
> Equal to the Father as touching his Godhead; / less than the Father as touching his Manhood.
> Who although he be God and man, / yet he is not two, but is one Christ [...][253]

These verses immediately precede those sung in the Christmas Eve service as described by Williams and quoted above.

The Wheel

Placed centrally in Williams's deck, the Wheel symbolizes the transition between the first part of the deck and the second, besides presenting a central mandala image. Williams describes it as a vision of Lothair Coningsby, Nancy's father (the ambitious civil servant). He sees it first as an image of futility, which as the Wheel of Fortune it obviously is: "as if bound upon a great wheel, spinning round, with lives bound to it" (GT 238; ch. 15) and, "—as the wheel turned: it didn't go quickly, but it was always revolving, and he had been on it for so long, so many years" (GT 238; ch. 15). This is the wheel of karma. Then, by an intensification of his vision, he sees:

> Wheels within wheels—there had been some phase of glory, angels or something, wheels full of eyes, cycles in cycles all vigilant and intelligent, revolving. (GT 238; ch. 15)

But the vision fades (as it had for Dante)—and he sees only "a vague wheel of innumerable hands, all intertwined and clasped and turning, turning faster and faster, turning out of mud and into the mist, hands falling from it, helplessly clutching. ..." (GT 238; ch. 15).

Illus. 68 Temperance. Illus. 69 Strength. Illus. 70 Justice.
Illus. 71 Wheel of Fortune. Marseilles Tarot. B.P. Grimaud. No date.

This motif—"the helpless hands that formed the Wheel" (GT 264; ch. 16)—appears once more, briefly, as Nancy and Henry behold the transfiguration of Sibyl Coningsby when she stretches out "a golden hand"—Williams compares it to "the hand of the Juggler" and "the hand of the Fool"—it is "the center of all things, the power and the glory, the pain glowing with a ruddy passion veiled by the aureate flesh—the hand of all martyrs, enduring; of all lovers, welcoming; of all rulers, summoning." The figures of the Tarot come rushing toward "the hand that, being human, was so much more than symbol" (GT 264; ch. 16). The hand of Sybil is revealed, briefly, as the hand of incarnate Deity: as are all our hands, as is all flesh.

The Hanged Man

That revelatory card is followed immediately in Williams's deck by what for many modern readers is the most compelling image of the Tarot. He first describes the card of the Hanged Man as showing "two other shapes who bore between them a pole or cross on which hung by his foot the image of a man" (GT 29; ch. 2). The "other shapes" are Williams's own invention. In a description of the dance of the Tarot images, as the Lovers moved, "before them rose the figure of the Hanged Man and they disjoined to pass on either side and went each under his cross" (GT 116; ch. 7). The "pole or cross" which is what supports the Hanged Man in Waite's deck but not in any traditional one, early or late, is identified with the Cross of Christ, and both Nancy and her father experience visions of this card. Nancy sees:

> there, with light full on it, thrown up in all its terrible detail, gaunt, bare, and cold, was a man, or the image of a man, hanging by his hands, his body thrust out from the pole which held it, his head dropping to one side, and on it a dreadful tangled head-dress [...] it was the wrong way up—the head should have been below; it was always so in the cards, the Hanged Man upside down. (GT 63; ch. 4)

Later she recalls it "as if it were a supernatural riddle, the shock of seeing the crucifix with its head above its feet, and the contrast with the Hanged Man of the cards" (GT 103; ch. 7). This explicitly Christian image is contrasted with Lothair's terrible (but accurate) vision of Henry, in which the identification of the Hanged Man as a traitor is present, though Williams probably did not know directly of this early meaning of the card. Lothair Coningsby (his name means "famous warrior"—but since this is explained by Williams as an obsession of its bearer—"Names had for him a horrid attraction, largely owing to his own [...] disastrous name" (GT 8; ch. 1)[254]—it probably has no symbolic content beyond a certain irony) sees that:

> Henry was, in the ridiculous reflections of the mist, hanging in the void, his head downwards, his hands out of sight behind him somewhere, his leg—one leg—drawn up across the other; it was the other he was hanging by. (GT 242; ch. 15)

This is an exact description of the posture of the Hanged Man in the *Waite-Smith* deck and in the traditional deck as well.

Left: Illus. 72 Hanged Man. Marseilles Tarot. B.P. Grimaud. No date.

Right: Illus. 73 Hanged Man. *Rider-Waite Tarot*®. Pamela Smith (artist) and Arthur Waite. 1909. © 1971 U.S. Games Systems. Illus. reproduced by permission of U.S. Games Systems. Further reproduction prohibited.

Death

Displaced by Williams from his unvarying position as the thirteenth card to place number fourteen, is "Death with the sickle" (GT 136; ch. 8). This attribute—"the stretched sickle of the image of Death" (GT 262; ch. 16)— identifies him: "the swift ubiquitous form of a sickle-armed Death" (GT 29; ch. 2). He is always "the naked figure of a peasant Death, his sickle in his right hand" (GT 90; ch. 5). A naked peasant, not a skeleton: Henry asks Aaron in seeking to identify the original Tarot deck" "and Death—is not Death a naked peasant, with a knife in his hand, with his sandals slung at his side?" (GT 26; ch. 2). There are certain images of Death used in Symbolist art (a style concurrent with Art Nouveau, which much influenced the style of Pamela Colman Smith's drawings) of which this would be a good description. The *Visconti-Sforza* deck makes him a dreadfully emaciated figure, and variations on the traditional deck usually make him a frank skeleton. The *Waite-Smith* deck has no influence here, for it makes Death a splendidly-armored skeleton on horseback. This is the only place where Death has a knife for Williams (unless he bears both knife and sickle, always a possibility for a peasant). When Aaron and Henry plot to kill Nancy's father, Aaron remarks dryly, "Death is one of the Greater Trumps" (GT 99; ch. 6). This is echoed by Nancy's agonized cry to Sybil about her father and Henry:

> "There's just Death between them, and I'm in the middle of it."
>
> Then," Sybil said, "there's something that isn't death, at least. And you might be more important than Death, mightn't you? In fact, you might be life perhaps." (GT 164; ch. 10)[255]

The Devil

A similar refusal to treat a card as merely malign, or as ultimately and irreversibly malign, is seen in Williams's descriptions of "the devil—if it is a devil?" (GT 110; ch. 7). He is called "the Devil" in some places, but he remains "a horned mystery bestriding two chained victims" (GT 29; ch. 2). Becoming explicit, Williams describes him as "a more ominous form still, Set of the Egyptians, with the donkey head, and the captives chained to him, the power of infinite malice" (GT 90; ch. 5), and again, as "the fearful shape of Set who was the worker of iniquity ruling over his blinded victims" (GT 178; ch. 11). Elsewhere he speaks of "the two victims who were dragged prisoners to the power of Set in the Tarot paintings" (GT 212; ch. 13). Set is the adversary and murderer of Osiris, the "corn god" who is resurrected year by year as Horus." The relationship of this pair of divinities to the king in Egyptian thought has been discussed already. By calling the Devil by Set's name, Williams relates him with his theme of Joanna as Isis distractedly seeking her son Horus: and as we know, she is to find him, in the person of Nancy, who bears a "gipsy name." The Devil, who is the Adversary, is always defeated in a fully Christian cosmology—or rather he plays his part (as in Job) and is ultimately incorporated into the necessary wholeness of divine action. The description given by Williams of the card corresponds to its traditional appearance, though the donkey-head seems to be Williams's contribution, for in the esoteric cards the Devil is goat-like (after Éliphas Lévi's famous illustration) and the exoteric cards show him as a leering (but horned) visage (or two).

Illus. 74 Death. Illus. 75 Devil. Illus. 76 Tower of Destruction.
Marseilles Tarot. B.P. Grimaud. No date.

The Tower

This card becomes an image of the purgatorial experience by which Henry is purified of his attempt upon the life of Nancy's father, so that he can be restored to her love. That passage, which is much too long to quote here in its entirety, is profoundly visionary:

> the Great Tower which reached almost out of sight, so loftily that it grew up and then always—just as his dimmed eyes strained to see the rising walls—tottered and swayed and began in a horrible silence to fall apart, but never quite apart. (GT 193; ch. 12)

The motif of "the Tower that fell continually" (GT 178; ch. 11) is its chief characteristic: it is "a tower that rose and fell into pieces, and then was re-arisen in some new place" (GT 29; ch. 2), and "a tower that continually fell into ruin and was continually re-edified" (GT 116; ch. 7). Williams opens the novel with Mr. Coningsby's peevish phrase, "Perfect Babel" (GT 3; ch. 1), and follows it with Nancy's pert rejoinder, "But Babel never was perfect, was it?" (GT 3; ch. 1). He uses the identification of the Tower with that of Babel as a symbol of pride and conflict: "the Tower that each had raised—the Babel of their desired heavens—had fallen in the tumult of their conflicting wills and languages" (GT 139; ch. 8). As an image of the defeat of overweening pride, or rather of the malign use of power and the desire to wrest from Heaven what can only be achieved by prayer and grace, the tower is the fit instrument of Henry's purgation.

The Star

The three celestial captives of Eternity are given unequal treatment by Williams; the Star is described only as "the woman who wore a crown of stars" (GT 29; ch. 2). The *Waite-Smith* deck shows the Empress as so crowned, but the context of the above description shows that Williams means the Star card by it. The traditional deck shows a kneeling woman pouring out water; her head is against a sky filled with large stars, so perhaps Williams's image is a poetic expression of this form.

The Moon

In his first mention of this card, Williams refers to "the twin beasts who had each of them on their heads a crescent moon" (GT 29; ch. 2). There are two beasts—they appear to be dogs—on the traditional card, but their heads do not bear crescents. He gives a very complete description of the traditional card (which in the *Waite-Smith* deck is simply a re-drawing of the traditional form rather than an occult inflation as in many of the others): this is one of the most mysterious of all the real Tarot cards and Williams's explanation of its meaning is a profound one. The two towers, the two dogs, and the "other creature—in a coat of shell" are as he describes them:

> For there, high between two towers, the moon shines, clear and perfect, and the towers are no longer Babels ever rising

> and falling, but complete in their degree. Below them again, on either side of a long and lonely road, two handless beasts—two dogs, or perhaps a wolf and a dog—sit howling, as if something which desired attainment cried out unprofitably to the gentle light disseminated from above; and again below, in the painting of mysterious depths, some other creature moves in the sea, in a coat of shell, clawed and armed, shut up in itself, but even itself crawling darkly towards a land which it does not comprehend. The sun is not yet risen, and if the Fool moves there he comes invisibly, or perhaps in widespread union with the light of the moon which is the reflection of the sun. (GT 226; ch. 14)

This card furnishes the title for Chapter 14, "The Moon of the Tarots."

Illus. 77 Star. Illus. 78 Moon. Illus. 79 Sun.
Marseilles Tarot. B.P. Grimaud. No date.

The Sun

Similarly, the Sun entitles Chapter 16, "Sun, stand thou still upon Gideon." In his description of the three celestial cards, which includes "the women who wore a crown of stars" and "the twin beasts who had each of them on their heads a crescent moon," this card becomes "the twin children on whose brows were two rayed suns in glory" (GT 29; ch. 2). The two children" appear—they are of various ages including adult—in the traditional Tarot, though the *Visconti-Sforza* deck has them as two putti. Williams describes them in detail:"

> It was the nineteenth card—that named the Sun—and was perfectly simple; the sun shone full in a clear sky, and two children—a boy and a girl—played happily below. Sybil smiled again as she contemplated them. "Aren't they the loveliest things?" she breathed, and indeed they were—so vivid, so intense, so rapturous under that beneficent light [...] (GT 17; ch. 1)

The light is diagnostic for Williams: he describes "the two children playing together under an unshaped sun, themselves shedding the light by which they played" (GT 262; ch. 16), and in a visionary sequence in the chapter named for the card, he makes "the sunlight shed itself about the whole house, and in the sunlight [...] seriously engrossed, two small strange children played" (GT 265; ch. 16). He explains the meaning of this card too: "Sybil stood there, and from her the sun of the Tarots ruled, and the holy children of the sun, the company of the blessed, were seen" (GT 17; ch. 1). Finally, in the summary of the deck which begins, "They [...] are the truths," he calls it "The Benign Sun of Wisdom" (GT 110; ch. 7).

The Last Judgement

The first image of this card emphasized equally the trumpeting angel and the resurrected, who for Williams is seen as a skeleton: "The heavenly form of judgement who danced with a skeleton half freed from its grave-clothes, and held a trumpet to its lips" (GT 29; ch. 2). Apparently Williams has transferred the traditional skeleton image from the card of Death to the card of the Last Judgement, for to a Christian, the final word on the skeleton is that it is to be the seed of the new body of the Resurrection. He changes the image slightly in the following passage: "he came to the pictures which were called (XX) The Last Judgment—where a Hand thrust out of a cloud touched a great sarcophagus and broke it, so that the skeleton within could arise" (GT 112; ch. 7). Whose hand it is, he reveals soon after: "Yet a tomb lay in their path, and the Fool—surely the motionless Fool!—stretch out its hand and from within it rose a skeleton" (GT 116; ch. 7). It is Nancy who sees this early revelation of the Fool's identity. Williams's pun on the words "trumpet" and "trumps" is suggested in the following passage: "the trumpets cry in the design which is called the Judgment, and the tombs are broken" (GT 226-27; ch. 14), which precisely describes the conventional card. He follows the defeat of the supernatural storm with a summary of his interpretation of the Triumph of Eternity:

> But if the Tarots hold, as has been dreamed, the message which all things in all places and times have also been dreamed to hold, then perhaps there was meaning in the order as in the paintings; the tale of the cards being completed when the mystery of the sun has opened in the place of the moon, and after that the trumpets cry in the design which is called the Judgment, and the tombs are broken, and then in the last mystery of all the single figure of what is called the world goes joyously dancing in a state beyond moon and sun, and the number of the Trumps is done. (GT 226-27; ch. 14)

The World

We first see this card as "the single figure who leaped in a rapture and was named the world" (GT 29; ch. 2). This describes both traditional and occult versions of the card: it is the singleness of the figure which is diagnostic: "and (XXI) The World—where a single singing form, as of a woman, rose in a ray of light towards a clear heaven of blue, leaving moon and sun and stars beneath her feet" (GT 112; ch. 7). This reveals to us Williams's conception of the structure of this part of the deck, as given in the passage quoted above. He refers finally to "the girdle of the woman who danced alone" (GT 262; ch. 16), and in both traditional occult versions the nude figure does trail a flowing ribbon of cloth about herself. The Tetramorphs, which usually appear on this card, are not mentioned, and in some ways Williams's description calls to mind the very early cards where a lady surmounts a globe.

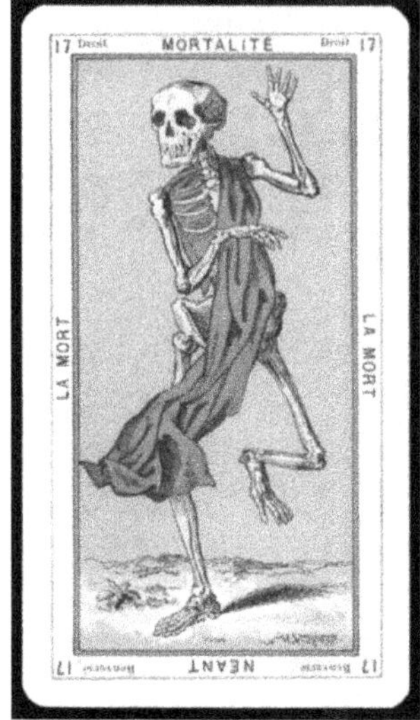

Top left: Illus. 80 Death. *Grand Jeu de Oracle des Dames*. Etteilla. France, 1870. Published as *The Book of Thoth*, © 2003 Lo Scarabeo. Illus. reproduced by permission of Lo Scarabeo.

Top middle: Illus. 81 Judgement. Bottom: Illus. 83 World. Marseilles Tarot. B.P. Grimaud. No date.

Top right: Illus. 82 World. *Golden Tarot of the Renaissance* (Estensi Tarot). Seventeen cards, including the World, based on originals of the "Charles VI" or "Gringonneur" Tarot, Italy, late 1400s. © 2004 Lo Scarabeo. Illus. reproduced by permission of Lo Scarabeo.

The Fool

The above quoted-summary of the last cards "among the one and twenty illuminations of the Greater Trumps" (GT 226; ch. 14) is concluded as follows:

> Save only for that which has no number and is called the Fool, because mankind finds it folly till it is known. It is sovereign or it is nothing, and if it is nothing then man was born dead. (GT 227; ch. 14)

As we have seen, the Fool, whether as a card or as the golden image, dominates the novel. He is neither mendicant, idiot, nor jester:

> She picked up the last card, numbered nought, and exhibited it. It might have needed some explanation, for it was obscure enough. It was painted with the figure of a young man, clothed in an outlandish dress of four striped colors, black and grey and silver and red; his legs and feet and arms were bare, and he had over one shoulder a staff, carved into serpentine curves, that carried a round bag, not unlike the balls with which the Juggler played. The bag rested against his shoulder, so that as he stood there he supported as well as bore it. Before him a dragon-fly, or some such airy creature, danced; by his side a larger thing, a lynx or young tiger, stretched itself up to him—whether in affection or attack could not be guessed, so poised between both the beast stood. The man's eyes were very bright. He was smiling, and the smile was so intense and rapt that those looking at it felt a quick motion of contempt—no sane man could be as happy as that. He was painted as if pausing in his stride, and there was no scenic background; he and his were seen against a flatness of dull gold. (GT 18-19; ch. 1)

This Fool is Williams's own, though it owes something to the *Waite-Smith* version; he frees it of the precipice and other unheeded menace: the dragon-fly appears nowhere else. The bag and staff are traditional. The attendant beast seems to be diagnostic of the card and the golden image alike, though he later has its own traits, to be discussed below. Of "The Fool and his tiger," Williams writes: "the tiger's quite life-like. So's the Fool" (GT 82-83; ch. 5). He reveals something of its mysterious meaning very late in the book:

> In the last of the Tarot cards, in the unnumbered illumination, she had seen something like that—a beast rearing against the Fool; in the midst of the images, rigid in the center of the base, she had seen it, a beast rearing against the fool. It had not then seemed to be attacking exactly; rather it had seemed as if poised in the very act of a secret measure trodden with its controlling partner among the more general measure trodden by

all the shapes. The Fool and the tiger, the combined and single mystery—" (GT 232-33; ch. 14)

As T.S. Eliot puts it in "Gerontion," "In the juvescence of the year / Came Christ the tiger."[256]

"Unnumbered:" this is another major trait: "that which has no number and is called the Fool, because mankind finds it folly till it is known. It is sovereign or it is nothing [...]" (GT 227; ch. 14). Williams's Fool is above all sovereign. This is symbolized by the Fool as an image, first by its apparent stillness: "the motionless Fool" (GT 116; ch. 7)—"It was still, it alone in the middle of all that curious dance did not move, though it stood as if poised for running. The lynx or other great cat by its side was motionless also" (GT 29-30; ch. 2). But this stillness is only apparent:

> "And the Fool who doesn't move?" she said after a pause.
>
> "All I can tell you of that," he said grimly, "is that it is the Fool who doesn't move. There are tales and writings of everything but the Fool: he comes into none of the doctrines or the fortunes. I've never yet seen what he can be."
>
> "Yet Aunt Sybil saw him move," she said. (GT 111; ch. 7)

This is "the vivid figure of the Fool" (GT 266; ch. 16) which dominates the novel:

> For a moment, as she ran, she thought she saw another form, growing out of the driving snow—a tall figure that ran down on the white stairs of the flakes, and as it touched earth circled round the overwhelmed man. Before it a gleam of pale gold, as of its own reflection, since no break in the storm allowed the sinking sun to lighten the world, danced in the air, on the ground, on hands that were stretched out towards the victim. They seemed to touch him, as in the Sistine Chapel the Hand of God forever touches the waking Adam, and vanished as she reached it. Only, for a moment again, she saw that gleam of flying gold pass away into the air [...] (GT 145-46; ch. 9)

Top: Illus. 84 Fool. *Golden Tarot of the Renaissance* (Estensi Tarot). Seventeen cards, including the Fool, based on originals of the "Charles VI" or "Gringonneur" Tarot, Italy, late 1400s. © 2004 Lo Scarabeo. Illus. reproduced by permission of Lo Scarabeo. Further reproduction prohibited.

Bottom left: Illus. 85 Folly. *Grand Etteilla Egyptian Gypsies Tarot.* Based on an eighteenth-century Etteilla deck. B.P. Grimaud. No date.

Bottom right: Illus. 86 Fool. Marseilles Tarot. B.P. Grimaud. No date.

This is the moment of rescue, when Henry's plan to murder Lothair is set aside by the Fool, lightly, through the agency of an old lady (Sybil) and a kitten.

> She knew where the golden light came from among the images; it came from the figure of the Fool who moved so much the most swiftly, who seemed to be everywhere at once, whose irradiation shone therefore so universally upward that it maintained the circle of gold high over all, under which the many other rays of color mingled and were dominated now by one, now by another. It had been, this afternoon, as if some figure—say, the Fool himself—had come speeding down from his own splendid abode of color to her brother's side ... (GT 161; ch. 10)

It is Sybil alone who fully understands the role of the Fool, insofar as he can be understood. She tells Nancy, "'never mind the storm; it's nothing, it's under the feet of the Fool [...]'" (GT 161; ch. 10). This is Williams's own answer to the discomfort some critics have felt at the ease with which the most malignant difficulties are set aside in his novels, for to him, everything is "under the feet of the Fool." This is, perhaps, the meaning of the "Fool and his tiger, the combined and single mystery," for Williams's Fool is a whole, a union of opposites, that image of God for which Jung pled in so many of his works, and perhaps most poignantly of all in *Memories, Dreams, Reflections*:

> The myth must ultimately take monotheism seriously and put aside its dualism, which, however much repudiated officially, has persisted until now and enthroned an eternal dark antagonist alongside the omnipotent Good. Room must be made within the system for the philosophical *complexio oppositorum* of Nicholas of Cusa and the moral ambivalence of Jacob Boehme; only thus can the One God be granted the wholeness and the synthesis of opposites which should be His.[257]

That the Fool dances is essential to his being. This is of course not an invention of Williams: Gerardus van der Leeuw (1963) writes of the medieval concept of dance, "the most eloquent example of such a dance of mystic contemplation is the image of the dancing Christ, which was current in Gnostic circles during the early centuries of our era."[258] He continues, "Medieval mysticism takes up this theme and describes the whole of life of the Lord in the form of a dance;" this can be seen in a fifteenth-century Shrove Tuesday song:

> Jesus, he must dance the lead,
> And the Virgin Mary;
> All must pay his rhythm heed
> To reach God's sanctuary.[259]

A contemporary theologian adds, "Modern theology has increasingly rejected the notion of an unmoved mover [...] and has come to speak of a dancing God, a God whose perfection is in process, whose life is involved in the relativities of relationship."[260] This understanding is of course no new thing in theology—to the Elizabethan mind, for instance, "the universe itself is one great dance comprising many lesser dances," as E.M.W. Tillyard (1967) tells us, and "It was creative love that first persuaded the warring atoms to move in order. Time and all its divisions are a dance."[261] This motif is developed in the poem *Orchestra* (1596) by Sir John Davies, which several writers on Williams have suggested as a source for his dancing golden images of the universals, and a quotation from it appears as the epigraph of the present paper.

We have already seen how the Juggler is identified as "neither God nor not God" (123; ch. 8)—and Williams relates him directly to the Fool:

> [...] of all the figures there was none left but the Juggler who appeared suddenly right under her eyes and went speedily up a single path which had late been multitudinous, and ran to meet the Fool. They came together; they embraced; the tossing balls fell over them in a shower of gold—and the golden mist covered everything." (116-17; ch. 7)

This apocalyptic image is repeated as Nancy remembers her visions: she "had lain awake for a long time, seeing only that last wild rush together of the Fool and the Juggler, that falling torrent of balls breaking into a curtain of golden spray, which thickened into cloud before her" (119-20; ch. 8)

Nancy and Sybil alike are granted visions of the Fool and his dance, for they are "Ladies whose understanding is of Love,"[262] as

Dante calls such women in *La Vita Nuova*. The Love they understand is that lord of terrible aspect whom Dante described:

> I thought a flame-coloured cloud appeared in my room, and in it I saw the figure of a lord, terrifying to anyone who should look at him. […] He said many things to me, of which I understood little, amongst them being: "I am your Lord."[263]

VII. The Sovereign Fool

Illus. 87 "The Dance of the Golden Images." Bonnie Callahan.
First pub. *Mythlore* 16.3 (#61) (1990), cover picture.

The figure of the Fool is so complex, so rich in resonance, that I will bring to bear upon it the remarkable insights of William Willeford's *The Fool and His Scepter* (1969) which might have been written as a direct commentary. Willeford is discussing Shakespeare's Fools and the great comic Fools of the twentieth century as specific examples, but he quotes and commends Charles Williams's use of the image.

According to Willeford, the traditional Fool wears feathers, as in the *Visconti-Sforza* Tarot and as in the court jester's costume, because of the bird-spirit association,[264] thus suggesting their ultimate, if remote, origin in the shaman. The earliest representation of a shaman associated with a bird is thought to be the tableaux in Lascaux cave, which shows an ithyphallic man who not only bears a bird's head upon his shoulders, but has next to him a staff with a bird at the top of it.[265] Fools and clowns derive from "phallic ritual and ceremonies of Dionysus."[266] Thus the Fool's "bauble" is probably a phallus[267] but it is also a scepter, which implies "that the fool has powers in some way equivalent to those of the king."[268] I would suggest that these powers go back much before the development of the concept of kingship, and that the king's scepter as an instrument of power derives from the shaman's staff or wand, an example of which is described above. The cock, whose comb sometimes adorns a Fool's head, is itself phallic, of course.[269] We have already seen, and Willeford reminds us again, that the conqueror carried a phallus painted red, which he showed to the people.[270]

But there is more: the common baggy, big-bellied clown costume suggests that "lumpishness" which equals chaos—"shapeless, yet material."[271] The word *follis* is Latin for "bellows or windbag," Willeford tells us, which, in the plural form of *folles,* means "puffed cheeks"; while in Italian, *buffare* means "puff."[272] He calls to mind a relationship between spirit, wind, blowing, and the Fool, all of which motifs span a range from the shaman who performs his miracles by blowing or sucking, to the Holy Spirit who is "a rushing mighty wind."[273] Again, the Fool's "motley," made of "particoloured bits and pieces" is characteristic, especially familiar to us in Harlequin's costume where it reverts to a symmetrical pattern. The shaman's coat of rags, tags, dependent amulets, masks, and mannequins come to mind here—"The multifarious appendages are attached either to the shaman's coat itself or to the belt. Some of them are animal and human figures, considered to be the shaman's helping spirits; others are disks of copper or iron, small bells, strips of leather or the skins of small animals, ribbons, rods, etc. Each of these objects has a symbolic significance."[274] —or again, "The shaman's dress consists of the skin of a wild goat or reindeer; the outside is almost covered with a multitude of twisted handkerchiefs of various sizes, which represent snakes [...]"[275] —these and other descriptions given by Andreas Lommel in *Shamanism, The Beginnings of Art* (1967) show the element of *assemblage* in shamanistic garb. One thinks of the striped garb of Williams's Fool; Willeford quotes E.W. Ives: "checked, striped, speckled, pied, patches, or parti-coloured coats were all admissible."[276]

Willeford speaks of the bells of the Fool. (It is curious how little sound Williams uses in his books—his golden figures only hum.) The bells for Willeford "present signs from another level of being,"[277] as they do in the Mass or in Hindu temples. I cannot help but think of the *ephod* or woven garment of the high Priest of Israel, who bore bells so that persons outside the Holy of Holies could hear him moving about within. It has been suggested—Willeford thinks somewhat fancifully—that the bells came from the same source. As the account in Genesis (28: 31–35) has it,

> And thou shalt make the robe of the ephod all of blue. And there shall be an hole in the top of it, in the midst thereof; it shall have a binding of woven work round about the hole of it, as it were the hole of an havergeon, that it be not rent. And beneath upon the hems of it thou shalt make pomegranates of blue, and of purple, and of scarlet, round about the hem thereof; and bells of gold between them round about: A golden bell and a pomegranate, a golden bell and a pomegranate, upon the hem of the robe round about. And it shall be upon Aaron to minister: and his sound shall be heard when he goeth in unto the holy place before the LORD, and when he cometh out, that he die not.

The relationship between this description and that of the shaman on the one hand, and of the belled and parti-coloured Fool on the other, is most tempting.

In keeping with the shamanist and Dionysian aspects of the Fool—which are expressed by Williams in his tiger companion, there are the animal elements—the asses' ears, coxcomb, and feathers as already mentioned, and foxtails, and calfskin. These Willeford relates to animal mummers and ultimately to religious ritual: Paleolithic representations of shamans in animal-skin costumes, accounts of Siberian shamans (like the ones given above), and images of Dionysus in his fawn-skin are well known. In *The Bacchae* of Euripides, the Chorus sings, "He wears the holy fawn-skin,"[278] and, interestingly enough, Pentheus mocks the god by calling him "one of those charlatan magicians, / with long yellow curls smelling of perfumes," and threatens "I'll stop his pounding with his wand and tossing / his head."[279]

Willeford goes on in a Dionysian vein to discuss the fact that both babbling and silence herald contact with the divine, or "possession."[280] Wine was "essential to the Saturnalia,"[281] which took place during the intercalary period and hence was outside normal time, and sacrificial victims were "made drunk to show their transcendence of the profane condition and their connection with the gods."[282] The babbling is that of the Fool as idiot, as Enid Welsford (1968) thinks he originally was:[283] Panofsky's relation of the Fool to the idiot has been discussed above.

Returning to the bauble, Willeford says it often was a mirror, an other-fool or double, an image of projection. It could argue with him, even stick out its tongue at him, breaking down the difference between reality and reflection.[284] We have seen that at Lascaux, the shaman and his staff have matching bird's-heads. The bauble is thus the Shadow, to use a Jungian term, and paired clowns or twin clowns sometimes appear, suggesting the primordial pair of mythology, from whom the rest of creation evolves.[285] We get a hint here of the embracing Juggler and Fool in their "shower of golden balls."

Willeford, quoting M. Willson Disher's description of the clown, says the clown is "neither wholly real nor unreal"[286]—as Williams says, "Neither God nor not God." Willeford speaks of imagination as "a radical reconstitution of experience in the interests of immediacy, totality, and a kind of meaning which is otherwise lacking,"[287] adding that such imagination is essential to symbolism in the Goethian sense. He quotes Goethe's saying in *Maximen and Reflexionen*, No. 1113:

> Symbolism transforms the phenomenon into idea and the idea into image; in the image the idea remains infinitely effective and unattainable and even when expressed in all languages remains inexpressible.[288]

Willeford recalls Jung's teaching that a symbol which crosses the threshold of consciousness has at first a numinous quality, but that this dynamism is lost in time, just as an experience of God loses its immediacy when it is turned into theology, only to be recovered by contact with new materials emerging from the unconscious.[289] One may see here again the Juggler (conscious order) and the Fool (unconscious?) embracing.

Willeford finds a relationship between the Fool and the Devil, Death, Fortune, the Saint, and Sexuality in medieval Christian drama. But most especially he sees the Fool as symbolizing that "self," which for Jung is "the matrix and organizing principle of consciousness."[290] Following other writers, Willeford "sees magical phenomena as belonging to a field of energy derived from the archetype [... and ...] this field of energy as constituting a dimension of experience and a characteristic mode of psychic functioning"[291] This is exactly what happens to Nancy when she rides in the Car—she has "fallen into such a magical field, with the dynamism of the archetypal constellation having usurped the controlling functions of ego-consciousness."[292] Readers who wish to check Williams's descriptions of alternative states of consciousness can find them validated and corroborated in either of Carlos Castanedas's books on his experiences as an apprentice to a Yaqui shaman. Castanedas' mentor, Don Juan, speaks of the "controlled folly" by which he is able to perceive or "see" the world in various unforgettable passages in *A Separate Reality*. As Willeford writes, "The fool [...] readmits the magical power of chaos."[293] Magical seeing is a special kind of apperception" which is that perception characterized by clearness, and by the relating of what is now present to previously acquired knowledge. He also writes:

> In one sense the modern Western nostalgia for "the primitive" is an expression of our cultural and psychological situation; in another it is extremely ancient. The notion of being completely *in* the world and not separated by the human condition with its burden of culture is as archetypal as is the notion of being

> radically divided from the world. This condition of being *in* the natural world—and out of culture—is often conceived as primitive, and the fool is one of the recurrent figures in which it is expressed.[294]

As Williams says of the Fool, "He was smiling, and the smile was so intense and rapt that those looking at it felt a quick motion of contempt—no sane man could be as happy as that" (GT 19; ch. 1).

Willeford considers magical thought in five categories: first is similarity, in which like produces like, an effect resembles its cause, and like things are identical. Second is contact or contagion, in which things once in contact remain in contact. Third is the concept of *pars pro toto*, in which a part of a thing *is* that thing (this is related to both the previous categories). Fourth is magical affinity, in which what affects one member of a group affects the others. Fifth is magical cause and effect, in which things can be influenced by supernatural and irrational events and thus set up a different sequence from that of natural cause and effect. Magic, in being based upon a universe operating according to the above principles, is "coercive:" it really can affect things. Willeford uses the term "fundamental apperception" for that "mystical participation" which deceives us into thinking that our everyday experiences are objective when they are really subjective. This causes "projection," the experience that our psychic life takes place outside of ourselves.[295] The archetypes are the "transpersonal, unconscious factors that actively shape our experience."[296]

It is as archetype, operating according to magical laws, that the Fool is identified with so many different roles. The "fool is like a chunk of chaos in which the archetypal divine child is present but unborn, his form and meaning hidden."[297] On the medieval stage, the devil's comic or fool element was a preservation of pagan wholeness, which included him as part of an "unconscious totality," rather than forcing him into the "dualism" that Willeford, like Jung, sees in official church doctrine which made the devil completely evil. Thus in medieval drama the devil and the personified Vice—Folly is a Vice—competed comically, in a pattern which evolved into the two-comic routine of today.

As we have seen, the Fool is closely linked with Dionysian rites. Dionysus is the god of "the irrational and of natural fertility;"[298] he is "a destructive but also highly creative link between man and the sources of natural life."[299] Thus, Williams's Fool is at home in the storm, for it is "under the feet of the Fool." As Willeford says, "the disorder of which he [Dionysus] is spirit is largely contained in his show, he serves the boundary of which he is the enemy; and in doing this, he sometimes even demonstrates an authority proper to the central figure of the established order."[300] The clown functions as a border between chaos and order—between waste land and kingdom[301]—like the triumphator who "enters" the city of Rome through an arch, a ceremonial door, and brings his dynamism in. "He [the clown] is impelled by the dynamism of chaos; they [his foils] are impelled by what they take to be the necessity of reinforcing the wall against the outside and of neutralizing what has broken through it into the world they govern."[302] Williams makes the forcing of the door to Aaron's house by the irresistible snow a high point of chaos in his novel: "At last those crashing buffets had torn lock and bolt from the doorpost; the door was flung back, and the invading masses of snow and wind swept in" (GT 210; ch. 13). The invasion takes the form of a dance—"the floor of the hall was covered before anyone could speak; the wind—if it were not rather the dance of searching shapes—swept into every corner" (GT 210; ch. 13). Of course it is Sybil who succeeds in shutting the door again, at least momentarily, until finally the golden mist of the Tarots within and the snowy powers—also of the Tarots—without are united, and "The two powers intermingled—golden mist with wind and snow; the flakes were aureoled, the mist was whitened" (GT 219; ch. 13) It is the climax of invasion: "Dancing feet went by; golden hands were stretched out and withdrawn. The invasion of the Tarots was fulfilled" (GT 220; ch. 13).

And yet this terrific and overpowering event is soon to be resolved by Nancy, and we are given foretaste of that as she muses, "the Tarots themselves were not more marvelous than the ordinary people she had so long unintelligently known. By the slightest vibration of the light in which she saw the world she saw it all differently; holy and beautiful, if sometimes perplexing and bewildering, went the figures of her knowledge" (GT 221; ch. 14). No wonder critics find the resolution disappointingly easy; three chapters before the end, Nancy sees that "Nothing was certain, but everything was safe—that was part of the mystery of Love [...] Nothing mattered beyond the full moment in which she could live to her utmost in the power and according to the laws of the dance" (GT 221-22; ch. 14).

The *center* is both the "source of established order" and the source of "the mana which erupts spontaneously from it;"[303] like the dynamism-filled triumphator who brought Dionysian *mana* into the city, having established and furthered its order. Willeford comments on "the coexistence of the cults of Apollo and Dionysus at Delphi."[304] We have already seen that Zeus (Jupiter) and Dionysus are really Father and Son, different aspects of a single god. Willeford compares this relationship of motifs to the meteorite (the uncontrollable natural event) set into the well of the highly rational square *kaaba* traditionally built by Abraham at Mecca.[305] I would add that Christianity as an established order "built by hands" is continuously disturbed and revivified by the action of the Holy Spirit.

This brings us to Willeford's theory on the relationship of the Fool to the King, which for him is central. He explains that "the title 'king' draws its resonance from an archaic pattern of belief, according to which the kingship is only secondarily a political office and is primarily magical and religious."[306] This is "the context from which the fool draws his highest symbolic value."[307] Perhaps we can find light here upon Moakley's intuition of a relationship between Fool and King. Briefly, the King embodied the fertility of the crops, and his potency enhanced them. In some cultures, although by no means all, as Frazer and others have thought, he was even killed to prevent his weakness from weakening the kingdom. In Egypt, as we have seen, he was re-crowned periodically to re-establish his power, with a ceremonial procession. In Mesopotamia (as described above) he reenacted the marriage of god and goddess with a priestess and a procession occurred there too. "The King is not only the magician, prophet, and lawgiver; he is also the hero, sometimes meeting with a tragic fate."[308] King David (and his son, King Solomon) embody this complex to Jews and Christians alike.

Now, when the triumphator, who was temporarily decked as a king—indeed, as Jupiter the king of the gods—was hailed by the cry *triompe* which was the name of a song for Dionysus and perhaps the name of the god himself, he was being addressed by the invocation of that god whose primary trait was to manifest himself. He was then accompanied by scatalogical jesting and phallic revelry. The Fool is thus the King's "shadow," the "rest of him." In the corn festival of which Moakley is reminded, the Fool himself becomes a mock King who dies in the King's palace—he is the King's double.

Willeford explains, "It is finally not the king as sun that is supreme but the planetary system that governs the rising and setting of the sun [...] the waxing and waning of the moon and all the figurations of the stars."[309] These motifs occur in the Tarot, of course, and in Williams's novel as well. Thus the magical character of jokes about the ultimate impotency—the human status of the King, compared to the apparent all-power of his royal status are revealed in evocations of his place in the divine plan:

> [T]he Roman conqueror habitually returned to Rome to receive a triumph. He rode in a chariot at the close of the procession, surrounded by dancing gold-crowned clowns and satyrs, who made obscene gestures and coarse jokes [...] While the conqueror held a dried cockerel's comb as an amulet against the evil eye, a gold-crowned slave holding the Crown of Jupiter Capitolinus above the victor's head whispered again and again, "O Conqueror, look behind you, and remember you are mortal."[310]

In the fifteenth century this slave, Willeford tells us, was depicted in the jester's trappings.[311]

The King's paraphernalia, whether he bears the spear or sword of a hero,[312] or the scepter as a world tree or world axis with a flower or leaf at its tip,[313] is phallic, as is the Fool's bauble[314] (read Williams's description again: "a staff, carved into serpentine curves, that carried a round bag,"), although, according to Willeford, these motifs may contain a feminine element as well, for the Fool of the Tarot carries a bag (female) as well as a staff (male).

Willeford speaks of "the archetypal experience" in the way that Williams would use "the Beatrician experience," saying that its "numinosity [...] gradually fades."[315] These experiences become part of the "collective unconsciousness," to use Jolande Jacobi's term which Willeford borrows. Thus "the self [king] and the ego [hero?] compose a system by which consciousness is brought to birth and organized within the larger field of the psyche (which is unconscious as well as conscious), and within and without this system the fool has a life-furthering role."[316] The Fool is thus the "archaic ego component"[317] which precedes ego and draws it back to its origin, the self. This idea Willeford calls "a working hypothesis in the exploration of certain psychopathological states that are characterized by loss or diminution of the powers of the ego," such as sickness, exhaustion, and other forms of stress, "and by the emergence of kinds of psychic functioning that we can crudely describe as magical."[318]

Willeford continues, "the fool is finally as much a symbol of the self as the king is, the fool presenting us with the dynamism and meaning that exceed our grasp of the totality and centrality of the self that belong to the self nonetheless."[319] This is exactly what the Fool stands for in Williams's Tarot, and perhaps in all Tarots. Willeford states: "In the lore about the Tarot cards the fool is sometimes regarded as the last card, sometimes as the first, and sometimes as being outside the sequence of the cards and forming a link between the last and the first, making a linear arrangement of the cards into a wheel."[320] This, "the position of the fool card in the Tarot pack, positionless, hovering between an ending and a beginning,"[321] is for Willeford an image of his entire interpretation of the role of the Fool and of his meaning, just as it is for Williams. Willeford concludes his book by describing Christ, tormented by the Roman soldiers and garbed in the mock robes of the Saturnalia, as the ultimate Fool, who is also God.

In the final version of his novel, Williams makes the meaning of his Tarot clear:

> The chaos of the hall was a marvel of new shape and color; the faces of those who stood around were illumined from within. It was Christmas night, but the sunlight shed itself about the whole house, and in the sunlight, between Sybil and Joanna, seriously engrossed, the small strange children played. The mystery which that ancient seer had worked in the Greater Trumps had fulfilled itself, at that time and in that place to so high a point of knowledge. Sybil stood there, and from her the sun of the Tarots ruled, and the holy children of the sun, the company of the blessed, were seen at least by some of the eyes that watched. For Amabel saw them and was ignorantly at peace; and Aaron saw them and was ashamed; and Nancy and Henry saw them, and Nancy laughed for mere

> joy of seeing, and when he heard it Henry felt his heart labor as it had never done before with the summons and the power; and Sybil saw them and adored, and saw beyond them, running down the stairs between herself and Nancy as if he were their union, and posed behind Joanna as if he supported and protected her, the vivid figure of the Fool. He had come from all sides at once, yet he was but one. All-reconciling and perfect, he was there, running down the stairs as he had run down the storm. (GT 265-66; ch. 16)

"He was but one"—"all reconciling and perfect"—"One altogether, not by confusion of substance, but by unity of person." As Otto writes "*At the beginning stands always the god.* By Him first are created the goal and the road to that goal; by Him, too, the suffering He is supposed to alleviate. It was not because man had wishes that a God appeared to man to grant him fulfillment, but the needs and the wishes, like the granting of the needs and wishes, flowed from the reality of the godhead."[322]

> Nancy, her finger pointing to the first of those great verses, [Rise to adore the mystery of love] whispered a question, "Is it true?" Sybil looked at the line, looked back at Nancy, and answered in a voice both aspirant and triumphant, "Try it darling." (GT 123; ch. 8)

In Williams's Tarot, as in his world, everything is under the feet of the Fool.

NOTE: Heartfelt thanks are due to Mrs. Stephanie Walker, Prof. J.R. Christopher of Tarleton State College, and Prof. Robert Ellwood of UCLA, for their meticulous reading and correction of the final version of this paper.

Notes

[1] C.S. Lewis, *English Literature in the Sixteenth Century, excluding Drama* (London: Oxford UP, 1954) 6.
[2] Lewis, *English Literature* 7.
[3] Lewis, *English Literature* 6.

Notes

[4] The present essay is an attempt to repay a great personal debt to Williams: *The Greater Trumps* was the very first-read of his books for me, and it introduced me to him and to the Tarot simultaneously. I first thought to outline his use of occult motifs in all his novels, but chose his Tarot as a specific example. The path on which this choice has led me has been one of continual astonishment and ever-deepening respect for his amazingly subtle and complex mind and for the riches of his novels, which this paper cannot begin to exhaust. The courtesy of Dr. Daniel Luzon Morris who sent me my first exoteric deck, the Marseille Tarot, and of Gracia-Fay Ellwood who sent me my first esoteric deck, the *Waite-Smith* Tarot, are hereby acknowledged and thanked as well.

[5] William Lindsay Gresham, "Preface" (1949), *The Greater Trumps* by Charles Williams (1950; New York: Noonday Press, 1962) viii.

[6] Edmund Fuller, "Many Dimensions; the Images of Charles Williams," *Books with Men Behind Them* (New York: Random House, 1962) 210.

[7] Richard Cavendish, *The Black Arts* (New York: Capricorn Books, 1968) 100.

[8] Editor's note: Eucatastrophy is a term coined by J.R.R. Tolkien. In "On Fairy Stories," he refers to it as the "good catastrophe" that marks the turning toward a happy ending that is part of all fairy-tales (85-86). Tolkien writes, "In its fairytale—or otherworld—setting, it is a sudden and miraculous grace: never to be counted on to recur [...] it denies (in the face of much evidence, if you will) universal final defeat and in so far is *evangelium*, giving a fleeting glimpse of Joy, Joy beyond the walls of the world, poignant as grief" (86). J.R.R. Tolkien, "On Fairy-Stories," *The Tolkien Reader* (New York: Ballantine Books, 1966) 33-99.

[9] Gunnar Urang, "Fantasy and the Ontology of Love," *Shadows of Heaven* (Philadelphia: United Church Press, 1971) 52.

[10] Urang 92.

[11] Urang 92.

[12] Urang 92.

[13] Urang 170.

[14] Fuller 210.

Notes

[15] Gresham, "Preface" (1949), *The Greater Trumps* ix.

[16] Alice Mary Hadfield, "The Relationship of Charles Williams' Working Life to his Fiction," *Shadows of Imagination*, ed. Mark R. Hillegas (Carbondale: Southern Illinois UP, 1969) 126.

[17] Alice Mary Hadfield, *An Introduction to Charles Williams* (London: Robert Hale, 1959) 81.

[18] Hadfield, *An Introduction to Charles Williams* 86.

[19] Hadfield, *An Introduction to Charles Williams* 86.

[20] T.S. Eliot, "Introduction," *All Hallow's Eve* by Charles Williams (New York: Bard Books, Avon Books, 1969) xii.

[21] Eliot, "Introduction," *All Hallow's Eve* by Charles Williams xi.

[22] W.R. Irwin, "Christian Doctrine and the Tactics of Romance: The Case of Charles Williams," *Shadows of Imagination*, ed. Mark R. Hillegas (Carbondale: Southern Illinois UP, 1969) 140.

[23] Hadfield, *An Introduction to Charles Williams* 79.

[24] George P. Winship, Jr., "The Novels of Charles Williams," *Shadows of Imagination*, ed. Mark R. Hillegas (Carbondale: Southern Illinois UP, 1969) 113-14.

[25] Mary McDermott Shideler, *The Theology of Romantic Love* (New York: Harper and Bros., 1962) 159-60.

[26] Shideler, *The Theology of Romantic Love* 63.

[27] R.J. Reilly, *Romantic Religion: A Study of Barfield, Lewis, Williams and Tolkien* (Athens: University of Georgia Press, 1971) 183-84.

[28] Reilly 184.

[29] Reilly 184.

[30] Reilly 184.

[31] Reilly 184.

[32] Shideler 175-76. Shideler cites the passage from Williams's *The Greater Trumps* (London: Faber & Faber, 1954) 196; ch. 14.

[33] Eliot, "Introduction," *All Hallow's Eve* by Charles Williams xiv.

[34] Charles William, *The Figure of Beatrice* (London: Faber and Faber, 1943) 188.

[35] See next note on this term.

[36] Anne Ridler, "Introduction," *The Image of the City and Other Essays* by Charles Williams (London: Oxford UP, 1958) xxiv. Yeats

Notes

himself left the Isis-Urania temple and "followed Dr. Felkin, who founded the order of the Stella Matutina" (Ridler, "Introduction" xxiii-xxiv). Waite himself adds, "In 1914 I put an end to the Isis-Urania or Mother Temple [...] Of a new Rite which arose, as if from the dead ashes, there [...] is no story to tell, either by myself or another. May that most sacred centre give up no outward form." A.E. Waite, *Shadows of Life and Thought* (London: Selwyn and Blount, 1938) 229. This is the "new Rite," or "later unnamed order" to which Anne Ridler refers.

[37] Hadfield, *An Introduction to Charles Williams* 79.

[38] Ridler, "Introduction" xxiv-xxv.

[39] Ridler, "Introduction" xxvi.

[40] Ridler, "Introduction" xxv. A major authority on Jewish mysticism, Gershom Scholem, writes, "In English literature on the subject A.E. Waite's *The Secret Doctrine in Israel* represents a serious attempt to analyze the symbolism of the Zohar. His work [...] is distinguished by real insight into the world of Kabbalism; it is all the more regrettable that it is marred by an uncritical attitude toward facts of history and philology [...] [Waite had no Hebrew]." Gershom Scholem, *Major Trends in Jewish Mysticism* (1941; New York: Schocken Books, 1965) 212.

[41] Ridler, "Introduction" xxv.

[42] Ridler, "Introduction" xxiv.

[43] T.S. Eliot, "The Waste Land," *The Waste Land and Other Poems* (New York: Harcourt, Brace, and Co., 1934) lines 43-59.

[44] T.S. Eliot, "The Waste Land," "Note on line 46," pp. 47-48. The "hooded figure in the passage of the disciples to Emmaus" is described in lines 360-64, p. 43.

[45] Editor's note: A more recent summary and discussion of this subject may be found in Catherine Waitinas, "Tarot as 'Secret Tradition' in T.S. Eliot's *The Waste Land*: 'These fragments I have shored against my ruins," *Tarot in Culture, Volume Two* (Clifford, ON: Valleyhome Books, 2014) 367-410.

[46] Anthony Burgess, "*The Waste Land* Revisited," *Horizon* (Winter 1972): 106.

Notes

[47] Charles Moorman, *Arthurian Triptych* (Berkeley: University of California Press, 1960) 138-39. His brackets.

[48] Jessie L. Weston, *From Ritual to Romance* (1920; Garden City, NY: Doubleday Anchor Books, 1957) 77.

[49] A section from Waite's *The Holy Grail* detailing the correspondences between the Grail hallows and Tarot suits is reprinted as "Waite's Last Word on the Tarot," in Arthur Edward Waite's *The Pictorial Key to the Tarot* (New Hyde Park, NY: University Books, 1959) vii-viii. Editor's note: Weston uses the term "Pentangles," but in the passage reproduced in *The Pictorial Key*, Waite uses "pentacle."

[50] Weston 78-79.

[51] Weston 79.

[52] Weston 80.

[53] Gertrude Moakley, "Introduction," *The Pictorial Key to the Tarot* by Arthur Edward Waite (New Hyde Park, NY: University Books, 1959) xvi-xvii.

[54] By a nice piece of synchronicity, I saw both the film of *Nightmare Alley*, which used the Waite deck, and a rather inferior recent film, *The Hanged Man*, which used the Swiss deck in a Mardi Gras setting, during the period when I was preparing this article.

Editor's note: The film referred to here is one based on Dorothy Hughes's novel *Ride the Pink Horse* (1946). This novel was made into a film noir (1947) of the same title directed by Robert Montgomery. There are no Tarot scenes in the novel or this film. The second film based on the novel was directed by Don Siegal and titled *The Hanged Man* (1964). It includes a Tarot reader and two shots of the Hanged Man card from the French version of the *1JJ Swiss* deck.

[55] Scholem, *Major Trends in Jewish Mysticism* 205. Christian theosophists would be Jacob Boehme and William Blake.

[56] Scholem, *Major Trends in Jewish Mysticism* 206-07.

[57] Scholem, *Major Trends in Jewish Mysticism* 207-08.

[58] Scholem, *Major Trends in Jewish Mysticism* 214.

[59] Scholem, *Major Trends in Jewish Mysticism* 215.

[60] Steven Runciman, *The Medieval Manichee* (New York: Viking Press, 1961) 187.

[61] Runciman 179.

Notes

[62] Runciman 187.

[63] C.G. Jung, *The Archetypes and the Collective Unconscious*, CW, vol. 9, Bollingen Series XX, second edition (Princeton, NJ: Princeton UP, 1968) 38.

[64] Jung, *The Archetypes and the Collective Unconscious* 38.

[65] Arthur Edward Waite, *The Pictorial Key to the Tarot* (1910; New Hyde Park, NY: University Books, 1959) 59.

[66] Catherine Perry Hargrave, *A History of Playing Cards and a Bibliography of Cards and Gaming* (1930; New York: Dover Publications, 1966) 1-2.

[67] Roger Tilley, *Playing Cards* (London: Weidenfield and Nickolson, 1967) 15-16. Editor's note: In the 1973 Octopus Books edition of *Playing Cards*, this information appears on page 11.

[68] Tilley 19. Octopus Books edition 15.

[69] Tilley 29-30. Octopus Books edition 22-23.

[70] Quoted from the translation given in an article by E.A. Bond, Chief Librarian of the British Museum, Athenaeum (January 19, 1878), in Tilley *Playing Cards* 26. Octopus Books edition 19.

[71] Quoted from the translation given in an article by E.A. Bond, Chief Librarian of the British Museum, Athenaeum (January 19, 1878), in Tilley *Playing Cards* 22. Octopus Books edition 15.

[72] Hargrave, *A History of Playing Cards* 224.

[73] Hargrave, *A History of Playing Cards* 224.

[74] Hargrave, *A History of Playing Cards* 224. Editor's note: In the paragraph following this citation, Patterson originally wrote from and cited a passage in Hargrave (226) which identifies Marziano da Tortona as an artist and indicates that he was paid for producing a minchiate deck in 1415. It is now known that Marziano da Tortona was not an artist and the deck he is associated with is not the one indicated in Patterson's text. I have simply deleted the passage as the information it contains no longer furthers Patterson's thesis. See Stuart K. Kaplan, *The Encyclopedia of Tarot* II (Stamford, CT: US Games, 1986) 147-48.

[75] Tilley *Playing Cards* 29. Octopus Books edition 22.

[76] Tilley *Playing Cards* 29. Octopus Books edition 22.

[77] Tilley *Playing Cards* 32. Octopus Books edition 25-26.

Notes

[78] Tilley *Playing Cards* 32. Octopus Books edition 26.
[79] Douglas C. McMurtrie, *The Book: The Story of Printing and Bookmaking* (New York: Oxford UP, 1962) 102.
[80] McMurtrie, *The Book* 101.
[81] McMurtrie, *The Book* 102.
[82] I am indebted for this idea and for McMurtrie as a source to Mrs. Stephanie Walker.
[83] Editor's note: Patterson relied on Hargrave and Tilley as her sources on Tarot and thus mistakenly believed that the "Tarot of Charles VI," also called the "Gringonneur" Tarot, was created in 1392. The back of the 1962 Noonday Press edition of the novel also states that Tarot "is first mentioned in history in 1393." I have corrected this error and explained the correction in the "Introduction to 'The Triumph of Love.'"
[84] Hargrave, *A History of Playing Cards* Plate 32.
[85] Waite, *The Pictorial Key to the Tarot* 43.
[86] Waite, *The Pictorial Key to the Tarot* 44.
[87] Waite, *The Pictorial Key to the Tarot* 45.
[88] Erwin Panofsky, *Meaning in the Visual Arts* (New York: Doubleday Anchor Books, 1955) 155. On Macrobius, see Panofsky 153.
[89] Panofsky 152.
[90] Panofsky 158-59.
[91] Vincent Cronin, "The Humanists," *Horizon* (Winter 1971): 89.
[92] Cronin 89.
[93] Waite, *The Pictorial Key to the Tarot* 52.
[94] Waite, *The Pictorial Key to the Tarot* 53.
[95] Waite, *The Pictorial Key to the Tarot* 53.
[96] Waite, *The Pictorial Key to the Tarot* 55.
[97] Waite, *The Pictorial Key to the Tarot* 56.
[98] Quote attributed to Gérard Encausse (Papus) in Jean-Paul Clébert, *The Gypsies*, trans. Charles Duff (Harmondsworth, UK: Penguin, 1963) 156.
[99] Clébert, *The Gypsies* 120.
[100] Clébert, *The Gypsies* 121.
[101] William Lindsay Gresham, "The Romany Trade," *Monster Midway* (Toronto: Clarke Irwin, 1953) 116.

Notes

[102] In 1967 I went to a Tarot reader—at that time it was difficult to obtain a deck of Tarots and I had never seen one—I cut the cards and she arranged them, according to a spread which I was then too ignorant to recognize. She told me to ask questions, which she answered on the basis of the spread before her. One question turned on my sister's marriage and because of the presence of the Four of Staves (she was using the *Waite-Smith* deck, as I remember that it showed a group of women dancing around four staffs between which garlands were suspended), she interpreted this as a card favourable to marriage. Her answers were all general and all based upon my questions, to which she related the cards. She was not a Gypsy, but a devout Roman Catholic born in Waterloo County. I think it only fair to report that her interpretations proved to be correct.

[103] Editor's note: see my discussion about this date in relation to the "Gringonneur" Tarot in "Introduction to 'The Triumph of Love.'"

[104] Gertrude Moakley, *The Tarot Cards Painted by Bonifacio Bembo for the Visconti-Sforza Family: An Iconographic and Historical Study* (New York: The New York Public Library, 1966) 10. I am indebted to Professor Virgil Burnett who introduced me to Gertrude Moakley's ideas and brought her book all the way from France so I could read it.

[105] Hargrave, *A History of Playing Cards* 227. Editor's note: I have made some minor corrections to the presentation of Hargrave's list and altered this paragraph slightly to identify the source Moakley says she used more clearly.

[106] Moakley, *The Tarot Cards* 61-62. Moakley cites Hargrave, *A History of Playing Cards* 227.

[107] Moakley, *The Tarot Cards* 62.

[108] Moakley, *The Tarot Cards* 76.

[109] Editor's note: According to Stuart Kaplan, "what appears to be the oldest list of standard trumps is contained in a late-fifteenth-century manuscript of a sermon against gambling" by a priest who "describes and condemns the use of dice and ordinary cards in the four suits of cups, coins, swords and staves. He then lists the names of the triumphi [...]" In this list, *L'amore* comes before *Lo Caro triumphale*. Kaplan, *Encyclopedia of Tarot* (Stamford, CT: U.S. Games, 1978) 2-3.

[110] Moakley, *The Tarot Cards* 63.

Notes

[111] Moakley, *The Tarot Cards* 113.
[112] William Willeford, *The Fool and His Scepter* (Northwestern UP, 1969) 75.
[113] Moakley, *The Tarot Cards* 63.
[114] Moakley, *The Tarot Cards* 52.
[115] Moakley, *The Tarot Cards* 44.
[116] Moakley, *The Tarot Cards* 45.
[117] Moakley discusses this poem in *The Tarot Cards* 45-46.
[118] Moakley, *The Tarot Cards* 62.
[119] Moakley, *The Tarot Cards* 13-16; undocumented prelude. Moakley's arrangement set in a list would look as shown here.
[120] Hargrave 226.
[121] Moakley, *The Tarot Cards* 62-63.
[122] Moakley, *The Tarot Cards* 62-63.
[123] Moakley, *The Tarot Cards* 64.
[124] Moakley, *The Tarot Cards* 35.
[125] Emile Mâle, *The Gothic Image* (New York: Harper Torchbooks, 1958) 98.
[126] Mâle 99.
[127] Mâle 104.
[128] Mâle 108.
[129] Moakley, *The Tarot Cards* 70.
[130] Moakley, *The Tarot Cards* 71-72.
[131] Moakley, *The Tarot Cards* 72-74.
[132] Moakley, *The Tarot Cards* 72.
[133] Moakley, *The Tarot Cards* 73-74.
[134] Moakley, *The Tarot Cards* 74.
[135] Moakley, *The Tarot Cards* 74-75.
[136] Leroy F. Vaughn, *Parade and Float Guide* (Minneapolis: T.S. Denison and Co., 1956) 29.
[137] Moakley, *The Tarot Cards* 76.
[138] Moakley, *The Tarot Cards* 77.
[139] Moakley, *The Tarot Cards* 78.
[140] Mâle 121.
[141] Mâle 122.
[142] Moakley, *The Tarot Cards* 79-80.

Notes

[143] Moakley, *The Tarot Cards* 86-87.
[144] Mâle 95.
[145] Mâle 96.
[146] Phyllis Hartnoll, *A Concise History of the Theatre* (London: Thames and Hudson, 1968) 42-43 (fig. 37). The illustration shows "The Triumph of Isabella" (Brussels, 1615) with Diana riding in a car of four wheels, attended by her nymphs.
[147] Moakley, *The Tarot Cards* 88.
[148] The French suits developed in the early fifteenth century: they are Coeurs (Hearts), Carreaux (Diamonds), Trèfles (Clubs), and Picques (Spades), looking just like the familiar suits. See Hargrave 41. Waite relates Cups to Hearts, Wands to Diamonds, Swords to Spades, and Pentacles to Clubs: see Waite, *The Pictorial Key* viii. Eden Gray gives a more convincing series: Cups (Hearts), Wands (Clubs), Swords (Spades), Pentacles (Diamonds). Eden Gray, *The Tarot Revealed* (New York: Bell Publishing, 1960) 5.
[149] Moakley, *The Tarot Cards* 95-96.
[150] Hargrave Pl. 35. The same deck has a very diabolical-looking Fool, whose leg is gnawed by a lion, under the number XV, where the Devil usually is found; he has no title, as Death does not. The whole deck has a charming and somewhat bowdlerized look to it. Pl. 36.
[151] Moakley, *The Tarot Cards* 15.
[152] Moakley, *The Tarot Cards* 94.
[153] Moakley, *The Tarot Cards* 96-97.
[154] Moakley, *The Tarot Cards* 98.
[155] Moakley, *The Tarot Cards* 98.
[156] Moakley, *The Tarot Cards* 99.
[157] Hartnoll 42-43.
[158] Hartnoll 44-45.
[159] Moakley, *The Tarot Cards* 100.
[160] Moakley, *The Tarot Cards* 106-07.
[161] Moakley, *The Tarot Cards* 108.
[162] Moakley, *The Tarot Cards* 109.
[163] Moakley, *The Tarot Cards* 110.
[164] Moakley, *The Tarot Cards* 111.
[165] Moakley, *The Tarot Cards* 112.

Notes

[166] C.G. Jung, "Mandalas," *The Archetypes and the Collective Unconscious*, CW, vol. 9, Bollingen Series XX, second edition (Princeton, NJ: Princeton UP, 1968) 388.
[167] C.G. Jung, "Concerning Mandala Symbolism," *The Archetypes and the Collective Unconscious*, CW, vol. 9, Bollingen Series XX, second edition (Princeton, NJ: Princeton UP, 1968) 377-78.
[168] Jung, "Concerning Mandala Symbolism" 361.
[169] Jung, "Concerning Mandala Symbolism" 357.
[170] Jung, "Concerning Mandala Symbolism" 357.
[171] Moakley, *The Tarot Cards* 113-15.
[172] E.O. James, *Seasonal Feasts and Fasts* (London: Thames and Hudson, 1961) 279.
[173] James 279-80.
[174] Moakley, *The Tarot Cards* 114.
[175] Mâle 120.
[176] Willeford 170.
[177] Willeford 251; note 16 to chapter 9.
[178] William and Ceil Baring-Gould, *The Annotated Mother Goose* (New York: Bramhall House, 1962) 84. The Baring-Gould's quote is from G.M. Trevelyan's English Social History: "All through the Tudor reigns, the 'beggars coming to town' preyed on the fears of dwellers in lonely farms and hamlets [...]" (85).
[179] Moakley, *The Tarot Cards* 13.
[180] Gertrude Moakley, "Notes on the Tarot as a Game," *The Pictorial Key to the Tarot* by Arthur Edward Waite (New Hyde Park, NY: University Books, 1959) 322.
[181] Moakley, "Notes on the Tarot as a Game" 320.
[182] Gershom Scholem, *On the Kabbalah and its Symbolism* (New York: Schocken Books, 1965) 122.
[183] Wylie Sypher, *The Four Stages of Renaissance Style* (Garden City, NY: Double Day/Anchor, 1955) 51.
[184] Sypher 51.
[185] Sypher 52.
[186] Moakley, *The Tarot Cards* 44.
[187] H.S. Versnel, *Triumphus* (Leiden: E.J. Brill, 1970) 11, 54.

Notes

[188] Versnel 38. In Christian liturgies the part of the consecration of the sacred elements which invokes the Holy Spirit is called the *epiclesis*.
[189] Versnel 196.
[190] Versnel 55.
[191] Versnel 300.
[192] Versnel 270.
[193] Versnel 262.
[194] Versnel 258.
[195] Versnel 293.
[196] Versnel 296.
[197] Versnel 292.
[198] Versnel 95.
[199] Versnel 78.
[200] Versnel 80. Editor's note: Jupiter is spelled Iuppiter in this source.
[201] Versnel 75.
[202] Versnel 56-57.
[203] Versnel 57.
[204] Willeford 162.
[205] Versnel, *Triumphus* 380.
[206] Willeford, *The Fool and His Scepter* 162.
[207] Versnel, *Triumphus* 356.
[208] Versnel 371.
[209] Versnel 387.
[210] Versnel 207.
[211] Versnel 207.
[212] Versnel 210.
[213] Versnel 215.
[214] Versnel 228.
[215] Versnel 228.
[216] Versnel 245.
[217] Versnel 246.
[218] Versnel 249.
[219] Robert Payne, *The Roman Triumph* (London: Robert Hale, 1962) 217.

Notes

[220] Dante, *Purgatory* in *The Comedy of Dante Alighieri*, trans. Dorothy L. Sayers (Harmondsworth, UK: Penguin, 1955) Canto XXIX, II, 93-95, p. 300.

[221] Dante, Purgatory, Canto XXIX, II, 100-01, p. 301.

[222] Dante, Purgatory, Canto XXIX, II, 106-08, p. 301.

[223] Dante, Purgatory, Canto XXIX, II, 130-32, p. 301.

[224] Panofsky says regarding the motif of the three eyes of Prudence, "This co-ordination of the three modes or forms of time with the faculties of memory, intelligence and foresight, and the latter's subordination to the concept of prudence, represent a classical tradition which preserved its vitality even when Christian theology had elevated prudence to the status of a cardinal virtue" (149). Prudence expresses this "tripartition" (150) by holding a disc of three sectors, a brazier with three flames, or a triple mirror, or she possesses three heads (150-51). Irwin Panofsky, "Titian's Allegory of Prudence: A Postscript," *Meaning in the Visual Arts* (New York: Doubleday Anchor Books, 1955).

[225] Dante, *Purgatory* in *The Comedy of Dante Alighieri*, trans. Dorothy L. Sayers, 305, note for line 107.

[226] Payne, *The Roman Triumph* 225.

[227] James A. Leith, *The Idea of Art as Propaganda in France, 1750–1799* (Toronto: University of Toronto Press, 1965) Plates between pages 76 and 77. Leith discusses the symbols of revolutionary allegories on pages 108-09.

[228] Walter F. Otto, *Dionysus, Myth and Cult*, trans. Robert B. Palmer (Bloomington: Indiana UP, 1965) 156.

[229] Otto 157-58.

[230] Otto 164.

[231] Otto 162.

[232] Readers who know of Robert Graves's writing of Dionysian cult, based upon R.G. Wasson's theories, will be aware of his conclusion that the ecstasy of the God was induced by consuming the juice of the *amanita muscaria* (fly-agaric)—either from dried pieces freshened with wine or in a secondary form in the urine of persons who have already eaten the "divine mushroom." I consulted a number of books on this thesis, including Robert Graves's own rather fantastic *The*

Notes

White Goddess; R.G. Wasson's perfectly serious *Soma, Divine Mushroom of Immortality*; and John Allegro's wildly over-wrought *The Sacred Mushroom and the Cross*. The whole investigation was fascinating but so distantly related to the Tarot that I can only allude to it here. For a study of the use of hallucinogenic materials, and the attitude toward them and their relationship to the divine (of which they are clearly conceived to be vehicles), consult Carlos Castaneda's superb studies, *The Teachings of Don Juan* and *A Separate Reality*. The pine forests of Greece did play host to the fly-agaric, so readers who want to see the Tarot as being based upon a mushroom cult will no doubt please themselves. Allegro mentions the Dionysian symbolism of the Triumph in this connection. The real point is that the god (God) manifests himself in myriad ways, including through mushrooms; the mere contemplation of one of these lovely fungi (one thinks of the red-leaded face of the triumphator) is a visionary experience. Robert Graves, "Mushroom," *Man, Myth, and Magic* [encyclopedia] 1905-1910.

[233] Otto, *Dionysus, Myth and Cult* 166.
[234] Otto 168.
[235] Otto 169-70.
[236] Otto 136.
[237] Otto 136.
[238] Otto 92.
[239] Otto 86.
[240] Otto 90.
[241] Otto 90.
[242] Otto 85.
[243] Otto 197-98.
[244] Otto 29.
[245] Dom Gregory Dix, *The Shape of the Liturgy* (London: Dacre Press, 1945) 274-75.
[246] S.J. Jean Daniélou, *Primitive Christian Symbols*, trans. Donald Attwater (London: Compass Books, Burnes and Oates, 1964) 142.
[247] Daniélou 142. This is why it is thought that the sign of the Cross originated as a Tav or Taw sign: the Tav, "the last letter of the Hebrew alphabet, signifies God, as does the Greek *omega*" (140).

Notes

Danielou states that "in Christ's time the *taw* of the Hebrew alphabet was represented by the sign + or X. It is in this form that we meet it in Palestinian ossuaries of the first century A.D., and there we may possibly have the oldest Christian representation of the cross. It signified the name of Yahweh" (141). He explains: "In a Greek environment this symbolism became unintelligible, and the cross was therefore interpreted in another way. In the form + it was regarded as a representation of the instrument of Jesus' suffering; in the form x it was taken for the first letter of Χρισto'ς [Christos]" (142). In the estoteric Tarot, the Fool is given the Hebrew letter Tav or Taw as Card 22. The Hanged Man depends from a T-shaped tree (the latin letter T is derived from that of tau, the nineteenth letter of the Greek alphabet).

[248] Canon J. Stafford Wright, *Christianity and the Occult* (London: Scripture Union, 1971) 67.

[249] It would be splendid, in attempting to design a deck based upon Williams's Tarot, to make the figures of the Suit of Deniers into a magnificent African court, perhaps like that of an Oba of Ife, with his gorgeous entourage, of which we know much from the bronze sculptures of the period.

[250] See Williams, *The Greater Trumps* 14-15; ch. 1, for the order of the Tarot Trumps.

[251] The Emperor and Empress and other Tarot pairs are referenced on p. 116; ch. 7.

[252] C.S. Lewis, "Williams and the Arthuriad," Charles Williams and C.S. Lewis. *Arthurian Torso* (London: Oxford UP, 1952) 105.

[253] *Book of Common Prayer*, "The Creed of St. Athanasius," vv. 30-34 (Toronto: Anglican Book Centre, 1959) 697.

[254] Lothair thinks of Nancy as a "gipsy name" (8). Williams attributes Lothair's and Sibyl's names to their godmother's liking for Disraeli. Perhaps Williams is suggesting that Nancy is the bearer of a Gypsy (Egyptian) name: Horus. In *Memories, Dreams, Reflections* (New York: Vintage Books, 1963), Jung describes the African sunrise, in which the first brilliant irradiation of the darkness is the moment of God's presence, the epiphany of Horus (268-29; ch. ix). This image

Notes

of enlightenment may be related to the concept of Grace, which is what Nancy's name (it is a diminutive of Anne) literally means.

[255] See *Song of Solomon* 8:6—"love is strong as death."

[256] T.S. Eliot, "Gerontion," *The Waste Land and Other Poems* 19.

[257] Jung, *Memories Dreams, Reflections* 338.

[258] Gerardus van der Leeuw, *Sacred and Profane Beauty: The Holy in Art* (New York: Holt, Rinehart and Winston, 1963) 29.

[259] Van der Leeuw, *Sacred and Profane Beauty* 30.

[260] Sam Keen, "Manifesto for a Dionysian Theology," *New Theology* No. 7: *The Recovery of Transcendence*, eds. Martin E. Marty and Dean G. Peerman (Toronto: Collier-Macmillan, 1970) 94.

[261] E.M.W. Tillyard, *The Elizabethan World Picture* (London: Chatto and Windus, 1967) 97.

[262] Dante, *The New Life*, trans. William Anderson (Harmondsworth, UK: Penguin, 1964) 64.

[263] Dante, *The New Life* 40.

[264] Willeford, *The Fool and His Scepter* 3, and also 239 note 1.

[265] Andreas Lommel, *Shamanism and the Beginnings of Art* (Toronto: McGraw-Hill, 1967) 128-29.

[266] Willeford 11, quoted from Thelma Niklaus, *Harlequin* (New York, Brazillier, 1956) 18.

[267] Willeford 240, note 6.

[268] Willeford 240, note 6.

[269] Willeford 12.

[270] Willeford 251, note 16.

[271] Willeford 16.

[272] Willeford 10.

[273] Willeford 16.

[274] Lommel 112.

[275] Lommel 112.

[276] Willeford 242, note 28. Quoted from E.W. Ives, "Tom Skelton—A Seventeenth Century Jester," *Shakespeare Survey* 13 (Cambridge: Cambridge UP, 1960) 103.

[277] Willeford 23.

Notes

[278] Euripides, "The Bacchae," trans. William Arrowsmith, *The Complete Greek Tragedies*, Vol. IV, *Euripides*, eds. David Grene and Richard Lattimore 548.

[279] Euripides, "The Bacchae" 552.

[280] Willeford 28-29. The noise and silence are typical of mushroom cult behaviour but obviously the drug effects of the mushroom are desired *because* they cause these certain signs of possession.

[281] Willeford 29.

[282] Willeford 29.

[283] Enid Welsford, *The Fool His Social and Literary History* (London: Faber and Faber, 1968) 55.

[284] Willeford 37-38.

[285] Willeford 41-42.

[286] Willeford 54; quoted from M. Willson Disher, *Clowns and Pantomimes* (London: Constable, 1923) 28-29.

[287] Willeford 65

[288] Willeford xvii.

[289] Willeford 120-21. See also 170-71.

[290] Willeford 120. The quoted passage may be found in C.G. Jung, *Aion*, trans. R.F.C. Hull, CW, Vol. 9, Part 2, Bollingen Series XX, second edition (Princeton, NJ: Princeton UP, 1968) 198, par. 310.

[291] Willeford 112.

[292] Willeford 112.

[293] Willeford 114.

[294] Willeford 79.

[295] Willeford 106.

[296] Willeford 112.

[297] Willeford 121.

[298] Willeford 131.

[299] Willeford 131.

[300] Willeford 133.

[301] Willeford 134.

[302] Willeford 135.

[303] Willeford 143.

[304] Willeford 143-44.

[305] Willeford 144.

Notes

[306] Willeford 151.
[307] Willeford 151.
[308] Willeford 153.
[309] Willeford 161.
[310] Willeford 162.
[311] Willeford 162.
[312] Willeford 167.
[313] Willeford 168.
[314] Willeford 170.
[315] Willeford 170.
[316] Willeford 172.
[317] Willeford 172.
[318] Willeford 173.
[319] Willeford 173.
[320] Willeford 212.
[321] Willeford 217.
[322] Otto, *Dionysus, Myth and Cult* 29.

2. The Jewels of Messias: Images of Judaism and Anti-semitism in the Novels of Charles Williams

In "The Jewels of Messias" Patterson details Williams's use of racial stereotyping. The occultists of Williams's milieu and of the preceding decades romanticized Judaism by developing various correspondences between the Hebrew alphabet and Tarot—a subject explored in "The Triumph of Love." Such romanticism may be regarded as the flip side of the overtly negative and derogatory views of Judaism in Williams's novels explored in this paper.

"The Jewels of Messias" was first published in Mythlore *6.2 (Spring 1979): 27-31. It was published after "Images of Judaism and Anti-Semitism in the Novels of Dorothy L. Sayers" (1978), available in* Detecting Wimsey: Papers on Dorothy L. Sayers's Detective Fiction *by Nancy-Lou Patterson.*

In the novels of Dorothy L. Sayers, Jews are depicted for the most part as private persons going about their business; social and economic beings, rather than religious;[1] but in the novels of Charles Williams, the man whom Sayers called "the dead master," it is their religious identity which is emphasized. In his essay, "The Jews," he speaks of the "Jewish mystery,"[2] and of "that extreme courtesy with which [Christians] should carry themselves towards Jews, especially towards orthodox Jews." As to the unorthodox (as well as for unorthodox Christians), "it is a matter of merely behaving as decently as possible."[3] In his description of the relations between Jews and Christians, Williams says, the Jew sees "a preposterous blasphemy," which is "fundamentally from his own people," while the "Christian is confronted by the rejection of the Faith by that from which the Faith sprang."[4] The matter is one "between fathers and children."[5] It is a "mystery of radical exchange."[6]

In a comment which may be used to judge both Sayers and Williams, Joshua Trachtenberg wrote in 1939:

> [...] where Jews are concerned [...] the vision of the world has been obscured by darkly bias-tinted spectacles. If, on the one

> hand, Christological and anti-Semitic prejudices have revealed only an infamous horde of blasphemers and parasites, on the other, a historical perspective limited by Scripture has disclosed an exalted band of prophets, hounded and persecuted as prophets must be for their vision and temerity. Between these two extremes—which have alike doomed Jews to the unhappiest of extremes—a normal people, with all the faults and virtues of humanity, has pursued its normal course through history, however abnormal were the conditions against which it struggled.[7]

In addition to the "normal" pursuits of daily life, normal Jewish religious activity has included both synagogue and home. In addition, the "folk religion" of Judaism has included, in the two thousand years since New Testament times, "on the periphery of the religious life, the practices of magic, which never broke completely with the tenets of the faith, yet stretched them almost to the breaking point."[8] Trachtenberg sees these practices, which emerge in his study of *Jewish Magic and Superstition* as remarkably innocent and benign, railed against by the rabbis. Nonetheless, as Trachtenberg says, "many medieval Christians looked upon the Jew as the magician *par excellence*."[9] As he says, "the striking feature [...] of Jewish sorcery is that it adhered not to certain specific Jews [...] but rather to the entire people, *en masse*. Consequently, every innocent Jewish act which by its strangeness laid itself open to suspicion was considered a diabolical device for working magic against Christians."[10] Ritual handwashing, casting a clod of earth at funerals, hunting for leaven on the eve of Passover: all these benign little ceremonies were seen as evil magic. The blessed wine of Sabbath was considered to have occult powers. The *mezuzah* was of course both feared and desired. Jewish doctors were thought to have special talent in magic healing[11] and Jewish druggists were seen as purveyors of magic potions and poisons.[12] Trachtenberg points out the survival into the twentieth century of these notions and of their ugliest form—the suspicion of ritual murder—so that Montague Summers could write of "the dark and hideous traditions of Hebrew magic [... in which] the blood of the victim [...] was used for magical purposes."[13] As this grotesque idea continued in the modern era, it stretched back into the past: "a host of popular magical works was attributed to Solomon and other fabled

Jewish masters. Juvenal's jibe that the Appian Way swarmed with fortune-telling Jewesses who would sell you any sort of dream at cut prices, was the kind of information that was bound to make and retain its impression,"[14] Trachtenberg writes.

There was, in fact, a Jewish magical tradition. In the period when Jewish mysticism took shape, partly under the influence of Hellenistic gnosticism, theosophical ideas developed which Trachtenberg described in terms that Williams himself might have used:

> Searching out the secret springs of the universe, the mystic brings to light awesome and puissant truths, which his more practical and profane confidants feel promptly impelled to profane for their own greater glory and might.[15]

Jewish medieval writings of course include references to events like those that Christian writers attribute to witches. They shared the common European heritage. Thus Menahem Ziyuni wrote in 1430 "There are men and women [...] who possess demonic attributes; they smear their bodies with a secret oil ... and instantly fly off like the eagle."[16] But this is not specifically Jewish magic. Rather, "the primary principle of medieval Jewish magic was an implicit reliance upon the Powers of Good, which were invoked by calling upon their names, the holy Names of God and His angels."[17] This calling upon the Name is the central act in several of Williams's novels.

Magical power required that one read and pronounce the sacred words, letters, and numbers, and for the most part the powers called upon were benign, divine, and not malignant. In other words, Jewish magic consisted in invoking power, a practice only a hair removed from actual prayer, rather than in commanding or wielding it oneself. As said above, these practices of folk religion were continually preached against by the rabbis of the period, not because they thought that devils were being contacted (as the Christian clergy believed) but because they recognized the dilution and attenuation of genuine religious life such activities represented. Needless to say, their efforts went unrewarded, and wonder-working was attributed to rabbis and to holy men in the folk tales of Eastern European Judaism—for instance, in the stories of the Golem—as well as by Christian writers.

Probably the direct route from all this to the fantasies of Charles Williams is through the person of Eliphas Zahed Levi (whose real name was Alphonse Louis Constant). Born in Paris in 1810, he was not a Jew; he studied for the Roman Catholic priesthood and became a deacon. He was, Francis King (1970) suggests, "a convert to the half-religious, half-political doctrines of that lunatic fringe of extremist 'French royalism'"[18]—after he had worked out his own version of the doctrines of these groups, he "completely romanticised the whole magical and alchemical tradition, the interpretation of the tarot cards, and what little he knew of the Hebrew Qabalah."[19] His writings, which King calls "nineteenth century Gothic," made him "responsible for the surfacing [...] of the whole under ground magical tradition."[20] The spirit of Levi imbues the whole nineteenth and early twentieth-century development of magical thought and practice. The Order of the Golden Dawn, which profoundly influenced Charles Williams was, in a sense, his spiritual child.

The fact that none of this is actually Jewish, let alone Jewish magic, must not be forgotten, but the followers of these groups often were not aware of it. Some of them became passable students of Jewish mysticism. Ridler tells us in her introduction to *The Image of The City* of Williams's admiration for Arthur E. Waite's *The Secret Doctrine in Israel* (1913), which she calls "a study of a Jewish mystical work, the *Zohar* [that] includes much of the lore which is found in Golden Dawn teachings."[21] Gershom G. Scholem (1941) refers to the "brilliant misunderstandings and misrepresentations of Alphonse Louis Constant, who has won fame under the pseudonym of Eliphas Levi, to the highly coloured humbug of Aleister Crowley and his followers, the most eccentric and fantastic statements" which have been made about Kabbalism.[22] In his view, Arthur E. Waite had a "fine philosophical intuition and natural grasp" of the Kabbalah, but "lacked all critical sense as to historical and philological data in this field."[23] Williams, who was quite enraptured by it all, seems to have accepted everything into his passionate mind and from it fashioned high fantasies of his own, in a sort of "twentieth-century Gothic" style, as we shall see.

In the first-written (but much later published) novel of his series of fantasy thrillers, *Shadows of Ecstasy* (1933), there is found dead, presumably of suicide, "a certain Simon Rosenberg who, among his interests in railways and periodicals and fisheries and dyeworks, in South African diamonds and Persian oils and Chinese silks, in textiles and cereals and patent medicines, rubber and coffee and wool [...]" (SE 21; ch. 2) had included a profound devotion to his wife recently dead. "[H]e'd developed a mania for making [for her to wear] the most wonderful collection of jewels in the world" (SE 26; ch. 2). Someone who had known her says, "she looked not merely like the sun, the moon and the eleven stars [...]" but "She was a magnificent creature, tall and rather large and dark," so that in her jewels she resembled "the New Jerusalem turned upside down so that the foundations showed" (SE 26; ch. 2).

Rosenberg has relatives who inherit this treasure. The character Considine (who is the villain in the novel) says of them:

> They are strict Jews, living in London because they are too poor to return to Jerusalem. They live in London and they abominate the Gentiles of London. They are fanatically—insanely, you would say—devoted to the tradition of Israel. They live almost without food [...] studying the Law and nourished by the Law. (SE 33; ch. 2)

Asked if the jewels are important to "Israel," Considine continues,

> [...] it was a Jew who saw the foundations of the Holy City splendid with a beauty for which the names of the jewels were the only comparison. We think of jewels chiefly as wealth, but I doubt if John of the Apocalypse did, and I doubt if the Rosenbergs will. Perhaps he saw them as mirrors and shells of original color. (SE 33; ch. 2)

There is general public unrest over the situation. "No-one could believe that the two aged and devoted students of Kabbalistic doctrine were fit persons to control the vast interests of the Rosenberg estate" (SE 55; ch. 4). Williams well depicts the ugliness of a crowd gathered outside their lodgings in London:

> He caught fragments of talk: "Say they're going to bribe the negroes"; "know all about those bloody niggers"; "great jewels like turnips—been buying them for months"; "lousy old Jews"; "Christ Almighty"; "bloody Jews." (SE 160; ch. 9)

The mood grows uglier still:

> Another call went up: "Come out, you bloody Jews!"; "Come out and bring us the jewels!"; "Come out and we'll show you what we'll do to the niggers!" [...] A woman of sixty nearby said with a sensuous shudder to her neighbor, "They do say that Jews eat babies." "Ah," said the neighbor, "foreigners'll do anything." (SE 160-61; ch. 9)

The gentle old scholars grow stern under this assault. Nehemiah Rosenberg confronts his persecutors: "Sons of abomination, what have we to do with you? Defilers of yourselves, who are you to come against the Holy One of Israel?" (SE 161; ch. 9).

There is stone-throwing: Nehemiah is killed. Ezekiel turns to the body; Williams says "He [...] intoned over it a Hebrew prayer" (SE 165; ch. 9). Taken under the protection of Considine (who has his own malignant intentions toward him), "Ezekiel still sat, lost in meditation in antique words [...] brooding over the manner in which the High and Holy One had in the secret story of Joseph or of David, in the hidden sayings of Ruth or Esther, signified the return of Israel to His pardon" (SE 226; ch. 12). He, too, is killed.

> He was dragged violently from his chair, but he clung to the sacred treasure [...] His face, as he lifted it, was full of a scorn deeper than time, the scorn of his God for the spoilers of the holy places. He saw the distorted face of a greedy Gentile above him, and before the bullet searched his brain he spat at it once. (SE 247; ch. 13)

In the first-published of his novels, *War in Heaven* (1930), a less benign, but equally fanatical, view of Jewish religious behavior is given. Sir Giles Tumulty is advising Gregory Persimmons on the use of a magic ointment: "A Jew in Beyrout tried it and didn't get back. Filthy beast he looked, all naked and screaming that he couldn't find his way" (WH 64; ch. 5). Persimmons pursues the inquiry; he finds the shop and the ointment. On his first visit he is served by "a Greek of sorts," but on his second visit there is a "new-comer." He "was smaller than the Greek, and much smaller than Gregory; his movements were swift and his repose alert. His bearded face was that of a Jew" (WH 143; ch. 11).

The novel concerns the Holy Grail (the Cup of the Last Supper): when Persimmons asks the intentions of these two toward it,

"The others looked over at him, the Jew scornfully, the other with a faint amusement. The Greek said, 'Manasseh and I are going to destroy the Cup [...]'" Asked why, he learns, "'Because it has power,' the Jew answered, leaning over the counter and whispering fiercely, 'it must be destroyed. Don't you understand that yet? They build and we destroy'" (WH 144; ch. 11). Later in the novel there is another exchange over this motif:

> "Praise to our Lord," Gregory said. But Manasseh smiled and shook his head. "He is the last mystery," he· murmured, "and all destruction is his own destroying of himself." (WH 188; ch. 12)

Ultimately there is a terrible psychic conflict in which the would-be protectors and would-be destroyers of the Cup contend. The Cup is rescued by Prester John, and its temporary holder, the Archdeacon, dies.

Williams's use of Jewish characters in these two novels may be compared not only with Sayers's use, but with others. A totally negative image of a Jew in a shop, used for no reason except coloration, may be found in Bram Stoker's *Dracula*, where "We found Hildescheim in his office, a Hebrew of rather the Adelphi Theater type, with a nose like a sheep, and a fez. His arguments were pointed with specie [coins]—we doing the punctuation—and with a little bargaining he told us what he knew."[24] The scorn attributed to the Rosenberg brothers resembles that which C.S. Lewis (1958) thought he saw in the Old Testament Psalms, which he discusses in "The Cursings," a chapter in *Reflections on the Psalms*:

> One's first impression is that the Jews were much more vindictive and vitriolic than the pagans.
>
> If we are not Christians we shall dismiss this with the old gibe "How odd of God to choose the Jews." That is impossible for us who believe that God chose that race for the vehicle of His own Incarnation, and who are indebted to Israel beyond all possible repayment.[25]

He concludes:

> If the Jews cursed more bitterly than the Pagans this was, I think, at least in part because they took right and wrong more

> seriously. For if we look at their railings we find they are usually angry not simply because things have been done to them but because these things are manifestly wrong, are hateful to God as well as to the victim.[26]

Jews in relation to religion, mysticism, and magic, continued to form part of Williams's novels; in *The Place of the Lion* (1931), there is a mysterious language heard: "Hebrew it might have been or something older than Hebrew, some incantation whereby prediluvian magicians had controlled contentions among spirits or the language in which our father Adam named the beasts in the garden" (PL 13; ch. 16).

In *Many Dimensions* (1930), Prince Ali is meditating as he drives through London in search of the mislaid Tetragrammaton, a sacred stone which, having the Hebrew letters of the Divine Name inscribed upon it, is capable of teleportation. He muses:

> Suleiman ben Daood, he knew, was a historic figure—the ruler of a small nation which, in the momentary decrease of its two neighbours, Egypt and Assyria, had attained an unstable pre-eminence. But Suleiman was also one of the four great world-shakers before the Prophet, a commander of the faithful, peculiarly favoured by Allah. He had been a Jew, but the Jews in those days were the only witness to the Unity. (MD 13; ch. 1)

The stone had been set in a crown, and the Prince, speaking of it, tells the Persian ambassador to the Court of St. James, "It is undoubtedly the Crown." "'The Crown of a Jew?' the Ambassador murmured.'" The Ambassador, too, muses on the idea: "'It might perhaps be held that the Christians derive as much from Judah as we,' he said" (MD 14-15; ch. 1).

The frequent association by occultists of the Tarot with the Kabbalah was accepted by Williams. In *The Greater Trumps* (1932), Henry is gazing at the dancing golden images which are the prototypes, in the novel, for the original Tarot deck he now holds in his hands. He says to his fiancée Nancy:

> "But once," he went on,"—some say in Egypt long before the Pharaoh heard of Yussuf Ben-Yakoob, and some in Europe while the dreaming rabbis whispered in the walled ghetto over

> fables of unspeakable words, and some in the hidden covens of doctrine which the Church called witchcraft—once a dancer talked of the dance, not with words, but with images; once a mind knew it to the seventy-eighth degree of discovery, and not only knew it, but knew how it knew it, so beautifully in one secret corner the dance doubled and redoubled on itself." (GT 107-108; ch. 7)

The idea that the Tarot emerged in Egypt and was carried from thence by the Jews is not original with Eliphas Levi but he gave it the most vivid expression, and even hoped to find a "Jewish Tarot" someday. The Yussuf Ben-Yakoob of the above passage is Joseph, son of Jacob. The rabbis are here listed as representative of secret doctrine, kabbalistic magic as Levi and even Waite imagined it to be. Henry's father Aaron meditates on the Tarot too:

> [...] his hidden secret of the gipsies had been borne about the world, covered by wrappings and disguises [...] one band of all those restless companies possessed the mystery which long since some wise adept of philosophical truths had made in the lands of the east or the secret houses of Europe: Egyptian or Jew or Christian heretic—Paulician, Bogophil, or Nestorian—or perhaps still farther off in the desert circled empire of Abyssinia." (GT 176; ch. 11)

Aaron ponders "the dark fate that falls on all mystical presentations [...] The doom which struck Osiris in the secular memory of Egypt and hushed the holy, sweet, and terrible Tetragrammaton in the ritual of Judah, and wounded the Keeper of the Grail in the Castle of the Grail, and by the hand of the blind Hoder pierced the loveliest of all the Northern gods [...]" (GT 177; ch. 11)

The most vivid and specific use of the idea of Jewish magic, however, appears in Charles Williams's last novel, *All Hallows Eve* (1945). Richard describes one of the novel's main characters, the magus Simon Leclerc, to Jonathan, whose fiancée Betty is actually Leclerc's daughter. "We know [...] that his name is Simon Leclerc—sometimes called Father Simon and sometimes Simon the Clerk. We gather he's a Jew by descent, though born in France, and brought up in America" (AHE 35; ch. 2). Simon preaches "Love, with a hint of some secret behind, which Love no doubt could find out" (AHE 36;

ch. 2). The character of Simon is based upon Simon Magus, the magician of Acts 8.9-24, who is converted by Philip and then tries to buy the power of God with silver, earning a rebuke from Peter. When Clerk Simon enters the novel, Williams describes him:

> He was a tall man, with a smooth mass of grey—almost white—hair; his head was large; his face thin, almost emaciated. The face had about it a hint of the Jew—no more; so little indeed that Jonathan wondered if it were only Richard's account that caused him to think he saw it. But, considering more carefully, he saw it was there. The skin was dark [...] (AHE 51; ch. 3)

The Clerk goes out through the streets of London, and "As he went the Jewish quality in his face seemed to deepen; the occasional policeman whom he passed thought they saw a Jew walking by night" (AHE 59; ch. 3). Chesterton, Sayers, and Williams (to say nothing of Stoker) all accept the notion that Jews are: one, a race whose physiological traits are genetically "Jewish," and two, physically recognizable. The following long passage contains the central motif of the novel, presenting, under the guise of a fantasy or thriller, Williams's own theological conceptions: as Christ is a Jew, so the Anti-Christ (Simon Leclerc) must be a Jew:

> Indeed that august race had reached in this being its second climax. Two thousand years of its history were drawing to a close; until this thing had happened it could not be free. Its priesthood—the priesthood of a nation—had been since Abraham determined to one End. But when [...] that End had been born, they were not aware of that End. It had been proposed that their lofty tradition should be made almost unbearably august; that they should be made the blood-companions of their Maker, the own peculiar house and family of its Incarnacy—no more than the Gentiles in the free equality of souls, but much more in the single hierarchy of kindred flesh. But deception had taken them; they had, bidding a scaffold for the blasphemer, destroyed their predestined conclusion, and the race which had been set for the salvation of the world became a judgment and even a curse to the world and to themselves. Yet the oaths sworn in heaven remained. It had been a Jewish

> girl who, at the command of the Voice which sounded in her ears, in her heart, along her blood, and through the central cells of her body, had uttered everywhere in herself the perfect Tetragrammaton. What the high priest vicariously spoke among the secluded mysteries of the Temple, she substantially pronounced to God. Redeemed from all division in herself, whole and identical in body and soul and spirit, she uttered the Word and the Word became flesh in her. Could It have been received by her own people, the grand Judean gate would have been opened for all peoples. It could not. They remained alien—to It and to all, and all to them and—too much!—to It. The Gentiles, summoned by that other Jew of Tarsus, could not bear their vicarious office. Bragging themselves to be the new Israel, they slandered and slew the old, and the old despised and hated the bragging new. (AHE 59-60; ch. 3)

In Williams's fantasy, a new man, for whom "Jew and Christian alike had waited" (AHE 60; ch. 3) was born in Paris, "in one of those hiding places of necromancy which all the energy of the Fourteenth Louis had not quite stamped out." He had been reared by "that small college" (AHE 60; ch. 3) to the secrets of power which "were private to those who had the right by nature, as all art is, but these especially to the high-priestly race. Only a Jew could utter the Jewish, which was the final, word of power" (AHE 61; ch. 3).

Something of what he has come for, Simon recalls, has already been attempted. He meditates on his own version of the life of Christ, taught him by his magical training: for him, St. Joseph was a sorcerer, and Mary was deceived:

> The sorcerer who had attempted it had also been a Jew, a descendant of the house of David, who clothed in angelic brilliance, had compelled a woman of the same house to utter the Name, and something more than mortal had been born. But in the end the operation had failed. Of the end of the sorcerer himself there were no records; Joseph ben David had vanished. The living thing that had been born of his feminine counterpart had perished miserably. (AHE 61-62; ch. 3)

But Simon has "dared to risk the attempt again." His child, born to his own female accomplice, is Betty Wallingford. What the Clerk does not know is that Betty has been baptized by her nurse; set forever beyond his reach. Williams does not mean that she is beyond his reach because her baptism has made her no more a Jew; her gentile mother has made her that already. Williams means that Betty's baptism removes her from use as a magical instrument.

Toward the end of the novel, as Simon's efforts move toward their culmination, Williams explains the Clerk's weakness:

> He encouraged his mind into illusion. Illusion, to the magician as to the saint, is a great danger. But the master in Goetia has always at the centre of his heart a single tiny everlasting illusion; it may be long before that point infects him wholly, but sooner or later it is bound to do so. It was infecting Simon now. (AHE 212; ch. 10)

In the end he is defeated in the act of trying to recall three apparitions of himself into one: a "heavenly rain" begins to fall.

> It had been so when that other Jew ascended; such a cloud had risen from the opening of the new dimensions into which he physically passed, and the eyes of the disciples had not pierced it. But that Jew had gone up into the law and according to the law. Now the law was filling the breach in the law. (AHE 232; ch. 10)

Overcome, he passes into imbecility and hell.

Nobody, to my knowledge, has called Williams anti-Semitic. Yet, is not his Simon Leclerc, of necessity a Jew, more terrible than all the epithets and thoughtless images in Sayers? When one's masters stumble, and that is what Sayers and Williams have been to me, it is presumption to go on oneself. But having raised the matter, I must discuss it. Williams's intention is more noble; his lapse is of necessity more terrible than Sayers's. We are talking here about psychic matters: the use of images to convey meaning. Williams seems to have been quite heedless of the human implications of his imagery; he made Hell "a negress" in one of his plays. Regarded as a saint by his friends, he would have been horrified or perhaps merely amused at the reading I have given to his last novel. But what can one make of the sentence "the race which had been set for the salvation of the world became a judgement and even a curse to the world and to themselves"? It is likely that few readers even notice: Williams is "a thundering good read," most people gobble up his supernatural thrillers for the sake of the story, quite regardless of the theological or social implications. But the, error is there.

The making of a person or of a whole people into "the other"—the target against which to project the shadow of our own unacknowledged weaknesses: this is the pit continually set at the feet of writers who follow the *Way of the Affirmation of Images*. The powers with which writers of fantasy have to deal are real, but they are in each one of us. They should be evoked with caution, and they should never be attributed to anybody else.

Notes

[1] See Nancy-Lou Patterson, "Images of Judaism and Anti-Semitism in the Novels of Dorothy L. Sayers" (1978) available in the anthology *Detecting Wimsey: Papers on Dorothy L. Sayers's Detective Fiction* (2017).
[2] Charles Williams, "The Jews," *The Image of the City and Other Essays*, ed. Anne Ridler (London: Oxford UP, 1958) 161.
[3] Williams, "The Jews," 162.
[4] Williams, "The Jews," 162.
[5] Williams, "The Jews," 162.
[6] Williams, "The Jews," 163.
[7] Joshua Trachtenberg, *Jewish Magic and Superstition; A Study in Folk Religion* (1939; New York: Atheneum, 1970) vii.
[8] Trachtenberg vii-viii.
[9] Trachtenberg 1.
[10] Trachtenberg 2
[11] Trachtenberg 4.
[12] Trachtenberg 5.
[13] Trachtenberg 8.
[14] Trachtenberg 9.
[15] Trachtenberg 12.
[16] Trachtenberg 14.
[17] Trachtenberg 15.
[18] Francis King, *Ritual Magic in England* (London: Neville Spearman, 1970) 22.

Notes

[19] King 23.

[20] King 22.

[21] Anne Ridler, Introduction to *The Image of the City and Other Essays* by Charles Williams, ed. Anne Ridler (London: Oxford UP, 1958) xxv.

[22] Gershom G. Scholem, *Major Trends in Jewish Mysticism* (1941; New York: Schocken Books, 1965) 2.

[23] Scholem 2.

[24] Bram Stoker, *Dracula* (1897; New York: Modern Library) 386.

[25] C.S. Lewis, *Reflections on the Psalms* (London: Geoffrey Bles, 1958) 28.

[26] C.S. Lewis, *Reflections on the Psalms* 30.

3. Charles Williams

In "Charles Williams," Patterson provides a succinct chronologically organized overview of Williams's life, relationships, employment, and publications. Patterson's secondary sources included Carpenter (1978), Cavaliero (1983), Dawson (1964), Hadfield (1959), Heath-Stubbs (1955), Schideler (1962) and (1966), and Sibley (1982).

"Charles Williams" was first published in Modern British Essayists, *Second Series, edited by Robert Beum (Detroit: Gale, 1990) 316-25. This original edition of the paper had no footnotes. The editors of* Divining Tarot *added those included here, with apologies for the few sources that remain unidentified.*

Charles Williams thought of himself primarily as a poet: he published seven volumes of poetry between 1912 and 1944. He also wrote seven novels and fifteen plays. During his lifetime, however, his most frequently anthologized works were essays of literary criticism, chiefly about poetry, and his essays continued to be anthologized posthumously. In the late twentieth century Williams speaks as a significant and even prophetic voice of his own period, writing with intense awareness of the watershed in literary style and subject matter between the Edwardian era and the era dividing the two world wars.

Charles Walter Stansby Williams was born on the 20th of September, 1886, in Holloway, North London, to Walter and Mary Wall Williams. His parents were devout members of the Church of England. He called himself an "irrevocable bourgeois ... (although a Cockney bourgeois, let me add a little haughtily: there are degrees even in dust)." In 1894 the family moved to St. Albans, where Walter Williams, suffering from failing sight, opened a shop for artists' supplies. Williams attended St. Albans Grammar School, then began to commute daily to University College, London, where he studied Latin, French, and English history until a lack of family funds forced him to leave at eighteen. After four years assisting in the New Connexion Methodist Bookroom in London and attending classes at the Working Men's College on Crowndale Road. Williams became a proofreader at

Oxford University Press in 1908. In the same year he met Florence Conway, the daughter of a St. Albans ironmonger. In the context of their falling in love, Williams was set to proofing a translation of *The Divine Comedy*: this coincidence of life and art was the germ of his great theme of the Beatrician vision.

With his first volume of poetry, *The Silver Stair* (1912), Williams's literary career began. In 1914 he was declared unfit for military service due to the persistent trembling of his hands; thus, in addition to missing the Oxbridge education of his literary peers, he also missed the profound initiation of the trenches. He married Florence (whom he dubbed "Michal") on the 12th of April, 1917, in St. Albans Abbey. On the 21st of September he was installed into an offshoot of the Golden Dawn, an occult order much influenced by Christian occultist A.E. Waite. Publication of his *Poems of Conformity* (1917) coincided with these events.

The year 1920 brought a third book of poetry *Divorce,* and Williams's first essay in literary criticism, "The Hero in English Verse." He began as he was to continue: already poetry and theology appear hand in hand. The Hero, according to Williams, is "a poetic figure to symbolise Man,"[1] and he explores the theme of "humanity undergoing its doom"[2] in the works of Milton, Tennyson, Browning, Wordsworth, and Patmore. Williams's peculiar vocabulary—"Omnipotence" as a title of God, for example—begins to appear, as does his intention to better the *Idylls of the King* (1859-1885) with Arthurian poems after his own heart.

A son, Michael, was born in 1922. The following year Williams began lecturing at the London County Council Literary Institute. In his second essay, "The Commonwealth in English Verse" (1923), he explores the "ideal commonwealth,"[3] a precursor of his major theme of "the City." He finds that

> the way to that State lies perhaps where Mrs. Browning and Tennyson and Wordsworth would have looked for it, in and through the family, or let us say, marriage [...] For in the family the problems which perplex the State have to be solved, each happy family combines freedom with obedience, the individual with the Community.[4]

In his own life, perhaps Williams saw "the community, the desire for the establishment at all risks of a stable and permanent fellowship of men upon earth"[5] in the Oxford University Press, with its august publisher, Henry Milford, exemplified.

An eccentric but compelling lecturer, Williams had begun to acquire a following of students and admirers. He published his fourth volume of poetry, *Windows of Night*, in 1924. By this time an editor, he produced two introductions to literary works—"Notes on Possible Endings to *Edwin Drood*" (1927) and a "Prefatory Note" in *A Book of Longer Modern Verse* (1926)—and began to write the first of his occult novels, *Shadows of Ecstasy*, which was published in 1933. At forty, he fell in love with the Oxford University Press's new librarian, Phyllis Jones, whom he dubbed first "Phillida" and then "Celia." For her he wrote *An Urbanity* and *The Masque of the Manuscript*, both performed at Amen House in Warwick—where the Oxford University Press had moved in 1924—and privately published in 1927. Phyllis fell in love as well, but with someone else. During this intense period of unconsummated and unrequited love he wrote the preface to *A Book of Victorian Narrative Verse* (1927), which notes that in Victorian literature noble conduct was an end in itself and that "nobility cannot afford to be conscious of itself," lest, like Tennyson's Arthur, it risk "mere pomposity."[6] He laments that nobility has become "unfashionable," while "subtlety [...] irony, and bitterness" prevail.[7]

Two slight comic essays preface a major development in Williams's critical career. In "The One-Eared Man" (1928) he comments upon the absence of images in music; music, he says, is "the resolution of all knowledge into its simplest form."[8] To this abstract element he was to return. In "The History of Critical Music" (1928) he wittily imagines a music devoted to the criticism of other music. Williams carried out a similar exercise in his first volume of criticism, *Poetry at Present* (1930), in which each of sixteen essays on contemporary British poets is accompanied by a poem in the manner of that poet. The essays in *Poetry at Present* were seriously meant, however. Three of them were separately published; "John Masefield" (1929) preceded the book in the *Saturday Review of Literature,* probably because its subject had just been named Poet Laureate. In "Masefield," Williams detects "a substitution of loveliness for intensity."[9] In "T.S. Eliot" Williams comments wryly that "quite a large number of [Eliot's] lines are his own creation."[10] He pronounces "Mr. Eliot's poetic experience of life would seem to be Hell varied by intense poetry,"[11] and asks hopefully, "Can this hell be rather the place of purgation?"[12] (Williams became friends with Eliot in 1934.) "Robert Bridges" praises Bridges's poetry as "beauty in restraint."[13]

In 1931 Williams published an introduction to the *Poems* of Gerard Manley Hopkins; most critics think that Hopkins was the model for Williams's later poetic style. He praises Hopkins's "continual shocks of strength and beauty"[14] and says the poet's theories are only ways of "explaining to himself his own poetic energy."[15] The lectures Williams delivered to evening classes for the London City Council at the City Literary Institute and to many Evening Institutes in London formed the background for his second critical volume, *The English Poetic Mind* (1932). In 1933 his first biography, *Bacon,* appeared, as well as a brief biographical essay, "Lord Macaulay" (1933).

Williams's most seminal critical essay, "The Ostentation of Poetry," appeared as the introductory chapter of his third book of literary criticism, *Reason and Beauty in the Poetic Mind* (1933). His ideas, like so many in the twentieth century, are presaged by the *Biographia Literaria* (1817) of Samuel Taylor Coleridge. Chapter 18, "Language of metrical composition, why and wherein essentially different from that of prose," calls attention to the peculiar *"order"* of verse when compared "with the language of ordinary men."[16] Coleridge says that in poetry, as the "elements are formed into metre *artificially*, by a *voluntary* act [...] so the traces of present *volition* should throughout the metrical language be proportionately discernible."[17] The poet, according to Coleridge, states boldly: "I write in metre, because I am about to use a language different from that of prose."[18] In "The Ostentation of Verse" Williams observes that despite the trend away from strict patterns in poetry, patterns are still a "necessity." The difference between poetry and prose "is ostentatiously insisted on by the verse itself"; indeed, "The ostentation is part of the verse."[19] The poem exists in "neither the pattern nor the subject of which we are separately aware, but in the resultant whole."[20] Williams calls attention to the "flagrancy" of the "pattern,"[21] that is, of the abstract elements in poetry. These elements are "the decision of [the] writer,"[22] a "personal choice among impersonal patterns."[23] Williams follows Coleridge in saying that poetry is the willed and controlled use of metre and metaphor to create effects different from those of prose.

The ostentatious abstract element of poetry as defined by Williams appears again in F.W. Bateson's *English Poetry: A Critical Introduction* (1966), though without attribution: "It is only indeed by a process of abstraction that the poet can give meaning."[24] In the twentieth century, consciousness of the abstract element in art is central to the practice as well as the criticism of art: Williams's essay of 1933 is an important manifestation of this consciousness in its historical context. (The concept of poetic "ostentation," adumbrated by Coleridge, developed by Williams, and then further elaborated by Bateson, is thoroughly explored in Robert Beum's *Poetic Art of William Butler Yeats*, which sees ostentation or "verbal conspicuousness"[25] as the touchstone, the definitive feature of all poetry.)

In his introduction to *The New Book of English Verse* (1935) Williams bases his choices upon an "effort to avoid cant."[26] This important essay introduces his view that for Milton "the Satanic rebellion was not only wicked but silly."[27] Also included is an insight as profound as that of "The Ostentation of Poetry." Williams states of his era, "It is the moment of the close of the myths. English verse had carried in its tradition a continual use of the myths—of Achilles, Alexander, Arthur, of the fables and the religions, especially of that greatest of the myths [...] Christianity."[28] Now, the myths, "If they are ever used [...] are realised as states of awareness."[29] This recognition arises, Williams says, from "the conscious knowledge of our consciousness."[30] Consciousness of abstraction and consciousness of consciousness are the twin foci of twentieth-century criticism, and Williams contributed to the development of both concepts.

Two selections from *The English Poetic Mind* were anthologized in 1936 in Anne Bradby's (Ridler) *Shakespeare Criticism, 1919-35* (1936) indicating the importance of Williams's criticism in his own period. In the first of these passages, which are somewhat awkwardly excised from their original context, "*Troilus and Cressida* and *Hamlet*" are seen as embodying Shakespeare's struggle to make his poetry match the human experience of deciding and acting in a world where what is may change to what ought not to be: Williams's experiences with Phyllis Jones underlie this interpretation. Also in *Shakespeare*

Criticism, 1919-35 is the essay "Henry V," which discusses "the sublime Fourth Chorus" ("Now entertain conjecture of a time").[31]

In 1935 Williams received the highest compliment ever paid to his abilities as a playwright: he was invited to follow Eliot's masterpiece *Murder in the Cathedral*, performed that year at Canterbury Cathedral, with a play of his own. *Thomas Cranmer of Canterbury*, produced and published in 1936, is perhaps Williams's best play. In February of that year C. S. Lewis borrowed a copy of *The Place of the Lion* (1931) and wrote to a friend that it was "a really great book."[32] In March Williams received a letter expressing Lewis's delight in his novel,[33] and the next day he wrote to praise Lewis's *The Allegory of Love*, which he had proofread for the Oxford University Press.[34] The two men soon met for lunch in London, and their friendship ensued.

An essay, "Notes on Religious Drama," followed Williams's Canterbury play in 1937.[35] The major event of that year for Williams was the publication of *Descent into Hell*, his masterpiece, in which his theme of "Substitution" is embodied rather than argued. The ideas of "Co-inherence" (the oneness of all) and "Exchange" (bearing one another's burdens) to which he refers so often and so gnomically in his religious essays beginning in 1938 resonate through *Descent into Hell* in a profound display of power.

Also published in 1937 was "The New Milton," pointing out the "element of comedy"[36] in *Paradise Lost.* In a touching subtext Williams discusses Milton's blindness in terms clearly based on his own father's experience. The 1938 essay "Religious Drama," says trenchantly that plays dealing with dogmas are "almost all bad."[37] A lecture given in Paris, "On Byron and Byronism" was also published in 1938, as were the biographical essays "Queen Victoria" and "H.M.P." (on Helen M. Peacock). Another whimsical essay on music, "Sound and Variations," appeared the same year. Even this minor piece contains a significant aphorism: art "provokes true emotions, and consequently does not represent them."[38]

In 1938 Williams published the first of his two major volumes of Arthurian poetry, *Taliessin through Logres,* in which all he had learned about verse was applied in works of powerful originality. He also published his first volume of explicitly theological speculation, *He Came Down From Heaven.*

With the outbreak of World War II in 1939, Oxford University Press moved to Southfield House, Oxford. Although Williams's wife remained in London, she had forgiven his infatuation with Phyllis Jones. At Oxford, Williams lectured on Milton, and Lewis reports that he held the undergraduate audience spellbound as he spoke on chastity in *Comus*. His seminal essay "Sensuality and Substance" appeared in the journal *Theology* in 1939. Although theology was not a new theme for him, here it takes the central position as he discusses the sacrality of matter and of the human body; the "Affirmation of Images" (related to the "Affirmative Way" as opposed to the more commonly used "Negative Way" of mysticism); the holiness of the intellect; and the concept of "Romantic Theology." Blake and D.H. Lawrence are compared, and their heresies against these concepts are corrected. "Poetry," Williams says, "is sensual and intellectual, like sex."[39]

Also in 1939 Williams published his second volume of theological speculation, *The Descent of the Dove*. A related essay, "The Church Looks Forward" (1940), contains the pronouncement that theologians have worked out "the doctrine of our Lord as God" but that "The other doctrine of His Manhood [...] has still to be worked out and put into action."[40] Continuing the theme expressed in his earliest essays, he derives the subject of "The Image of the City in English Verse" (1940) from the vision of "the New Jerusalem" in Revelation and sees its most perfect literary expression in a line from *Henry V*: "The singing masons building roofs of gold."[41] An interview, "Taste in Literature" (1940), offers a rare example of his speaking style. In "The Recovery of Spiritual Initiative" (1940), an address to a group of sociologists, he says acerbically that the church is served by people "who blanket their messages by making heroic efforts to talk in a way nobody listens to."[42]

The introduction to *The English Poems of John Milton* (1940) includes a comment which probably contributed to C.S. Lewis's *Perelandra* (1943): "Obedience [...] is the proper order of the universe in relation to a universal law,"[43] and an analysis of Satan's sense of "injured merit"[44] which certainly contributed to Lewis's *A Preface to Paradise Lost* (1942). This essay contains Williams's most-quoted aphorism, "Hell is always inaccurate." Hell, as Williams personifies it, is unable to understand not only Heaven but ordinary human life.

Williams's second introduction of 1940, to Søren Kierkegaard's *The Present Age,* reports that this prophet attacked his "Age" for "its mediocrity, its insignificance, its solemn and imbecile hypocrisy." To Kierkegaard, "'The Crowd' meant [...] numbers, quantity, multiplication," whereas, Williams says, "there is only the individual and necessity. There and there only is Authority."[45]

Nine essays—the longest series published by Williams in any one year—appeared in 1941. Later included in *The Image of the City* are: "Charles Williams on *Taliessin through Logres,*" "Blake and Wordsworth," "The Redeemed City," and "Natural Goodness." "Charles Williams on *Taliessin through Logres*" sets forth the major symbols he added to the Arthurian canon: "the identification of the Empire of Byzantium [...] with the human organism"[46] and the magical, disciplinary, and measuring properties of the hazel rod (which have caused some observers to see a sadistic element in the poems). "Blake and Wordsworth" returns to Williams's study of "the feeling intellect";[47] comparing Blake's "prophetic books"[48] with Wordsworth's *The Prelude* (1850), he defines his doctrine of "Co-inherence" as "the exchange of pardon between all men and women."[49]

In "The War for Compassion" (1941) he sees World War II as being fought for "the restoration [...] of the natural rights of man" already existing before the church and calls on the church to search for "what remains of freedom in the most abandoned or the most oppressed."[50] In "Notes on the Way" (1942) [see note below], after commenting on words the war has coined (*quisling*) or debased (*appeasement*), he gives his only published reference to his exile in Oxford. Mourning "by Isis for my lovelier Thames," he laments that while unlike the Psalmist, "It is no Babylon that receives us, but friends and comfortable houses," even so, like Dante, he eats, "the salt bread" and "climbs the steep stairs of others."[51]

In "The Redeemed City," a major theological essay, he says of Britain: "There is no final idea for us but the glory of God in the redeemed and universal union—call it Man or the Church or the City."[52] In "Natural Goodness" he argues that the natural and the supernatural are not actually opposed and that "Matter and 'nature' have not, in themselves, sinned; what has sinned is spirit."[53]

The essay *Religion and Love in Dante: The Theology of Romantic Love* (1941) contains the heart of Williams's thought, which influenced his friend Dorothy L. Sayers in her translation for Penguin of *The Divine Comedy*. Dante's work begins with "nightmare"[54] and culminates in "the supernatural validity of that 'falling-in-love' experience" of Dante with Beatrice,[55] he says, discussing an idea he later developed most fully in *The Figure of Beatrice* (1943). *The Way of Exchange* (1941) declares that "exchange and substitution fills the phrase 'bear ye one another's burdens' with a much fuller meaning than is usually ascribed to it." For Williams, "Compacts can be made for the taking over of the suffering of troubles, and worries, and distresses, as simply and as effectively as an assent is given to the carriage of a parcel."[56] Williams's *Witchcraft* (1941) is still one of the best studies of its subject.

"Notes on the Way" (28 February 1942) comments that in Williams's Arthurian myth "there was imagined a union of geography, physiology, and metaphysics,"[57] and adds: "philosophic truths depend for the Church on the body. Torture and concentration camps and slavery are against the body."[58] The body was for Williams a measure of the real and was intrinsically innocent.

Williams had defined the Affirmation of Images in "The Church Looks Forward" as "Justice, Charity, Union. These [he said] are the three degrees of the Affirmation of the Images, and all of us are to be the images affirmed."[59] In a rare discussion of the Rejection of Images in "St. John of the Cross" (1942) he calls it one of the "darker metaphors," but an image nonetheless. He adds that "even the images must in the end be loved only because God loves them."[60] In "The Index of the Body" (1942) he reviews the uses in astrological and religious symbolism of the body as a figure for the cosmos, and "not merely the old spatial macrocosmic heavens, but the deep heavens of our inner being,"[61] in other words, of the Unconscious. C.S. Lewis used the phrase "deep heaven" with this meaning in *That Hideous Strength* (1945). Williams had joined Lewis's circle, "The Inklings," a group that met weekly for drink, conversation, and reading aloud from their works in progress.

By 1943 he was lecturing regularly at Oxford University, which gave him an honorary M.A. in that year. In "A Dialogue on Mr. Eliot's Poem" (1943) he imagines a conversation between Nicobar, Eugenio (evidently himself), Sophronisba and Celia on *Little Gidding* (1942), pronouncing these verses in Celia's voice "soliloquies from the heart's cloister."[62] The chidden Eugenio laments of his earlier, lower estimation of Eliot, "I have said so much that I do not clearly remember."[63] A second conversation between the four voices, "A Dialogue on Hierarchy" (1943), concludes that "we are not to suppose that the hierarchy of one moment is likely to be that of the next,"[64] and that "Equality is the name we give to the whole sum of such changes."[65] This idea also anticipates Lewis's *That Hideous Strength.*

Williams's introduction to *The Letters of Evelyn Underhill* (1943) remains essential to the understanding of Underhill. Expecting more because of their shared membership in an offshoot of the Golden Dawn, Williams finds her occult novels disappointing. From his own experience of "Impossibility," in which what is becomes what ought not to be, he understands her shock when Pius X condemned Modernism: "It is the details of the Impossibility that press home—the sordid, the comic, the agonizing,"[66] he says feelingly, echoing his painful encounter with "Celia." He finds that Underhill's *Mysticism* (1911), which he "must have read [...] within a year or two of its appearance," still has for him the "immediate sense of authority."[67]

Of all his theological essays, "What the Cross Means to Me" (1943) is the most accessible and the most profound: "It is credible that the Almighty God should [...] create beings to share His Joy [...] but it is not credible that a finite choice ought to result in an infinite distress."[68] The Cross demonstrates that "alone among the gods, He deigned to endure the justice He decreed."[69] Williams says, and adds of the Cross that "This is what Almighty God, as well as we, found human life to be."[70] Writing in the depths of World War II, he says, "It is finished; we too do but play out the necessary ceremony. As in bombings from the air, cancer, or starvation, for instance? Yes, I suppose so; if at all, certainly in those examples."[71] He concludes: "Not the least gift of the Gospel is that our experiences of good need not be separated from our experiences of evil."[72]

Williams's second volume of Arthurian poetry, *The Region of the Summer Stars*, was published in 1944, as was an essay related to his poetry, "Malory and the Grail Legend." Neither Tennyson nor William Morris "had the full capacity of the mythical imagination,"[73] he says, and he praises Malory's figure of Galahad as "that in the human soul which finds Christ."[74] The last year of his life saw the publication of his superb supernatural novel *All Hallows' Eve* and his final introductory essay, "On the Poetry of *The Duchess of Malfi*," a dark opinion of a darker work. In this triumphant novel and this dystopic essay the extremes of his extraordinary personality are encompassed. Williams died on 15 May 1945 from complications of surgery to correct a recurrent intestinal disorder. His death shocked his friends: Lewis wrote that when Williams died, it was the idea of death which had to change.

In his lifetime, Charles Williams enjoyed the approval of some distinguished peers. His earliest posthumous appreciation came from Lewis in *Arthurian Torso* (1948). Anne Ridler edited anthologies of his essays in 1958 and 1961; in her commentary on the first she wrote that his "literary criticism is 'creative criticism' of a kind that has been somewhat out of fashion since the analytical critics were in the ascendant." In *Charles Williams* (1966) Mary McDermott Shideler comments that his "non-fiction is more explosive and illuminating than his imaginative writings [...] because expository writings cannot be brushed off by alluding to fantasies or figures of speech."[75]

During the 1980s several books on Williams appeared, including Alice Mary Hadfield's second and indispensable biography. In *Charles Williams: Poet of Theology* (1983), Glen Cavaliero perceives that in the

> critical books one can see Williams moving towards an equation between literary method and personal apprehension. The 'why' of poetry was implicit in its 'how': the discovery, which must have come naturally to one who was steeped in an incarnational theology, was to have a lasting impact on his development both as theologian and as artist.[76]

At this distance, Williams's critical works emerge as vivid cultural artifacts, revealing a mind original, individual, personal, and intuitive, through which is refracted, as through a prism, the uncertain sunlight of his era.

Notes

[1] Charles Williams, "The Hero in English Verse," *Contemporary Review* 118 (1 Jul. 1920): 837.

Notes

[2] Williams, "The Hero in English Verse" 837.

[3] Charles Williams, "The Commonwealth in English Verse," *Contemporary Review* 124 (1 Jul 1923): 231.

[4] Williams, "The Commonwealth in English Verse" 235. See Williams's comments about Robert Browning's poetry on pages 230-31. See Williams's comments about Mrs. Browning's work on pages 234-35.

[5] Williams, "The Commonwealth in English Verse" 230.

[6] Charles Williams, Selected with an Introduction, *A Book of Victorian Narrative Verse* (1927; Oxford: Clarendon Press, 1931) iv-v.

[7] Charles Williams, Selected with an Introduction, *A Book of Victorian Narrative Verse* x.

[8] Charles Williams, "The One-Eared Man," *Dominant* I (Dec. 1927): 11-12.

[9] Charles Williams, "Masefield," *Saturday Review of Literature* 6 (1929): 1154; *Poetry at Present* (1930; Rpt. Freeport, NY: Books for Library Press, 1969) 114-27.

[10] Charles Williams, "T.S. Eliot," *Poetry at Present* 170.

[11] Charles Williams, "T.S. Eliot," *Poetry at Present* 166.

[12] Charles Williams, "T.S. Eliot," *Poetry at Present* 173.

[13] Charles Williams, "Robert Bridges," *Poetry at Present* 20.

[14] Charles Williams, "Introduction," *Poems of Gerard Manley Hopkins, Second edition*, ed. Gerald Roberts (1931; London: Oxford UP, 1940) xiv.

[15] Charles Williams, "Introduction," *Poems of Gerard Manley Hopkins, Second edition* xiii.

[16] Samuel Taylor Coleridge, *Biographia Literaria Volume II* (London: Oxford UP, 1817) 45.

[17] Coleridge 50.

[18] Coleridge 53.

[19] Charles Williams, "The Ostentation of Verse," *Reason and Beauty in the Poetic Mind* (1933; Folcroft, PA: Folcroft Library Editions, 1974) 3.

[20] Williams, "The Ostentation of Verse" 7.

[21] Williams, "The Ostentation of Verse" 10.

[22] Williams, "The Ostentation of Verse" 8.

Notes

[23] Williams, "The Ostentation of Verse" 9.

[24] Frederick W. Bateson, *English Poetry: A Critical Introduction, Second edition* (New York: Barnes & Noble, 1966) 41.

[25] Robert Beum's *Poetic Art of William Butler Yeats* (New York: F. Ungar, 1969) 9.

[26] Charles Williams, "Introduction," *The New Book of English Verse* (Gollancz, 1935) (Rpt. Miami, Florida: Granger Books, 1978) 7.

[27] Williams, "Introduction," *The New Book of English Verse* 8.

[28] Williams, "Introduction," *The New Book of English Verse* 16.

[29] Williams, "Introduction," *The New Book of English Verse* 17.

[30] Williams, "Introduction," *The New Book of English Verse* 17.

[31] Anne Bradby (Ridler), selected with an introduction, *Shakespeare Criticism,* 1919-35 (London: Oxford UP, 1936) 184.

[32] C.S. Lewis, letter to Arthur Greeves, of Feb. 26th, 1936, *They Stand Together: The Letters of C.S. Lewis to Arthur Greeves (1914–1963)*, ed. Walter Hooper (London: Collins, 1979).

[33] Walter Hooper, ed., *The Collected Letters of C.S. Lewis: Books, Broadcasts, and the War, 1931–1949* (San Francisco: Harper-SanFrancisco, 2004) 183-84. The letter Williams received from Lewis was dated March 11th, 1936.

[34] Walter Hooper, ed., *The Collected Letters of C.S. Lewis: Books, Broadcasts, and the War, 1931–1949* 184-85.

[35] Charles Williams, "Notes on Religious Drama," *Chelmsford Diocesan Chronicle* 23 (May 1937): 75-76.

[36] Charles Williams, "The New Milton," *The Image of the City and Other Essays* (London and New York: Oxford UP, 1958) 23.

[37] Charles Williams, "Religious Drama," *The Image of the City and Other Essays* (London and New York: Oxford UP, 1958) 55.

[38] Charles Williams, "Sound and Variations," *The Image of the City and Other Essays* (London and New York: Oxford UP, 1958) 53.

[39] Charles Williams, "Sensuality and Substance," *The Image of the City and Other Essays* (London and New York: Oxford UP, 1958) 72.

[40] Charles Williams, "The Church Looks Forward," *St. Martin's Review* (July 1940): 330.

Notes

[41] Charles Williams, "The Image of the City in English Verse," *The Image of the City and Other Essays* (London and New York: Oxford UP, 1958) 92.

[42] Glen Cavaliero, *Charles Williams: Poet of Theology* (1983; Eugene, OR: Wipf & Stock, 2007) 62.

[43] Charles Williams, Introduction, *The English Poems of John Milton* (1940; London: Oxford UP, 1971) xi.

[44] Charles Williams, Introduction, *The English Poems of John Milton* xii.

[45] Charles Williams, Introduction, *The Present Age* by Søren Kierkegaard, trans Alexander Dru and Walter Lowrie (London: Oxford UP, 1940) x.

[46] Charles Williams, "Charles Williams on *Taliessin through Logres*," *Poetry Review* (April 1941), published as "The Making of Taliessin" in *The Image of the City and Other Essays* (London and New York: Oxford UP, 1958) 181.

[47] Charles Williams, "Blake and Wordsworth," *The Image of the City and Other Essays* (London and New York: Oxford UP, 1958) 60.

[48] Williams, "Blake and Wordsworth" 660.

[49] Williams, "Blake and Wordsworth" 65.

[50] Charles Williams, "War for Compassion," *Sword of the Spirit* 20 (15 May 1941): 7.

[51] Charles Williams, "Notes on the Way," *Time and Tide* 23. Editor's note: Patterson's quotes do not seem to come from either the February or March parts of this article

[52] Charles Williams, "The Redeemed City," *The Image of the City and Other Essays* (London and New York: Oxford UP, 1958) 102.

[53] Charles Williams, "Natural Goodness," *The Image of the City and Other Essays* (London and New York: Oxford UP, 1958) 76.

[54] Charles Williams, *Religion and Love in Dante: The Theology of Romantic Love* (Westminster, UK: Dacre Press, 1941) 16.

[55] Charles Williams, *Religion and Love in Dante: The Theology of Romantic Love* 30.

[56] Charles Williams, *The Way of Exchange* (pamphlet) (James Clarke, 1941).

Notes

[57] Charles Williams, "Notes on the Way," *Time and Tide* 23 (28 Feb. 1942): 170.
[58] Williams, "Notes on the Way" 171.
[59] Charles Williams, "The Church Looks Forward," *St. Martin's Review* (July 1940) 332.
[60] Charles Williams, "St. John of the Cross," *Time and Tide* 23 (27 Jun. 1942): 522.
[61] Charles Williams, "The Index of the Body," *The Image of the City and Other Essays* (London and New York: Oxford UP, 1958) 85.
[62] Charles Williams, "A Dialogue on Mr Eliot's Poem", *Dublin Review* 212 (April 1943) 115.
[63] Charles Williams, "*A Dialogue on Mr Eliot's Poem*" 122.
[64] Charles Williams, "A Dialogue on Hierarchy," *The Image of the City and Other Essays* (London and New York: Oxford UP, 1958) 127.
[65] Williams, "A Dialogue on Hierarchy" 127.
[66] Charles Williams, *The Letters of Evelyn Underhill* (London: Longmans, Green, 1943) 15.
[67] Charles Williams, *The Letters of Evelyn Underhill* 17.
[68] Charles Williams, "The Cross," *The Image of the City and Other Essays* (London and New York: Oxford UP, 1958) 131. "The Cross" was first published as "What the Cross Means to Me" (1943).
[69] Williams, "The Cross" 132.
[70] Williams, "The Cross" 135.
[71] Williams, "The Cross," 138.
[72] Williams, "The Cross" 139.
[73] Charles Williams, "Malory and the Grail Legend," *The Image of the City and Other Essays* (London and New York: Oxford UP, 1958) 187.
[74] Williams, "Malory and the Grail Legend," 190 note.
[75] Mary McDermott Shideler, *Charles Williams: A Critical Essay* (Grand Rapids: Eerdmans, 1966) 41.
[76] Glen Cavaliero, *Charles Williams: Poet of Theology* (1983; Eugene, OR: Wipf & Stock, 2007) 29.

Appendix 1

Nancy-Lou Patterson's Tarot Collection

The following lists do not reflect the extraordinary size and breadth of Patterson's library, much of which has been dispersed. The Tarot-related items listed here are among those specifically set aside by her family as being of special importance to her.

Books

Butler, Bill. *Dictionary of the Tarot*. New York: Schocken Books, 1975. Hardcover. [The bookplate indicates Patterson acquired this volume in 1976.]

Gardner, Richard. *The Tarot Speaks*. 1971. London: Tandem, 1974. Paperback. Illus. with Marseilles-style cards. [Unsigned.]

Gray, Eden. *The Tarot Revealed*. Toronto: A Signet Mystic Book published by the New American Library of Canada, 1960. Paperback. Illus. with *Rider-Waite Tarot* cards. [Patterson signed the first page.]

—— *A Complete Guide to the Tarot*. Toronto: Bantam Books, 1970. Paperback. Illus. with *Rider-Waite Tarot* cards. [Unsigned.]

—— *Mastering the Tarot: Basic Lessons in an Ancient, Mystic Art*. Scarborough, ON: A Signet Classic book published by the New American Library of Canada, 1973. Paperback. Illus. with *Rider-Waite Tarot* cards. [Unsigned.]

Hargrave, Catherine Perry Hargrave. *A History of Playing Cards and A Bibliography of Cards and Gaming*. 1930. New York: Dover Publications. Toronto: General Publishing Co., Ltd, 1966. An unabridged republication of the work published by Houghton Mifflin Co. in 1930. Reprinted by permission of the United States Playing Card Company. Paperback. [Signed by Nancy-Lou Patterson on the title page.]

Kaplan, Stuart R. *James Bond 007 Tarot Book*. New York: U.S. Games Systems, 1973. Paperback. [Unsigned. Deck listed below.]

—— *Tarot Classic*. New York: Grosset & Dunlap, 1972. Hardcover [The bookplate indicates Patterson acquired this volume in 1972. Deck listed below.]

—— *Tarot Cards for Fun and Fortune Telling*. New York: U.S. Games Systems, Inc., 1970. Hardcover. [Patterson signed the front binding page vertically between two card illustrations, indicating she acquired the volume on September 6, 1972.]

McCormack. Kathleen. *Tarot: How to foretell your future in the cards*. No loc. Fontana Books, 1973. Paperback. Illustrated with what appear to be hand-drawn Marseilles-style cards. [Unsigned.]

Ouspensky, P.D. *The Symbolism of the Tarot: Philosophy of Occultism in Pictures and Numbers*. New York: Dover Publications; Toronto: General Publishing Co., Ltd., 1976. Paperback. [Patterson signed the title page, indicating that she acquired the volume during Septuagesima, 1977. Septuagesima Sunday is the ninth Sunday before Easter, but the term may apply to the period extending to the beginning of Lent on Shrove Tuesday.]

Papus. *The Tarot of the Bohemians: The Most Ancient Book in the World*. Trans. A.P. Morton. Third edition, revised with preface by Arthur E. Waite. Hollywood, CA: Wilshire Book Co., 1970.

Ussher, Arland. *The Twenty Two Keys of the Tarot*. Designs drawn by Leslie Mac Weeney. 1953. Dublin: Dolmen Press, 1969. Hardcover. [Patterson signed the front binding page indicating she acquired the volume in 1970.]

Waite, Arthur Edward. *The Key to the Tarot*. 1910. Hawthorne, Melbourne, Victoria, Aus.: Century Hutchinson Publishing Group, 1972. Paperback. [Unsigned. Deck listed below.]

—— *The Pictorial Key to the Tarot*. 1910. New Hyde Park, NY: University Books, 1959. Includes Gertrude Moakley's "Introduction" ix-xviii and "Note on the Tarot as a Game 317-22. Hardcover. [The bookplate indicates Patterson acquired this volume on the Feast of St. Gregory, 1969. Deck listed below.]

Tarot and Other Decks

America Playing Cards: Arts of Pre-Columbian America. Spain: Heraclio Fournier S.A., 1960?). Drawings and descriptions by Teodoro N. Miciano, Prof. of San Fernando High School of Fine Arts, Madrid. Booklets (English and Spanish versions) explain the cultural references in the images on the court cards: spades stand for North west Indians, the suit of diamonds "red Indians," the suit of hearts Aztecs, and the suit of clubs Incas. There are two jokers, one showing indigenous groups in North America and Mesoamerica, and the other those in South America. The cards all have gold corners.

Aquarian Tarot. David Mario Palladini. Morgan Press, 1970. These cards have solid blue backs. The *Aquarian Tarot* is now available through U.S. Games Systems.

Egyptian Tarot Cards. The box is white with a black label and no publishing information. The cards are printed on light-weight cream-colored construction paper. The deck appears to be the *Brotherhood of Light Tarot*, which was used to illustrate C.C. Zain's *The Sacred Tarot*, 1936. *The Brotherhood of Light Tarot* was created for this purpose by Gloria Beresford by redrawing and revising the Falconnier and Wegener 1896 Egyptian deck. This deck may be distinguished from its variants by the constellations that Beresford added.

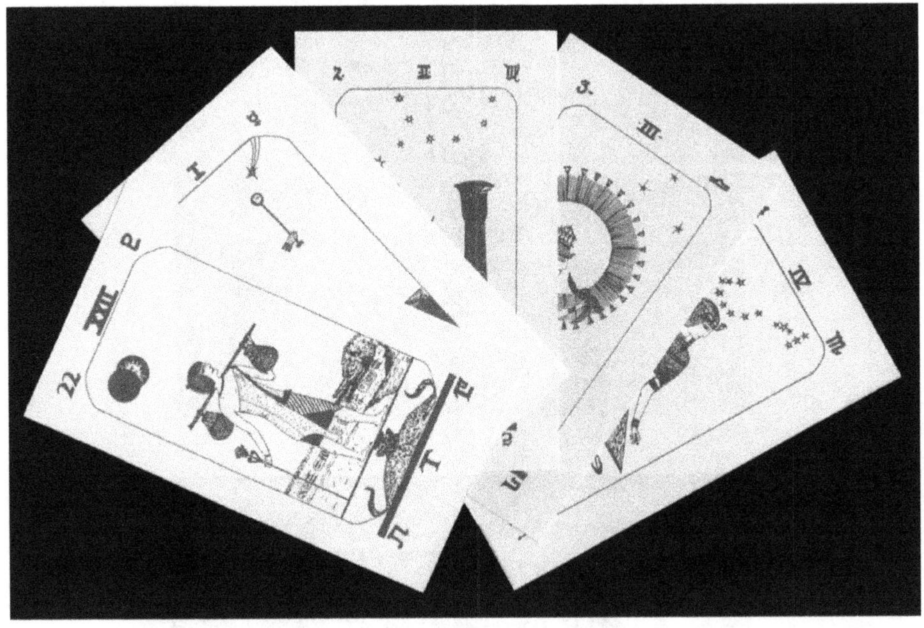

Giant Rider-Waite Tarot Cards 22 Major Arcana. Arthur E. Waite and Pamela Colman Smith (artist). New York: U.S. Games Systems, 1971.

The Goddess Tarot. Kris Walkherr. Stamford, CT: U.S. Games Systems. With instruction booklet, © 1997 U.S. Games Systems.

Grand Etteilla Egyptian Gypsies Tarot. Based on an eighteenth-century Etteilla deck. B.P. Grimaud. No date.

James Bond 007 Tarot. © 1973. Eon Productions Ltd. and Glidrose Publications, Ltd. With instruction booklet by Stuart R. Kaplan. Distributed by U.S. Games Systems.

The Jesus Deck. Rev. Ralph M. Moore. Switzerland: AGMueller, © 1972. A deck of 54 cards, including four suits with ten numbered cards and a king, queen, and jack in each, plus two jokers, and an instruction booklet.

Mountain Dream Tarot. Bea Nettles. © Bea Nettles 1975. Distributed by Light Impressions Corp., Rochester, NY.

Mulùk wanuwwàb the only arabic playing cards extant. Limited edition of 750 copies. No. 00584. Brussels and Louvain: Aurelia Books, 1972. Manufactured by Carta Mundi, Turnhout. Facsimile and reconstructed edition of fifteenth-early-sixteenth-century originals. Cards 19.9 x 7.4 cm. Booklet by Jan Bauwens with the card inscriptions translated by Prof. Tangi of the University of Istanbul. The deck includes four suits (coins, cups, swords, polo-sticks) with ten numbered cards and four court cards (King, Lieutenant, Second Lieutenant, and Assistant) in each. (Info. From "Mamluk Playing Cards," *The World of Playing Cards*. < http://www.wopc.co.uk/egypt/mamluk>.) [The explanatory booklet and chart are both missing from this copy.]

Playing Deck. Bergamo, Italy: Masenghini. No date. This four-suited Italian-style deck is smaller than most, being 5 x 8.5 cm. The simple suit images are set on a cream ground without borders. The card backs show a black-and-white three-dimensional cube pattern. No instruction booklet included.

Rider-Waite Tarot Cards. Arthur E. Waite and Pamela Colman Smith (artist). New York: U.S. Games Systems, 1971.

Tarock Deck. Heron. The deck is in a clear plastic case and is almost identical to the *Jeu de Tarot* deck listed below, except this copy does not include a card explaining the game rules, and two corners of each trump of the deck show the Heron logo. All four corners of each *Jeu de Tarot* trump show the number of the trump. The cards of this deck, but not those of the *Jeu de Tarot* deck, have gold corners, and the backs of the *Jeu de Tarot* cards are a deep burgundy with gold calligraphy and those of this deck are pink and black stripes in a plaid pattern.

The identification card indicates that this is a "héron" deck, but not that it is a Tarock Deck. However, in design the trump cards are similar, though not identical to, the AGMuller deck illustrated in Kaplan's *Encyclopedia of Tarot*, vol. I, p. 323. They may be a closer match to item 465—a deck released in 1970—in Felix Alfaro Fournier's *Playing Cards, 1st Supplement Fournier Museum* (Heraclio Fournier, S.A.–Vitoria).

Tarock Deck. Label: *Jeu de Tarot.* The identification card reads "Ce jeu vous est offert par les Cognacs Prince Hubert de Polignac et Héron maitres-Cartiers Boéchat." The box carries similar labeling. There is another added card giving rules for the game. The four suits include four double-ended court cards, and the trumps are numbered from one through twenty-two. Each trump includes a picture below the number identification on each half of the card, with a different picture on each half. The cards are almost identical to those of the Tarock Deck listed above.

Top: Tarock Deck (Heron)
Bottom: Adapted Heron Tarock Deck

Tarot Classic. Reproduced from an eighteenth-century deck. New York: U.S. Games Systems, © 1971.

Tarot of Marseilles. Two Decks.

—— B.P. Grimaud. © 1963. The cards have English language labels and are packaged with an instruction booklet in a red cardboard box. All of the cards are stamped © G.P. Grimaud 1963. The backs have the same mauve plaid checkered pattern that appears on the deck listed below.

—— B.P. Grimaud. No date. The cards have English language labels and are packaged with an instruction booklet in a green cardboard box. This deck is identical to that with a copyright date of 1963, except that the card stamp does not include a copyright date and the stamp does not appear at all on the numbered pips or on some of the trumps (The Tower of Destruction, Moon, and Sun). The backs show the same pale mauve pattern that appears on the deck listed above. There is a hand-written note in this deck box that reads "Dear Nancy-Lou: On seeing these, I immediately thought of you. You may already have a set—no harm! All your prophecies will be of double effect. Love. Dan."

Thoth Tarot. Aleister Crowley and Frieda Harris (artist). © 1944 Ordo Templi Orientis. U.S. Games Systems © 1978, 1983. Instruction booklet by James Wasserman with two essays by Harris and commentary and footnotes by Stuart R. Kaplan.

Visconti-Sforza Tarot. 2 versions. Facsimile and reconstructed edition created from hand-painted original produced in Milan c. 1450. Missing: Devil, Tower, 3 of Swords, and Knight of Coins.

—— *I Tarocchi Dei Visconti.* Bergamo Italy: Monumenta Longobardica © 1974. With booklet in Italian by Gabriele Mandel. The deck is in a box in a slipcase. The box opens like a book, with a recess for the cards. The booklet fits on top. The modern Devil and Tower cards are identical to those in the U.S. Games edition listed below.

—— *Visconti-Sforza Tarocchi Deck.* New York: U.S. Games Systems, © 1975. The modern Devil and Tower cards are identical to those in the Monumenta Longobardica edition listed above.

Visconti-Sforza Tarocchi. Facsimile and reconstructed edition created from hand-painted original produced in Milan c. 1450.
Top: Monumenta Longobardica © 1974. Bottom. U.S. Games Systems © 1975.
Illus. reproduced by permission of U.S. Games Systems.
Further reproduction prohibited.

Excerpt from Stuart R. Kaplan, *The Encyclopedia of Tarot*, Vol. I. Stamford, CT: U.S. Games Systems, Inc., 1978. 71-72.

The Devil This is one of the four cards lost from the extant Visconti-Sforza tarocchi pack. The first five hundred Visconti-Sforza decks reproduced in 1975 by Grafica Gutenberg and U.S. Games Systems, Inc., contained a composite line drawing of The Devil card from other popular tarot decks. The second edition of the reproduced Visconti-Sforza deck, also published in 1975, recreated the card of The Devil, shown here, as it may have appeared in the fifteenth century.

The figure of a fierce Devil—whose torso is half male and half female and whose lower body is animal—stands on a pedestal. The Devil is winged and has horns and ass's ears. It carries in its left hand a small club, while its right hand gives a sign. In front of The Devil, tied to the pedestal, are two smaller figures, both half animal and half human, one male and one female. They are clothed in loose green cloth. A heavy rope tied around their necks goes through a knot affixed to the pedestal. The male figure facially resembles The Devil. The female figure has a lighter skin tone.

The Falling Tower This is the second card missing from the trumps. In the first reproduction of five hundred Visconti-Sforza decks a line drawing of a popular Falling Tower card was substituted. In the second edition of the reproduced deck an artist recreated The Falling Tower card as it might have appeared at the time of the original Visconti-Sforza deck. A blazing red sun with scalloped rays appears in the upper right section of the card. One ray strikes the tower and separates the gold crown-shaped top from the stone battlement. Stones and debris fall to the ground, along with two figures dressed in garments similar to those worn by the two figures in The Lovers Card. However, the facial expressions of the falling figures are tense and fearful.

Note: New Devil and Tower cards by Luigi Scapini are included in the 1986 U.S. Games Systems edition of this deck. Other editions of this deck are now available from different publishing companies.

Xultun Tarot. Peter Balin. Arcana Publishing. © 1976 Peter Balin. [This copy of the deck includes two copies of the 3 of Staffs and only twenty of the twenty-two trumps. The instruction booklet and top part of the box are also missing.]

Appendix 2

Readings on Charles Williams in *Mythlore*

This list is for the reader looking for more papers on Charles Williams. It is extracted from the *Mythlore Index* (for issues 1-133) compiled by Janet Brennan Croft and Edith Crowe and excludes papers by Nancy-Lou Patterson, which may be found under her name in the bibliography.

Anderson, Angelee Sailer. "The Nature of the City: Visions of the Kingdom and its Saints in Charles Williams' *All Hallows' Eve.*" *Mythlore* 15.3 (#57) (1989): 16-21. Study of Williams's symbolic portrayal of the Kingdom of God in *All Hallows' Eve*. Discusses co-inherence, substitution, and the affirmation and rejection of changes.

Beach, Charles. "'Courtesy' in Charles Williams's *The Greater Trumps.*" *Mythlore* 19.1 (#71) (1993): 16-21. Describes the tradition of courtesy in medieval court and monastic communities. Refers to these traditions and Williams's writings to define courtesy as he saw it. Notes the different levels of courtesy as defined by Williams.

Beare, Rhona. "Charles Williams and the Angelicals." *Mythlore* 8.4 (#30) (1982): 31. Notes similarities between the angelicals that appear in *The Place of the Lion* and the Gnostic archons, which are also represented in animal form.

—— "Charles Williams and the Stone." *Mythlore* 8.3 (#29) (1981): 34. Relates Islamic and Jewish creation stories to the Stone of King Solomon (the Shekinah) in *Many Dimensions.*

Blasdell, Heather L. "'... And There Shall The Lilith Repose.'" *Mythlore* 14.4 (#54) (1988): 4–6, 12. Notes the attributes of Lilith in mythology, and demonstrates how Jadis and the Emerald Witch of Narnia, and Williams's Lily Sammile in *Descent Into Hell*, share these characteristics.

Bosky, Bernadette. "Even an Adept: Charles Williams and the Order of the Golden Dawn." *Mythlore* 13.2 (#48) (1986): 25-31, 34-35. Presents information on Williams's association with the Hermetic Order of the Golden Dawn and the Fellowship of the Rosy Cross. Gives the convoluted history of the Order and the tension between proponents of mysticism vs. ritual magic. Suggests the level of Williams's involvement and its significance to him.

—— "Grace and Goetia: Magic as Forced Compensation in *All Hallows Eve* [sic]." *Mythlore* 12.3 (#45) (1985): 19-23. Contrasts the free exchange and substitution of Williams's principle of co-inherence with the forced exchange of magic, as practiced by Simon the Clerk in *All Hallows' Eve*. Previously appeared as "Grace and Goetia: Magic as Forced Compensation in Charles Williams' *All Hallows' Eve*." *Mythcon XVI, Wheaton College, Wheaton, IL, 1985*. Ed. Diana Pavlac: Mythopoeic Society, 1985. 15–30.

—— Introduction. *The Masques of Amen House, together with Amen House Poems and with Selections from the Music for the Masques.* Charles Williams; music by Hubert J. Foss; introduction by Bernadette Lynn Bosky. Ed. David Bratman. Altadena: Mythopoeic Press, 2000. 1–30. An overview of Williams's literary works, personal life, and career, with particular emphasis on his work at the Oxford University Press, his love for Phyllis Jones, and the plays as part of the masque tradition. –has multiple listings in the index

Bratman, David, Judith Kollmann, Bernadette Bosky, David Samuelson, and Richard L. Purtill. "A Centennial Retrospective on Charles Williams." *Mythlore* 13.2 (#48) (1986): 13–21, 40. Edited transcript of a panel discussion (including audience contributions) at the 17th Mythopoeic Society Conference.

Browning, Lydia R. "Charles Williams's Anti-Modernist *Descent into Hell.*" *Mythlore* 31.1/2 (#119/120) (2012): 69–84. Focuses on the theme of community versus isolation. Ralph Waldo Emerson's essay "Self Reliance" is used as a key to understanding Lawrence Wentworth's increasing withdrawal from reality and "the city" of his fellow human beings, in contrast with the workings of co-inherence personified in the interactions of other characters.

Carter-Day, Deborah. "'Coinherence' [sic] and 'The Terrible Good': A Soul's Journey to Awareness and Responsibility." *Mythlore* 7.4 (#26) (1981): 27–30. Examines Williams's conceptions of co-inherence, exchange, and substitution as they are portrayed in *All Hallows' Eve*——particularly in the actions of Lester Furnival.

Christopher, Joe R. "Climbing Jacob's Ladder: A Hierarchical Approach to Imagistic Mysticism." *Mythlore* 3.3 (#11) (1976)/*Tolkien Journal* #18 (1976): 10–19. Discusses a number of poets and writers (including Lewis and Williams) related by similar philosophical and mystical traditions. Demonstrates how their work relates to Rudolph Otto's definition of the Imagistic Way and its stages.

—— "John Heath-Stubbs' *Artorius* and the Influence of Charles Williams." [Part III]. *Mythlore* 13.4 (#50) (1987): 51–56. Considers the influence of Williams on Heath-Stubbs's Arthurian poem cycle. Part I looks at zodiacal imagery. Part II examines particularly the symbolism of the Muses in *Artorius*. The conclusion primarily considers the influence of Williams and Eliot on Heath-Stubbs.

Cutsinger, James S. "Angels and Inklings." *Mythlore* 19.2 (#72) (1993): 57–60. Religious and philosophical discussion on the nature of angels, particularly as portrayed by Lewis, Tolkien, and Williams.

Doyle, Berry B. "The Ways of the Images in Charles Williams' *The Place of the Lion*." *Mythlore* 16.3 (#61) (1990): 15-19. Notes the importance of imagery to Williams, and shows how *The Place of the Lion* presents "three basic ways of how imagery is used and various examples of each way": perversion, affirmation, and rejection. Charts.

Duriez, Colin. "Tolkien and the Other Inklings." *Mythlore* 21.2 (#80) (1996): 360–63. Looks at Tolkien's relationship with the other Inklings, especially Lewis, Williams, and Barfield, in particular studying the affinities and differences between them and what Tolkien owes to them. "The Notion Club Papers" is discussed as an idealized portrait of the Inklings.

Ellwood, Gracia Fay. "Matters of Grave Import: The Third Heaven." *Mythlore* 8.4 (#30) (1982): 29–30. Discusses the concept of the Third Heaven in Charles Williams's Arthuriad.

Enright, Nancy. "Charles Williams and his Theology of Romantic Love: A Dantean Interpretation of the Christian Doctrines of the Incarnation and the Trinity." *Mythlore* 16.2 (#60) (1989): 22–25. Relates Williams's Romantic Theology to the precursors of Dante and Beatrice, and to the Christian doctrines of the Holy Trinity and the Incarnation.

GoodKnight, Glen. "The Social History of the Inklings: J.R.R. Tolkien, C.S. Lewis, Charles Williams, 1939–1945." *Mythlore* 2.1 (#5) (1970)/*Tolkien Journal* 4.2 (#12) (1970): 7–9. Overview of the formation and meetings of the Inklings; primarily discusses the WWII era. Discusses Williams as "catalyst" and focuses mainly on the effects of his membership and unexpected death on the group.

—— "Transcending the Images: Archaisms and Alternatives." *Mythcon II, Francisco Torres, Santa Barbara, CA, 1971*. Ed. Glen GoodKnight. Los Angeles: Mythopoeic Society, 1971. 3–5, 25. Discusses the medieval theological concepts of affirmation of images (romantic, seeking truth reflected in imagery) and rejection of images (mystical, seeking direct access to truth), building on Mary Schildeler's book on Williams, *The Theology of Romantic Love*, and liberally quoting from Jung and Lewis. Concludes that Lewis advocated a hybrid concept of transparent images; that ideally one should simultaneously contemplate both the image and the truth behind it, transcending dualism.

Gottlieb, Stephen A. "A Reading of Williams' Arthurian Cycle." *Mythlore* 4.2 (#14) (1976): 3–6. Detailed analysis of the symbolism and character of Williams's Arthurian poems, which are "about the unities and disunities in human history that ow around the themes of order versus disorder and identity versus false identity or lack of identity."

Hanger, Nancy C. "The Excellent Absurdity: Substitution and Co-Inherence in C.S. Lewis and Charles Williams." *Mythlore* 9.4 (#34) (1983): 14–18. Cites examples of Williams's notions of co-inherence and exchange in both his works and those of Lewis.

Haykin, Michael. "A Note on Charles Williams' *The Place of the Lion*." *Mythlore* 5.2 (#18) (1978): 37–38. Considers why Williams refers to a non-existent Gnostic tradition in a conversation between Anthony and Mr. Richardson. Is this mere error or purposeful?

Higgins, Sørina. "Is a 'Christian' Mystery Story Possible? Charles Williams's *War in Heaven* as a Generic Case Study." *Mythlore* 30.1/2 (#115/116) (2011): 77–90. Examines *War in Heaven's* radical upsetting of the detective novel norms promised in its first few paragraphs and shows how Williams uses and subverts these conventions and leads us to contemplate, instead of a mystery and its solution, an insoluble Mystery with a capital M.

Hopkins, Lisa. "Female Authority Figures in the Works of Tolkien, C.S. Lewis and Charles Williams." *Mythlore* 21.2 (#80) (1996): 364–66. The powerful, learned woman is a figure of fear in the works of Williams, seen as transgressing her proper role. In Lewis, legitimate authority figures are male, illegitimate ones are female, and gender roles are strictly demarcated. Tolkien, however, not only creates powerful and heroic women, but also suggests that the combination of authority and femininity can be particularly potent and talismanic.

Howard, Thomas. "Granting Charles Williams his *Doneé*." *Mythlore* 8.2 (#28) (1981): 13–14. Discusses the difficulty of objective criticism of Williams as a novelist because of his unusual, *sui generis* subject matter and treatment.

Hyles, Vernon. "On the Nature of Evil: The Cosmic Myths of Lewis, Tolkien and Williams." *Mythlore* 13.4 (#50) (1987): 9–13, 17. Examines the works of Tolkien, Lewis, and Williams for what they have to say about the nature of evil in their fiction, particularly as it relates to Christian scripture and eschatology.

Previously appeared in *Mythcon XVI, Wheaton College, Wheaton, IL, 1985*. Ed. Diana Pavlac. Altadena: Mythopoeic Society, 1985. 102–21.

Kawano, Roland M. "The Impact of Charles Williams' Death on C.S. Lewis." *Mythcon I, Harvey Mudd College, Claremont, CA, 1970*. Ed. Glen GoodKnight. Los Angeles: Mythopoeic Society, 1970. 27–28. Recounts the beginnings of the friendship of Lewis and Williams and Williams's later association with the Inklings until his death following complications from surgery in May 1945. Discusses the effect of his death on C.S. Lewis's thoughts about mortality and reprints his poem "On the Death of Charles Williams."

Kilby, C.S. "Tolkien, Lewis, and Williams." *Mythcon I, Harvey Mudd College, Claremont, CA, 1970*. Ed. Glen GoodKnight. Los Angeles: Mythopoeic Society, 1970. 3–4. A brief, early history of the Inklings: their primary members, their similarities in outlook, and their basic writings.

Kollmann, Judith. "Charles Williams and Second-Hand Paganism." *Mythlore* 11.2 (#40) (1984): 5–7, 20. Argues that unlike Lewis and Tolkien, who incorporate true pagan worldviews into their works as imperfect precursors of Christianity, Williams uses superficially pagan elements that are really a product of the Judeo-Christian world. Williams's portrayal of the pagan/occult is more negative, while showing the attractiveness of such power.

—— "*Eros*, *Philia*, and *Agape* in Charles Williams' Arthuriad." *Mythlore* 18.4 (#70) (1992): 9–14. Argues that Williams, in recasting the Grail legend into his own Christian metaphysics, used the three Grail knights to represent the three forms of love.

—— "The Figure of Beatrice in the Works of Charles Williams." *Mythlore* 13.2 (#48) (1986): 3–8. Keynote address, Mythcon 17. Notes the importance of the figure of Beatrice to Williams, and reviews his use of Beatrician figures in his novels and poems.

—— "The Legend of the Grail and *War in Heaven*: From Medieval to Modern Romance." *Mythlore* 10.4 (#38) (1984): 20–22, 44. Compares *War in Heaven* to its literary sources, particularly *Le Morte Darthur*. Notes the ways the former incorporates specific aspects of the Grail legend, as well as the differences Williams introduced to adapt the legend for a twentieth-century novel.

Lee, George. "And the Darkness Grasped it Not: The Struggle of Good and Evil in Charles Williams." *Mythlore* 6.1 (#19) (1979): 18–20. Discusses the "central theme" of the "struggle of good and evil" in three of Williams's novels.

Lenander, David. "*The Cocktail Party* After *All Hallows' Eve*: All Saints' Day Hangover." *Mythcon XVI, Wheaton College, Wheaton, IL, 1985*. Ed. Diana Pavlac. Altadena: Mythopoeic Society, 1985. 135–45. Discusses the mutual influence of Williams and Eliot, including as illustration a lengthy quote from Eliot's introduction to *All Hallows' Eve*. Considers Eliot's verse play *The Cocktail Party* for its "participation in the Christian mythopoeic genre of Charles Williams' novels," and discusses the importance of the character Julia Shuttlethwaite and her eventual revelation as one of the guardian angels.

Matthews, Janet. "Charles Williams: A Perspective Through the Eyes and Works of T.S. Eliot." *Mythcon XVI, Wheaton College, Wheaton, IL, 1985*. Ed. Diana Pavlac. Altadena: Mythopoeic Society, 1985. 161–94. Explores a number of themes and concerns paralleled in the works of Williams and Eliot—the Ways of Affirmation and Negation of Images, exchange, substitution, and co-inherence, and the image of the City—as well as their mutual admiration and influence. Speculates as to why Williams is not held is as high esteem as Eliot.

McKinley, Marlene Marie. "'To Live From a New Root': The Uneasy Consolation of *All Hallows' Eve*." *Mythlore* 16.1 (#59) (1989): 13–17. Analyzes Williams's view of love in *All Hallows' Eve*, noting the challenging and disquieting notion of giving up earthly attachments and definitions of the phrase to "live from a new root."

McLaren, Scott. "Hermeticism and the Metaphysics of Goodness in the Novels of Charles Williams." *Mythlore* 24.3/4 (#93/94) (2006): 5-33. Examines metaphysical symbols in three novels by Charles Williams: the Holy Grail in *War in Heaven*, the Stone of King Solomon in *Many Dimensions*, and the Tarot deck in *The Greater Trumps*.

Milburn, Michael. "Art According to Romantic Theology: Charles Williams's Analysis of Dante Reapplied to J.R.R. Tolkien's 'Leaf by Niggle.'" *Mythlore* 29.3/4 (#113/114) (2011): 57–75. Provides a grounding in Charles Williams's "romantic theology," which was heavily indebted to his reading of Dante, and the application of romantic theology to art, which Milburn demonstrates by examining Tolkien's "Leaf by Niggle" through this lens. Winner of the Alexei Kondratiev Award at Mythcon 41.

Nyman, Amy. "A Feminist Perspective in Williams' Novels." *Mythlore* 12.4 (#46) (1986): 3–10. Looks at women in the novels of Charles Williams from the perspective of feminism, especially feminist theology. Finds a wide range of female characters at various stages of spiritual development, androgyny and inclusiveness in regard to God. Previously appeared as "A Feminist Perspective in Charles Williams' Novels." *Mythcon XVI, Wheaton College, Wheaton, IL, 1985*. Ed. Diana Pavlac. Altadene: Mythopoeic Society, 1985. 229–46.

Pauline, Sister, C.S.M. "Mysticism in the Ring." *Tolkien Journal* 3.4 (#10) (1969): 12–14. Considers a large part of the appeal of *Lord of the Rings* to rest in its mysticism; that is, the way of seeing all things and actions as part of a larger whole. Uses Williams's concept of co-inherence to help explain this idea. Defines mysticism as distinct from allegory and complementary to science. Concludes with a discussion of reconciliation of opposites as a foundation of the mystical worldview, particularly in Eastern thought.

Pavlac, Diana Lynne. "More than a Bandersnatch: Tolkien as a Collaborative Writer." *Mythlore* 21.2 (#80) (1996): 367–74. It is commonly argued that the Inklings had no influence on Tolkien. This paper will show that they had a profound influence, so much so, that Lewis and Williams should be considered co-architects of Middle-earth.

Peoples, Galen. "The Agnostic in the Whirlwind: The Seven Novels of Charles Williams." *Mythlore* 2.2 (#6) (1970): 10-15. An overview of Williams's novels in publication order, with summaries and a discussion of common themes and style.

Pitts, Mary Ellen. "The Motif of the Garden in the Novels of J.R.R. Tolkien, Charles Williams, and C.S. Lewis." *Mythlore* 8.4 (#30) (1982): 3–6, 42. Considers the importance of the symbolism of the garden, especially from *Genesis* and medieval literature, in certain works of Lewis, Tolkien, and Williams.

—— "Ways of Passage: An Approach to *Descent Into Hell*." *Mythlore* 10.2 (#36) (1983): 9–12. Compares ways of descending into Hell described in Silvestris's *Commentary* with those in Williams's *Descent Into Hell*.

Price, Meredith. "'All Shall Love Me and Despair': The Figure of Lilith in Tolkien, Lewis, Williams, and Sayers." *Mythlore* 9.1 (#31) (1982): 3–7, 26. Examines Lilith-figures in Tolkien, Lewis, Williams, and Sayers, discussing how each demonstrates certain attributes of the archetypal temptress character.

Purdy, Margaret R. "Battle Hill: Places of Transition in Charles Williams' *Descent Into Hell*." *Mythlore* 7.2 (#24) (1980): 11–12. Notes that Williams uses many elements of the traditional ghost story in *Descent Into Hell*, especially in the story of the suicide. However, Williams "touches [the ghost story] with the numinous, giving its symbols a sacramental meaning."

Rateliff, John D. "'And Something Yet Remains to be Said': Tolkien and Williams." *Mythlore* 12.3 (#45) (1986): 48–54. Attempts to sort through Tolkien's comments on Charles Williams "to show that Tolkien's opinion of Williams underwent a radical change years after Williams' death." Concludes the two main reasons were the death of Lewis and the rise of scholarly criticism defining the Inklings as a literary circle. Previously appeared in *Mythcon XVI, Wheaton College, Wheaton, IL, 1985*. Ed. Diana Pavlac. Altadena: Mythopoeic Society, 1985. 271–86.

—— "The Lost Letter: Seeking the Keys to Williams's Arthuriad." *Mythlore* 34.1 (#127) (2015): 5–36. Mythcon 47 Guest of Honor address. The Arthuriad is dense with allusion and the reader often has a sense of missing much that goes on below the surface; as it happens, the reader is not wrong to be confused. Rateliff finds the keys that unlock this poetic sequence *à clef* in a relatively unknown letter Williams wrote in answer to a list of questions on the Arthuriad from C.S. Lewis, in the "gynecomorphical map" drawn to Williams's personal specifications which served as endpapers to the poetry, and in Williams's private life as revealed in letters and memoirs, in particular to personae he ascribed to certain women in his life. Includes illustrations.

Rauscher, Eric. "From Dubric to Taliessen: Charles Williams's Early Work on the Arthurian Cycle." *Mythlore* 23.1 (#87) (2000): 20–29. Explores the transformation of Dubric into Taliessen, focusing on how Dubric gradually recedes in importance in Williams's thinking about the Arthur story and is finally transformed into Taliessen.

Reynolds, George. "Dante and Williams: Pilgrims in Purgatory." *Mythlore* 13.1 (#47) (1986): 3–7. Analyzes *All Hallows' Eve* in terms of the symbolism and structure of Dante's *Il Purgatorio.* Asserts the importance of the purgatorial aspect, which not all critics recognize. Previously appeared in *Mythcon XVI, Wheaton College, Wheaton, IL, 1985*. Ed. Diana Pavlac. Altadena: Mythopoeic Society, 1985. 287–98.

Rose, Ellen Cronan. "A Briefing for *Briefing*: Charles Williams' *Descent Into Hell* and Doris Lessing's *Briefing For a Descent into Hell.*" *Mythlore* 4.1 (#13) (1976): 10–13. Asserts that "Doris Lessing's naming of her book and its protagonist was both intentional and ironic, and that it acknowledges her indebtedness to the form of Williams' fiction and her [...] futile gesture toward the Romantic amalgam of appearance and reality."

Ruskin, Laura A. "Three Good Mothers: Galadriel, Psyche, and Sybil Coningsby." *Mythcon I, Harvey Mudd College, Claremont, CA, 1970*. Ed. Glen GoodKnight. Los Angeles: Mythopoeic

Society, 1970. 12–14. Examines the imagery and functions of the Mother archetype in world mythology and the characters of Tolkien's Galadriel, Lewis's Psyche, and Williams's Sybil.

Russell, Mariann. "Elements of the Idea of the City in Charles Williams' Arthurian Poetry." *Mythlore* 6.4 (#22) (1979): 10–18. Sees Williams's Arthurian poems as a dialectic with a pa ern of thesis, antithesis, and synthesis, the last related to the idea of co-inherence. Examines Williams's characteristic image of the City as it appears in the Arthurian poems.

Schakel, Peter. "Dance as Metaphor and Myth in Lewis, Tolkien, and Williams." *Mythlore* 12.3 (#45) (1986): 4–8, 23. Guest of Honor address at Mythcon 16. Notes the occurrence of images of dance, including the cosmic dance, and their metaphorical usage. Concentrates on Lewis but includes examples from Tolkien and Williams. Previously appeared in *Mythcon XVI, Wheaton College, Wheaton, IL, 1985*. Ed. Diana Pavlac. Altadena: Mythopoeic Society, 1985. 5–14.

Shideler, Mary McDermo . "Excerpts from a Letter about Charles Williams." *Mythlore* 2.2 (#6) (1970): 6. Brief introduction to who Williams was and some remarks about his work.

Smith, Evans Lansing. "The Mythical Method of *Descent Into Hell*." *Mythlore* 20.2 (#76) (1994): 10–15. Considers Williams's *Descent Into Hell* as an excellent "example of the use of the mythical method [as defined by T.S. Eliot] as a metaphor of poesis, by which the fundamental forms of the imagination are catalyzed." Geometrical symbolism and the underworld journey link it to many modernist works.

Stolzenbach, Mary. "Machen's Hallows." *Mythlore* 11.3 (#41) (1985): 28, 38. Discusses one of Machen's rare stories that deal with "the good supernatural"— in this case, the Grail. Sees parallels between this story and works of Lewis and Williams (especially *War in Heaven*).

Veach, Grace L. "What the Spirit Knows: Charles Williams and Kenneth Burke." *Mythlore* 26.3/4 (#101/102) (2008): 117–28. Explores parallels between the philosophy of Kenneth Burke and the poetry of Charles Williams.

Versinger, Georgette. "The Commonplace Book: Charles Williams's Early Approach to the Arthurian Poetry." *Mythlore* 22.3 (#85) (1999): 39–54. Examines Williams's handwritten notebook, in which he jotted ideas and references for his Arthurian poetry, for clues about influences, style, themes, and characters.

Warren, Colleen. "Wentworth in the Garden of Gomorrah: A Study of the Anima in *Descent Into Hell.*" *Mythlore* 13.2 (#48) (1986): 41–44, 54. Views Wentworth's personal "descent into hell" "from a Jungian perspective [...] which reveals a man's obsession with his anima, or feminine archetype, his consequent repression of true selfhood, and his final dispossession of both, leading him ultimately to insanity, or, as Williams puts it, to hell."

Weinig, Sister Mary Anthony. "Exchange, Complementarity, Co-Inherence: Aspects of Community in Charles Williams." *Mythlore* 7.2 (#24) (1980): 27–29. Discusses Williams's ideas of exchange and co-inherence in relation to community, particularly church. Argues that Williams's works (fiction and non- fiction) exhibit not only a theology of romantic love "but also an ecclesiology and sacramental system."

White, Donna R. "Priestess and Goddess: Evolution of Human Consciousness in *The Greater Trumps.*" *Mythlore* 14.3 (#53) (1988): 15-19. Extracts a definition of fantasy from Barfield's theory of consciousness, and calls Williams a "master at [...] Barfieldian fantasy." Analyzes *The Greater Trumps* as "the best exemplum" of this kind of fantasy, "that explores some aspect of human consciousness by reviving a mythic mode of thought."

Williams, Charles. "Ballad of a Street Door." *Mythlore* 2.3 (#7) (1971): 18.

—— "*The Noises That Weren't There*. Chapter 1: The Noises That Weren't There." *Mythlore* 2.2 (#6) (1970): 17-21.

—— "*The Noises That Weren't There*. Chapter 2: The Voice of the Rat." *Mythlore* 2.3 (#7) (Autumn 1971): 17-23.

——"*The Noises That Weren't There*. Third and Final Chapter of the Unfinished Manuscript." *Mythlore* 2.4 (#8) (Winter 1972): 21-25.

Wilson, Simone. "The Arthurian Myth in Modern Literature." *Mythlore* 1.1 (#1) (1969): 30–32. Discusses Moorman's work, which analyzes how Arthurian legend is treated by Charles Williams, T.S. Eliot, and C.S. Lewis.

—— "The Empire of Charles Williams." *Mythlore* 1.4 (#4) (1969): 50–53. Outlines the geography of the Empire in Williams's Arthuriad, and the symbolic meaning of its parts.

Woods, Richard. "The Figure of Taliesin in Charles Williams' Arthuriad." *Mythlore* 10.1 (#35) (1983): 11–16. Discusses Taliesin as a historical personage and as a legendary and mythological figure, and specifically the sources for Williams's portrayal of Taliesin in his Arthurian poetry. Speculates on why Williams chose Taliesin as the "romantic focus" of his poems, how he conceived his role, and why he departed from traditional sources.

Yandell, Steven. "'A Pattern Which Our Nature Cries Out For': The Medieval Tradition of the Ordered Four in the Fiction of J.R.R. Tolkien." *Mythlore* 21.2 (#80) (1996): 375–92. Considers the fiction of Tolkien and the other Inklings (specifically Lewis and Williams) as influenced by a set of shared ideas. First, the concept of a creator and of individuals as sub-creators; the Medieval four-fold division of the world; and the tripartite nature of creation, whether by God or humans. Analyzes the narrative structure of *The Lord of the Rings* in light of these ideas. Concepts detailed in several charts and graphics.

Bibliography

Baring-Gould, William and Ceil. *The Annotated Mother Goose*. New York: Bramhall House, 1962.

Bateson, Frederick W. *English Poetry: A Critical Introduction.* 1950. Second edition. New York: Barnes & Noble, 1966.

Beum, Robert. *Poetic Art of William Butler Yeats.* New York: F. Ungar, 1969.

Book of Common Prayer. The Creed of St. Athanasius. Toronto: Anglican Book Centre, 1959.

Burgess, Anthony. "*The Waste Land* Revisited." *Horizon* (Winter 1972): 105-09.

Carpenter, Humphrey. *The Inklings*. London: Allen & Unwin, 1978. [Reviewed by Patterson in *Mythlore* 6.2 (#20) (1979): 34.]

Cavaliero, Glen. *Charles Williams: Poet of Theology*. Grand Rapids, MI: Eerdmans, 1983. [Reviewed by Patterson in *Mythlore* 10.3 (#37) (1984): 37.]

Coleridge, Samuel Taylor. *Biographia Literaria Volume II.* London: Oxford UP, 1817.

Cronin, Vincent. "The Humanists." *Horizon* (Winter 1971): 81-103.

Cavendish, Richard. *The Black Arts*. New York: Capricorn Books, 1968.

Clébert, Jean-Paul, *The Gypsies*. Trans. Charles Duff. Harmondsworth, UK: Penguin, 1963.

Daniélou, Jean. S.J. *Primitive Christian Symbols*. 1961. Trans. Donald Attwater. London: Compass Books, Burnes and Oates, 1964.

Dante [Alighieri]. *The New Life*. Trans. William Anderson. Harmondsworth, UK: Penguin, 1964.

—— *Purgatory* in *The Comedy of Dante Alighieri*. Trans. Dorothy L. Sayers. Harmondsworth, UK: Penguin, 1955.

Dawson, Lawrence R. Jr. "A Checklist of Reviews by Charles Williams." *Papers of the Bibliographical Society of America*, 55 (Second Quarter 1961): 100-117.

—— "Reflections of Charles Williams in Literature." *Ball State Teachers College Forum*, V (Winter 1964): 23-29.

Dix, Dom Gregory. *The Shape of the Liturgy*. London: Dacre Press, 1945.

Eliot, T.S. "Introduction." *All Hallow's Eve* by Charles Williams. New York: Bard Books, Avon Books, 1969.

—— *The Waste Land and Other Poems*. New York: Harvest Books, Harcourt, Brace, and Co., 1934.

Euripides. "The Bacchae." Trans. William Arrowsmith. *The Complete Greek Tragedies*. Vol. IV. *Euripides*. Eds. David Grene and Richard Lattimore. Chicago: University of Chicago Press. 529–609.

Fuller, Edmund. "Many Dimensions; the Images of Charles Williams." *Books with Men Behind Them*. New York: Random House, 1962.

Glenn, Lois. *Charles W.S. Williams—A Checklist*. Kent, OH: Kent State UP, 1975.

Graves, Robert, "Mushroom." *Man, Myth, and Magic* [Encyclopedia].

Gray, Eden. *The Tarot Revealed*. New York: Bell Publishing, 1960.

Gresham, William Lindsay. "Preface" (written 1949; first published 1950. Rpt. 1962). *The Greater Trumps* by Charles Williams (1932). 1950. New York: Noonday Press, 1962.

—— *Nightmare Alley*. 1946. New York: New York Review of Books, 2010. [Film of the same title, 1947.]

—— "The Romany Trade." *Monster Midway*. Toronto: Clarke Irwin, 1953.

Hadfield, Alice Mary. *An Introduction to Charles Williams*. London: Hale, 1959.

—— *Charles Williams: An Exploration of His Life and Work*. London: Oxford UP, 1983. [Reviewed by Patterson in *Mythlore* 10.4 (#38) (1984): 42-43.]

—— "The Relationship of Charles Williams' Working Life to his Fiction." *Shadows of Imagination*. Ed. Mark R. Hillegas. Carbondale: Southern Illinois UP, 1969. 125-38.

Hargrave, Catherine Perry. *A History of Playing Cards and a Bibliography of Cards and Gaming*. 1930. New York: Dover Publications, 1966.

Hartnoll, Phyllis. *A Concise History of the Theatre*. London: Thames and Hudson, 1968.

Heath-Stubbs, John. *Charles Williams*. London: Longmans, Green, 1955.

Hillegas, Mark R., ed. *Shadows of Imagination*. Ed. Mark R. Hillegas. Carbondale: Southern Illinois UP, 1969. [Reviewed by Patterson in *Mythlore* 7.1 (#23) (1980): 24.]

Hooper, Walter, ed., *The Collected Letters of C.S. Lewis: Books, Broadcasts, and the War, 1931–1949*. San Francisco: HarperSanFrancisco, 2004.

Irwin, W.R. "Christian Doctrine and the Tactics of Romance: The Case of Charles Williams." *Shadows of Imagination*. Ed. Mark R. Hillegas. Carbondale: Southern Illinois UP, 1969. 139-49.

James, E.O. *Seasonal Feasts and Fasts*. London: Thames and Hudson, 1961.

Jung, C.G. *Aion*. Trans. R.F.C. Hull. The Collected Works. Vol. 9 Part 2. Bollingen Series XX. Second Edition. Princeton, NJ: Princeton UP, 1968.

—— *The Archetypes and the Collective Unconscious*. Trans. R.F.C. Hull. The Collected Works. Vol. 9. Bollingen Series XX. Second Edition. Princeton, NJ: Princeton UP, 1968.

—— "Concerning Mandala Symbolism." *The Archetypes and the Collective Unconscious*. Trans. R.F.C. Hull. The Collected Works. Vol. 9. Bollingen Series XX. Second Edition. Princeton, NJ: Princeton UP, 1968. 355-84.

—— "Mandalas." *The Archetypes and the Collective Unconscious*. Trans. R.F.C. Hull. The Collected Works. Vol. 9. Bollingen Series XX. Second Edition. Princeton, NJ: Princeton UP, 1968. 387-90.

—— *Memories Dreams, Reflections*. New York: Vintage Books, 1963.

Keen, Sam. "Manifesto for a Dionysian Theology." *New Theology* No. 7: *The Recovery of Transcendence*. Eds. Martin E. Marty and Dean G. Peerman. Toronto: Collier-Macmiillan, 1970.

King, Francis. *Ritual Magic in England.* London: Neville Spearman, 1970.

Leith, James A. *The Idea of Art as Propaganda in France, 1750–1799*. Toronto: University of Toronto Press, 1965.

Lewis, C.S. *English Literature in the Sixteenth Century, excluding Drama*. London: Oxford UP, 1954.

—— "Williams and the Arthuriad." Charles Williams and C.S. Lewis. *Arthurian Torso*. London: Oxford UP, 1952.

Lommel, Andreas. *Shamanism, The Beginnings of Art*. Toronto: McGraw-Hill, 1967.

Mâle, Emile. *The Gothic Image*. New York: Harper Torchbooks, 1958.

McMurtrie, Douglas C. *The Book: The Story of Printing and Bookmaking*. New York: Oxford UP, 1962.

Moakley, Gertrude. "Introduction." *The Pictorial Key to the Tarot* by Arthur Edward Waite. New Hyde Park, NY: University Books, 1959. ix-xviii.

—— "Notes on the Tarot as a Game." *The Pictorial Key to the Tarot* by Arthur Edward Waite. New Hyde Park, NY: University Books, 1959. 317-22.

—— *The Tarot Cards Painted by Bonifacio Bembo for the Visconti-Sforza Family: An Iconographic and Historical Study*. New York: The New York Public Library, 1966.

—— "The Tarot Trumps and Petrarch's *Trionfi*: Some Suggestions on their Relationship." *Bulletin of the New York Public Library* (Feb. 1956): 55-69.

Moorman, Charles. *Arthurian Triptych*. Berkeley: University of California Press, 1960.

Otto, Walter F. *Dionysus, Myth and Cult*. Trans. Robert B. Palmer. Bloomington: Indiana UP, 1965.

Panofsky, Irwin. *Meaning in the Visual Arts*. New York: Doubleday Anchor Books, 1955.

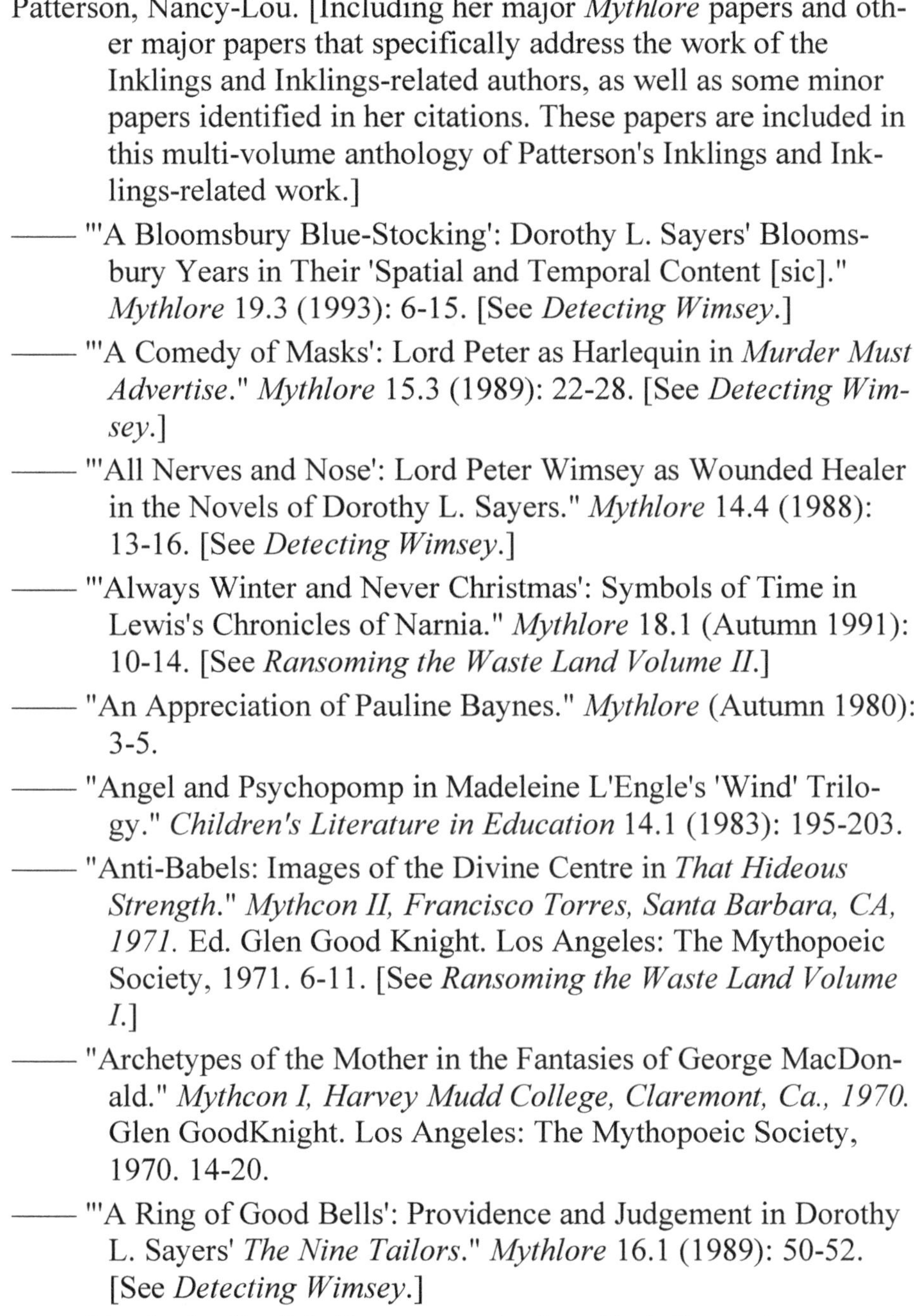

Patterson, Nancy-Lou. [Including her major *Mythlore* papers and other major papers that specifically address the work of the Inklings and Inklings-related authors, as well as some minor papers identified in her citations. These papers are included in this multi-volume anthology of Patterson's Inklings and Inklings-related work.]

—— "'A Bloomsbury Blue-Stocking': Dorothy L. Sayers' Bloomsbury Years in Their 'Spatial and Temporal Content [sic]." *Mythlore* 19.3 (1993): 6-15. [See *Detecting Wimsey.*]

—— "'A Comedy of Masks': Lord Peter as Harlequin in *Murder Must Advertise*." *Mythlore* 15.3 (1989): 22-28. [See *Detecting Wimsey.*]

—— "'All Nerves and Nose': Lord Peter Wimsey as Wounded Healer in the Novels of Dorothy L. Sayers." *Mythlore* 14.4 (1988): 13-16. [See *Detecting Wimsey.*]

—— "'Always Winter and Never Christmas': Symbols of Time in Lewis's Chronicles of Narnia." *Mythlore* 18.1 (Autumn 1991): 10-14. [See *Ransoming the Waste Land Volume II.*]

—— "An Appreciation of Pauline Baynes." *Mythlore* (Autumn 1980): 3-5.

—— "Angel and Psychopomp in Madeleine L'Engle's 'Wind' Trilogy." *Children's Literature in Education* 14.1 (1983): 195-203.

—— "Anti-Babels: Images of the Divine Centre in *That Hideous Strength.*" *Mythcon II, Francisco Torres, Santa Barbara, CA, 1971.* Ed. Glen Good Knight. Los Angeles: The Mythopoeic Society, 1971. 6-11. [See *Ransoming the Waste Land Volume I.*]

—— "Archetypes of the Mother in the Fantasies of George MacDonald." *Mythcon I, Harvey Mudd College, Claremont, Ca., 1970.* Glen GoodKnight. Los Angeles: The Mythopoeic Society, 1970. 14-20.

—— "'A Ring of Good Bells': Providence and Judgement in Dorothy L. Sayers' *The Nine Tailors.*" *Mythlore* 16.1 (1989): 50-52. [See *Detecting Wimsey.*]

—— "Art in the English Classroom: An Interdisciplinary Approach." *English Quarterly* 6.4 (Winter 1973): 345-49.

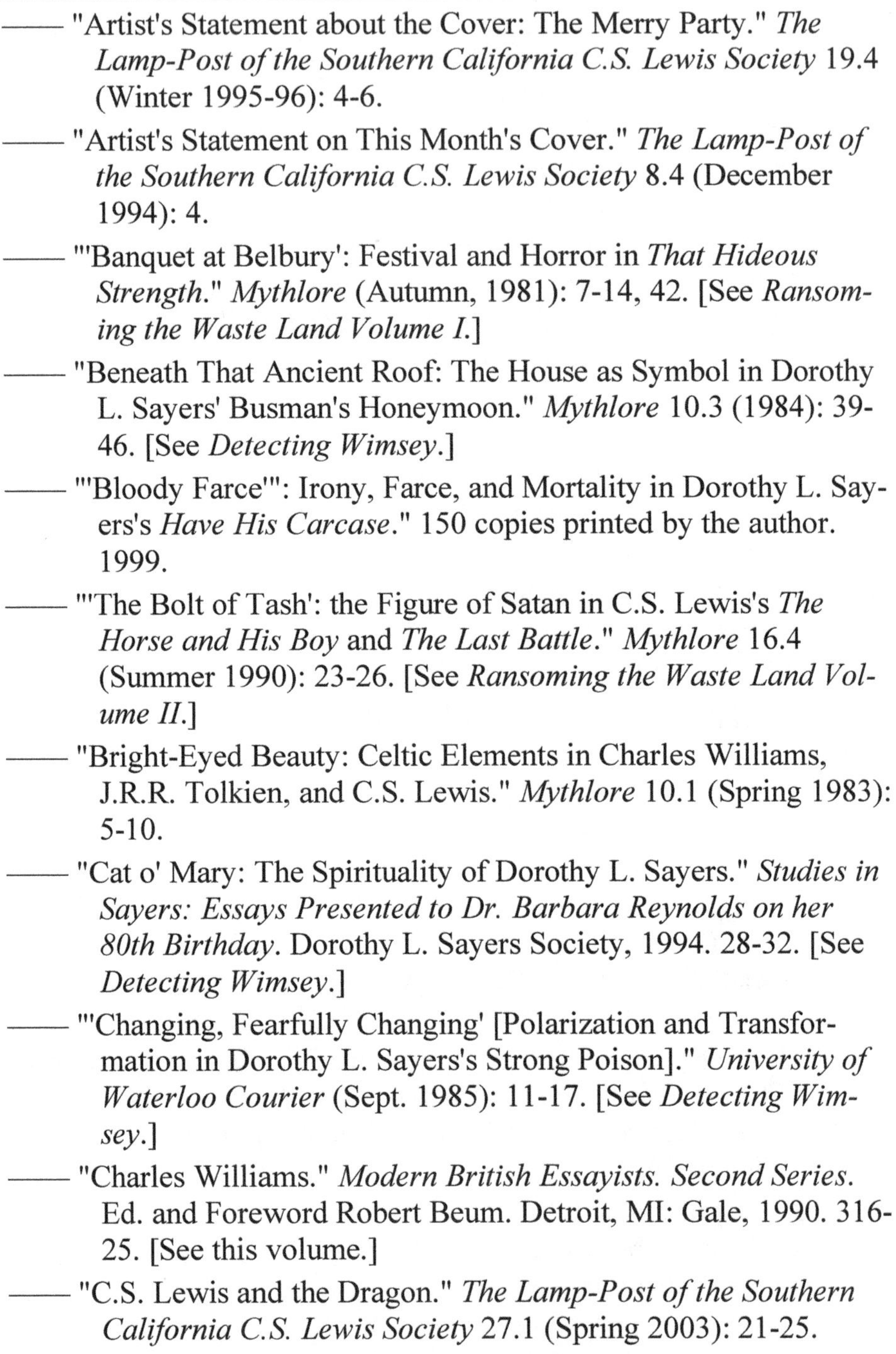

—— "Artist's Statement about the Cover: The Merry Party." *The Lamp-Post of the Southern California C.S. Lewis Society* 19.4 (Winter 1995-96): 4-6.

—— "Artist's Statement on This Month's Cover." *The Lamp-Post of the Southern California C.S. Lewis Society* 8.4 (December 1994): 4.

—— "'Banquet at Belbury': Festival and Horror in *That Hideous Strength*." *Mythlore* (Autumn, 1981): 7-14, 42. [See *Ransoming the Waste Land Volume I.*]

—— "Beneath That Ancient Roof: The House as Symbol in Dorothy L. Sayers' Busman's Honeymoon." *Mythlore* 10.3 (1984): 39-46. [See *Detecting Wimsey.*]

—— "'Bloody Farce'": Irony, Farce, and Mortality in Dorothy L. Sayers's *Have His Carcase*." 150 copies printed by the author. 1999.

—— "'The Bolt of Tash': the Figure of Satan in C.S. Lewis's *The Horse and His Boy* and *The Last Battle*." *Mythlore* 16.4 (Summer 1990): 23-26. [See *Ransoming the Waste Land Volume II.*]

—— "Bright-Eyed Beauty: Celtic Elements in Charles Williams, J.R.R. Tolkien, and C.S. Lewis." *Mythlore* 10.1 (Spring 1983): 5-10.

—— "Cat o' Mary: The Spirituality of Dorothy L. Sayers." *Studies in Sayers: Essays Presented to Dr. Barbara Reynolds on her 80th Birthday*. Dorothy L. Sayers Society, 1994. 28-32. [See *Detecting Wimsey.*]

—— "'Changing, Fearfully Changing' [Polarization and Transformation in Dorothy L. Sayers's Strong Poison]." *University of Waterloo Courier* (Sept. 1985): 11-17. [See *Detecting Wimsey.*]

—— "Charles Williams." *Modern British Essayists. Second Series.* Ed. and Foreword Robert Beum. Detroit, MI: Gale, 1990. 316-25. [See this volume.]

—— "C.S. Lewis and the Dragon." *The Lamp-Post of the Southern California C.S. Lewis Society* 27.1 (Spring 2003): 21-25.

—— "Death by Landscape." *Niekas* 45 (July 1998): 22-25.

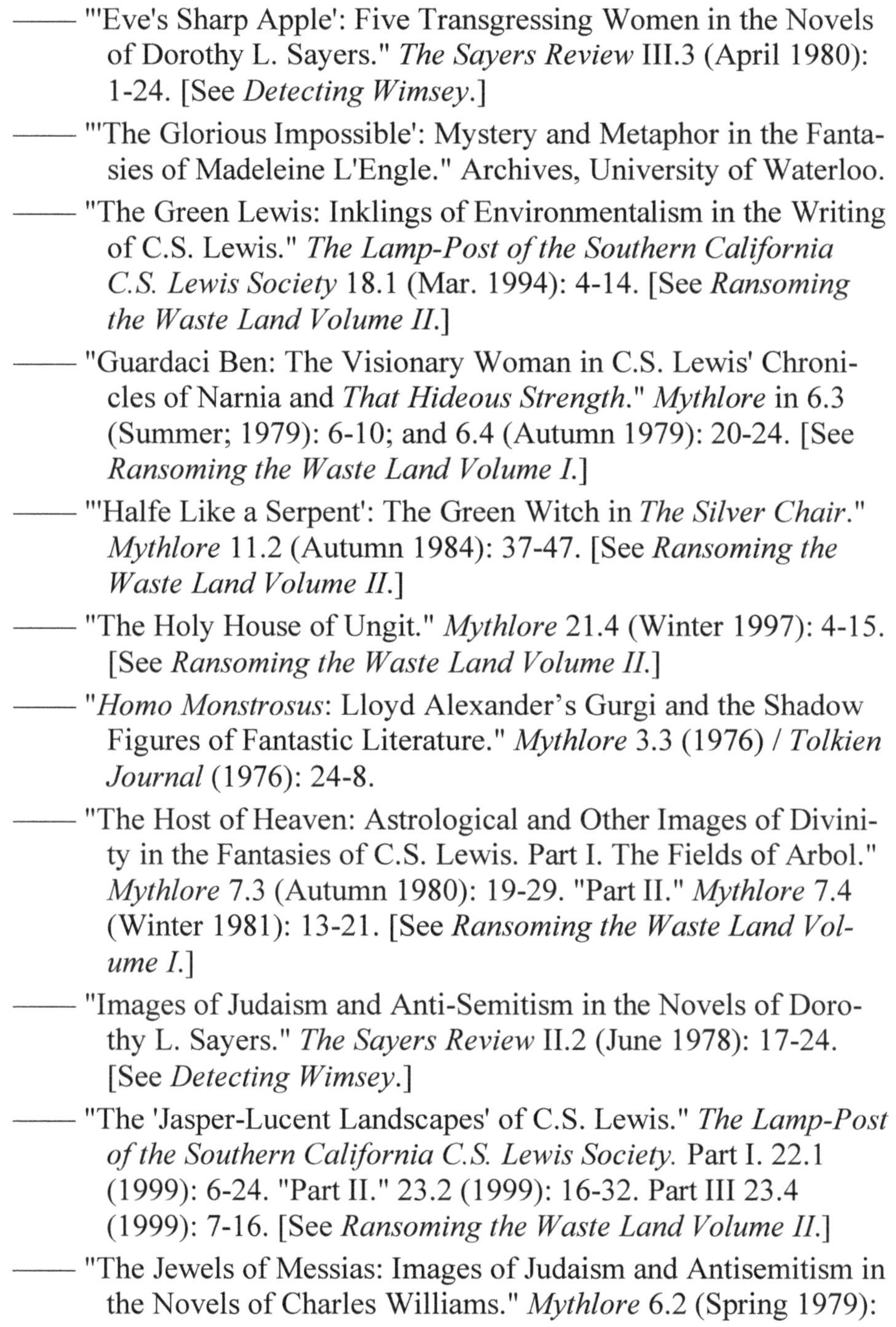

—— "'Eve's Sharp Apple': Five Transgressing Women in the Novels of Dorothy L. Sayers." *The Sayers Review* III.3 (April 1980): 1-24. [See *Detecting Wimsey*.]

—— "'The Glorious Impossible': Mystery and Metaphor in the Fantasies of Madeleine L'Engle." Archives, University of Waterloo.

—— "The Green Lewis: Inklings of Environmentalism in the Writing of C.S. Lewis." *The Lamp-Post of the Southern California C.S. Lewis Society* 18.1 (Mar. 1994): 4-14. [See *Ransoming the Waste Land Volume II*.]

—— "Guardaci Ben: The Visionary Woman in C.S. Lewis' Chronicles of Narnia and *That Hideous Strength*." *Mythlore* in 6.3 (Summer; 1979): 6-10; and 6.4 (Autumn 1979): 20-24. [See *Ransoming the Waste Land Volume I*.]

—— "'Halfe Like a Serpent': The Green Witch in *The Silver Chair*." *Mythlore* 11.2 (Autumn 1984): 37-47. [See *Ransoming the Waste Land Volume II*.]

—— "The Holy House of Ungit." *Mythlore* 21.4 (Winter 1997): 4-15. [See *Ransoming the Waste Land Volume II*.]

—— "*Homo Monstrosus*: Lloyd Alexander's Gurgi and the Shadow Figures of Fantastic Literature." *Mythlore* 3.3 (1976) / *Tolkien Journal* (1976): 24-8.

—— "The Host of Heaven: Astrological and Other Images of Divinity in the Fantasies of C.S. Lewis. Part I. The Fields of Arbol." *Mythlore* 7.3 (Autumn 1980): 19-29. "Part II." *Mythlore* 7.4 (Winter 1981): 13-21. [See *Ransoming the Waste Land Volume I*.]

—— "Images of Judaism and Anti-Semitism in the Novels of Dorothy L. Sayers." *The Sayers Review* II.2 (June 1978): 17-24. [See *Detecting Wimsey*.]

—— "The 'Jasper-Lucent Landscapes' of C.S. Lewis." *The Lamp-Post of the Southern California C.S. Lewis Society*. Part I. 22.1 (1999): 6-24. "Part II." 23.2 (1999): 16-32. Part III 23.4 (1999): 7-16. [See *Ransoming the Waste Land Volume II*.]

—— "The Jewels of Messias: Images of Judaism and Antisemitism in the Novels of Charles Williams." *Mythlore* 6.2 (Spring 1979): 27-31. [See this volume]

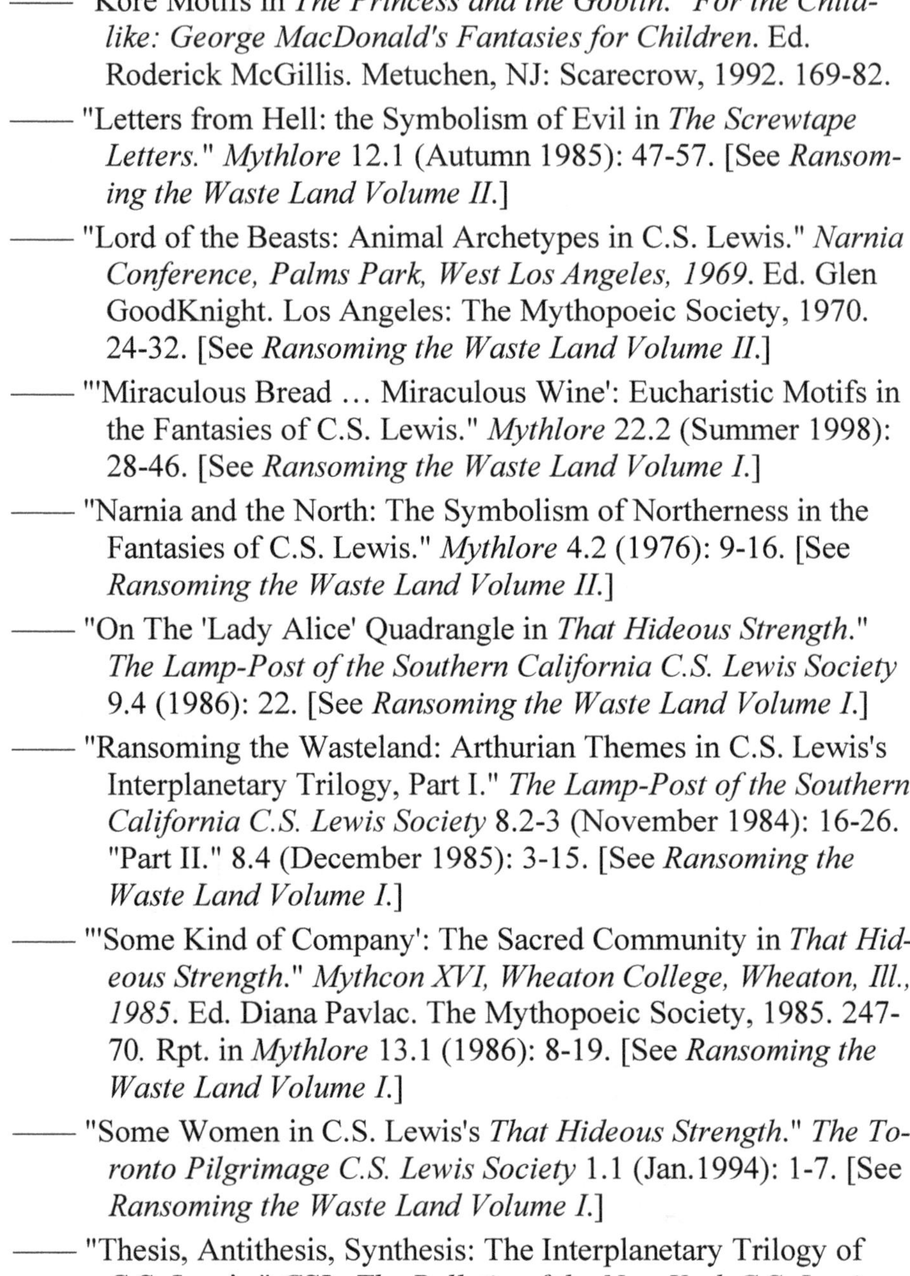

—— "Kore Motifs in *The Princess and the Goblin*." *For the Childlike: George MacDonald's Fantasies for Children*. Ed. Roderick McGillis. Metuchen, NJ: Scarecrow, 1992. 169-82.

—— "Letters from Hell: the Symbolism of Evil in *The Screwtape Letters*." *Mythlore* 12.1 (Autumn 1985): 47-57. [See *Ransoming the Waste Land Volume II.*]

—— "Lord of the Beasts: Animal Archetypes in C.S. Lewis." *Narnia Conference, Palms Park, West Los Angeles, 1969*. Ed. Glen GoodKnight. Los Angeles: The Mythopoeic Society, 1970. 24-32. [See *Ransoming the Waste Land Volume II.*]

—— "'Miraculous Bread … Miraculous Wine': Eucharistic Motifs in the Fantasies of C.S. Lewis." *Mythlore* 22.2 (Summer 1998): 28-46. [See *Ransoming the Waste Land Volume I.*]

—— "Narnia and the North: The Symbolism of Northerness in the Fantasies of C.S. Lewis." *Mythlore* 4.2 (1976): 9-16. [See *Ransoming the Waste Land Volume II.*]

—— "On The 'Lady Alice' Quadrangle in *That Hideous Strength*." *The Lamp-Post of the Southern California C.S. Lewis Society* 9.4 (1986): 22. [See *Ransoming the Waste Land Volume I.*]

—— "Ransoming the Wasteland: Arthurian Themes in C.S. Lewis's Interplanetary Trilogy, Part I." *The Lamp-Post of the Southern California C.S. Lewis Society* 8.2-3 (November 1984): 16-26. "Part II." 8.4 (December 1985): 3-15. [See *Ransoming the Waste Land Volume I.*]

—— "'Some Kind of Company': The Sacred Community in *That Hideous Strength*." *Mythcon XVI, Wheaton College, Wheaton, Ill., 1985*. Ed. Diana Pavlac. The Mythopoeic Society, 1985. 247-70. Rpt. in *Mythlore* 13.1 (1986): 8-19. [See *Ransoming the Waste Land Volume I.*]

—— "Some Women in C.S. Lewis's *That Hideous Strength*." *The Toronto Pilgrimage C.S. Lewis Society* 1.1 (Jan.1994): 1-7. [See *Ransoming the Waste Land Volume I.*]

—— "Thesis, Antithesis, Synthesis: The Interplanetary Trilogy of C.S. Lewis." *CSL: The Bulletin of the New York C.S. Lewis Society* 16.8 (June 1985): 1-6. [See *Ransoming the Waste Land Volume I.*]

—— "'This Equivocal Being': The Un-Man in C.S. Lewis's *Perelandra.*" *The Lamp-Post of the Southern California C.S. Lewis Society* 19.3 (Fall 1995): 6-24; 19.4 (Winter 1996) 7-19. [See *Ransoming the Waste Land Volume I.*]

—— "Trained Habit: The Spirituality of C.S. Lewis." *The Canadian C.S. Lewis Journal* 87 (Spring 1995): 37-53.

—— "Tree and Leaf: J.R.R. Tolkien and the Visual Image." *English Quarterly* 6.4 (Spring 1974): 10-26.

—— "The Triumph of Love: Interpretations of the Tarot in Charles Williams' *The Greater Trumps.*" *Mythcon III, Regency Hyatt House, Long Beach, Ca., 1972*. Ed. Glen GoodKnight. Los Angeles, CA: The Mythopoeic Society, 1974. 12-32. [See this volume.]

—— "The Unfathomable Feminine Principle: Images of Wholeness in *That Hideous Strength.*" *The Lamp-Post of the Southern California C.S. Lewis Society* 9.1-3 (1986): 3-38. [See *Ransoming the Waste Land Volume I.*]

—— "Why We Honor the Centenary of Dorothy L. Sayers (1893–1957)." *Mythlore* 19.3 (1993): 4-5. [See *Detecting Wimsey.*]

Payne, Robert. *The Roman Triumph*. London: Robert Hale, 1962.

Reilly, R.J. *Romantic Religion: A Study of Barfield, Lewis, Williams and Tolkien*. Athens: University of Georgia Press, 1971.

Ridler, Anne, ed. "Introduction." *The Image of the City and Other Essays* by Charles Williams. London: Oxford UP, 1958.

Runciman, Steven. *The Medieval Manichee*. New York: Viking Press, 1961.

Scholem, Gershom Gerhard. *Major Trends in Jewish Mysticism.* 1941. New York: Schocken Books, 1965.

—— *On the Kabbalah and its Symbolism*. New York: Schocken Books, 1965.

Shideler, Mary McDermott. "Essays of Explosive Clarity." *Charles Williams: A Critical Essay.* Grand Rapids, MI: Eerdmans, 1966. 41-46.

—— *The Theology of Romantic Love: A Study in the Writings of Charles Williams*. New York: Harper, 1962.

Sibley, Agnes. *Charles Williams*. Boston: Twayne, 1982. [Reviewed by Patterson in *Mythlore* 10.4 (#38) (1984): 41-42.]

Sypher, Wylie. *The Four Stages of Renaissance Style*. Garden City, NY. Double Day/Anchor, 1955.

Tilley, Roger. *Playing Cards*. London: Weidenfield and Nickolson, 1967.

Tillyard, E.M.W. *The Elizabethan World Picture*. London Chatto and Windus, 1967.

Trachtenberg, Joshua. *Jewish Magic and Superstition; A Study in Folk Religion*.1939. New York: Atheneum, 1970.

Urang, Gunnar. "Fantasy and the Ontology of Love." *Shadows of Heaven*. Philadelphia: United Church Press, 1971.

Vaughn, Leroy F. *Parade and Float Guide*. Minneapolis: T.S. Denison and Co., 1956.

Van der Leeuw, Gerardus. *Sacred and Profane Beauty: The Holy in Art*. New York: Holt, Rinehart and Winston, 1963.

Versnel, H.S. *Triumphus*. Leiden: E.J. Brill, 1970.

Waite, Arthur Edward. *The Pictorial Key to the Tarot*. 1910. New Hyde Park, NY: University Books, 1959.

—— *The Secret Doctrine in Israel*. 1913.

—— *Shadows of Life and Thought: A Retrospective Review in the Form of Memoirs*. London: Selwyn and Blount, 1938.

—— "Waite's Last Word on the Tarot." *The Pictorial Key to the Tarot*. New Hyde Park, NY: University Books, 1959. vii-viii.

Welsford, Enid. *The Fool His Social and Literary History*. London: Faber and Faber, 1968.

Weston, Jessie L. *From Ritual to Romance*. 1920. Garden City, NY: Doubleday Anchor Books, 1957.

Williams, Charles. *See also the novels listed in the front matter.*

—— *A Book of Victorian Narrative Verse*. Ed. Selected with an Introduction by Charles Williams. 1927. Oxford: Clarendon Press, 1931.

—— "A Dialogue on Mr. Eliot's Poem." *Dublin Review* 212 (Apr. 1943): 114-22.

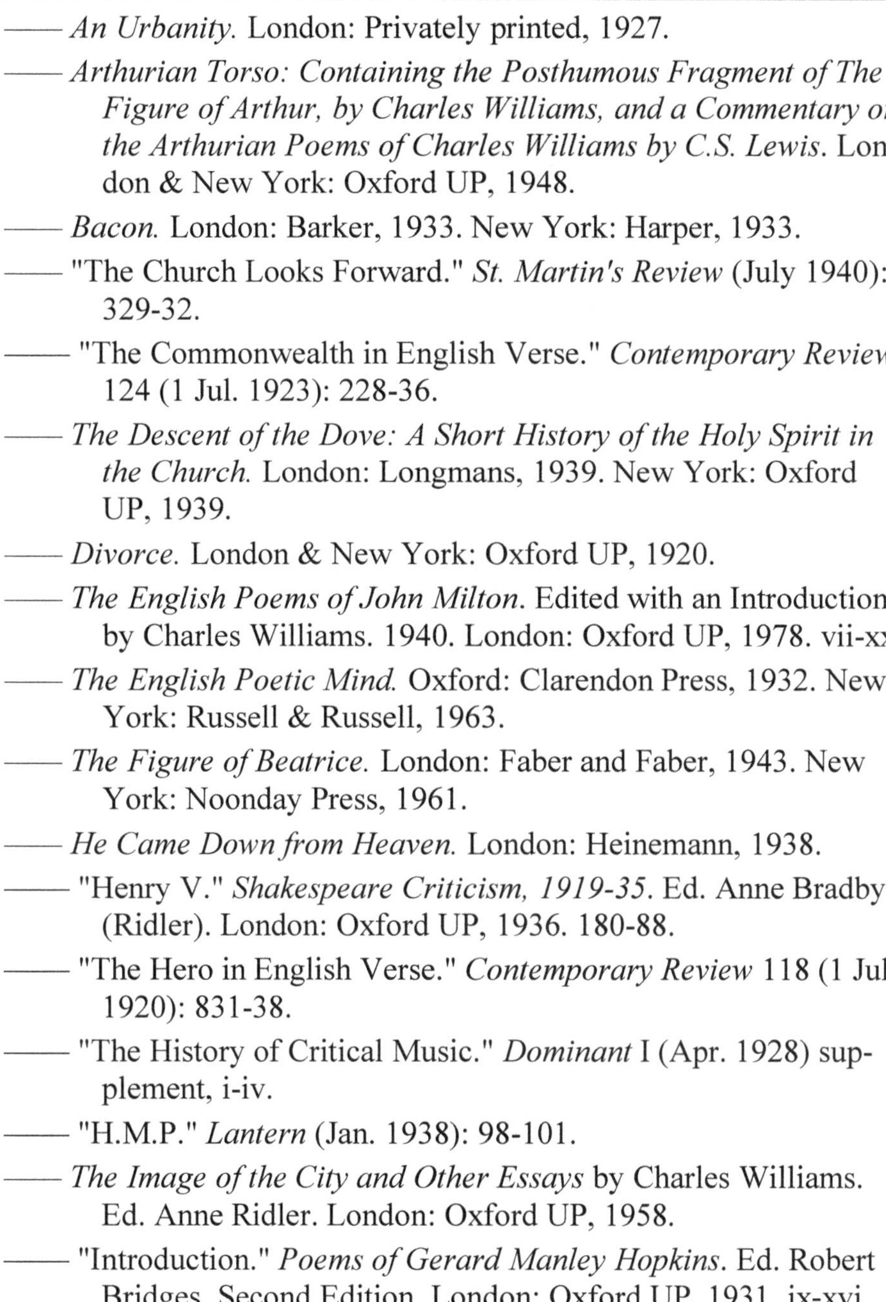

—— *An Urbanity.* London: Privately printed, 1927.

—— *Arthurian Torso: Containing the Posthumous Fragment of The Figure of Arthur, by Charles Williams, and a Commentary on the Arthurian Poems of Charles Williams by C.S. Lewis*. London & New York: Oxford UP, 1948.

—— *Bacon.* London: Barker, 1933. New York: Harper, 1933.

—— "The Church Looks Forward." *St. Martin's Review* (July 1940): 329-32.

—— "The Commonwealth in English Verse." *Contemporary Review* 124 (1 Jul. 1923): 228-36.

—— *The Descent of the Dove: A Short History of the Holy Spirit in the Church.* London: Longmans, 1939. New York: Oxford UP, 1939.

—— *Divorce.* London & New York: Oxford UP, 1920.

—— *The English Poems of John Milton*. Edited with an Introduction by Charles Williams. 1940. London: Oxford UP, 1978. vii-xx.

—— *The English Poetic Mind.* Oxford: Clarendon Press, 1932. New York: Russell & Russell, 1963.

—— *The Figure of Beatrice.* London: Faber and Faber, 1943. New York: Noonday Press, 1961.

—— *He Came Down from Heaven.* London: Heinemann, 1938.

—— "Henry V." *Shakespeare Criticism, 1919-35*. Ed. Anne Bradby (Ridler). London: Oxford UP, 1936. 180-88.

—— "The Hero in English Verse." *Contemporary Review* 118 (1 Jul. 1920): 831-38.

—— "The History of Critical Music." *Dominant* I (Apr. 1928) supplement, i-iv.

—— "H.M.P." *Lantern* (Jan. 1938): 98-101.

—— *The Image of the City and Other Essays* by Charles Williams. Ed. Anne Ridler. London: Oxford UP, 1958.

—— "Introduction." *Poems of Gerard Manley Hopkins*. Ed. Robert Bridges. Second Edition. London: Oxford UP, 1931. ix-xvi.

—— Introduction to *The Present Age*. By Søren Kierkegaard. Trans Alexander Dru and Walter Lowrie. London: Oxford UP, 1940. vii-xii.

—— "John Masefield." *The Saturday Review of Literature* VI.49 (Sat 28 Jun 1930): 1153-1155.

—— *The Letters of Evelyn Underhill*. Edited with an Introduction by Charles Williams. London: Longmans, Green, 1943. 7-46.

—— "Lord Macaulay." *Six Short Biographies*. Ed. R.C. Goffin. Oxford, 1933.

—— *The Masque of the Manuscript,* music by Foss. London: Henderson & Spalding, 1927.

—— "Notes on Possible Endings to Edwin Drood." In *The Mystery of Edwin Drood* by Charles Dickens. London: Oxford UP, 1927. 366-76.

—— "Notes on Religious Drama." *Chelmsford Diocesan Chronicle* 23 (May 1937): 75-76.

—— "Notes on the Way." *Time and Tide* 23 (28 Feb. 1942): 170-71.

—— "Notes on the Way." *Time and Tide* 23 (7 Mar. 1942): 194-95.

—— "On Byron and Byronism." *Bulletin of the British Institute of the University of Paris* (April 1938): 13-19.

—— "The One-Eared Man." *Dominant* I (Dec. 1927): 11-12.

—— "On the Poetry of *The Duchess of Malfi."* In *The Duchess of Malfi* by John Webster. London: Sylvan Press, 1945. xv-xxii.

—— "The Ostentation of Poetry." *Reason and Beauty in the Poetic Mind.* Oxford: Clarendon Press, 1933. Folcroft, Pa: Folcroft Library Editions, 1974.

—— *Poems of Conformity.* London & New York: Oxford UP, 1917.

—— *Poetry at Present.* Oxford: Clarendon Press, 1930. Freeport, NY: Books for Libraries Press, 1969. [Includes "Masefield" 114-27. "T.S. Eliot" 163-74. "Robert Bridges" 18-29.]

—— "Prefatory Note." *A Book of Longer Modern Verse.* Ed. Edward A. Parker. Oxford, 1926.

—— "Queen Victoria." *More Short Biographies.* Ed. R.C. Goffin. Oxford, 1938.

—— *The Region of the Summer Stars.* London: Nicholson & Watson, 1944.

—— *Religion and Love in Dante: The Theology of Romantic Love.* Westminister, UK: Dacre Press, 1941.

—— *The Silver Stair.* London: Herbert & Daniel, 1912.

—— "St. John of the Cross." *Time and Tide* 23 (27 Jun. 1942): 522.

—— *Taliessin through Logres.* London: & New York: Oxford UP, 1938.

—— "Taste in Literature." *Listener* 24 (26 Dec. 1940): 913-14.

—— *Thomas Cranmer of Canterbury.* London: Oxford UP, 1936.

—— "*Troilus and Cressida* and *Hamlet.*" *Shakespeare Criticism, 1919-35*. Ed. Anne Bradby (Ridler). London: Oxford UP, 1936. 188-208.

—— "The War for Compassion." *Sword of the Spirit* 20 (15 May 1941): 7.

—— *The Way of Exchange*. London: Clarke, 1941.

—— *Windows of Night.* London: Oxford UP, 1924.

—— *Witchcraft.* London: Faber & Faber, 1941. Cleveland: World, 1959.

—— ed., and Introduction. *The New Book of English Verse*. London: Gollancz, 1935. Rpt. Miami, Florida: Granger Books, 1978. 3-18.

Willeford, William. *The Fool and His Scepter*. Northwestern UP, 1969.

Winship Jr, George P. "The Novels of Charles Williams." *Shadows of Imagination*. Ed. Mark R. Hillegas. Carbondale: Southern Illinois UP, 1969. 111-24.

Wright, Canon J. Stafford. *Christianity and the Occult*. London: Scripture Union, 1971.

Index

0
ת
The Fool

www.ingramcontent.com/pod-product-compliance
Lightning Source LLC
Chambersburg PA
CBHW070635310726
48982CB00001B/288

* 9 7 8 1 9 8 7 9 1 9 0 8 0 *